BEYOND THE EAGLE

An Intervibrational Perspective On Woman's Spiritual Journey

ELLEN
CHAMBERS

with

GRACE WALKING STICK

and

SEVEN OTHER WOMEN IN SPIRIT

DEDICATION

To the women
who have walked before us,
leaving trails of inspiration
as guideposts;

And to the women
who walk with us,
showering smiles
of encouragement and strength.

Library of Congress Catalog Card Number 88-51319
ISBN 0-9621017-0-2

Published by Wild Violet Publishing, P.O. Box 1311, Hamilton, MT 59840.

ACKNOWLEDGEMENTS

Our deepest appreciation to all who have contributed to this project from the many vibrations and in the myriad of ways. And to those who will carry it beyond the present into the Dreams. You know who you are, and we are grateful.

PREFACE

In the far north the White Eagle has lived, although few have known her or even seen her. She represents the outer limits of physicalness on this planet. Her purposes and behavior were unprecedented, as she lived in solitude, unbound to any male bird. Unencumbered by the demands of others, she was able to soar in the freedom of her own choices. (Some might say she was an albinized Golden Eagle, genetically inferior to and consequently rejected by her species.) However, we recognize her uniqueness, thus the limitlessness of her potential, so use her as a symbol for yours.

There are many worlds that await you because you are a woman. These worlds are far more expansive than the levels of physical reality some of us have only begun to know. *Beyond the Eagle* is intended to be a catalyst for your journey. We cannot take you where you will go, but we can offer our perspectives on the potential of woman. We can tell you stories and philosophies of our travels. You too can soar and live as the White Eagle, until even her territory is too small for your wings. So please take our love and our words to help you go beyond the eagle.

INTRODUCTION

Beyond the Eagle was born of the union of the Dreams of several women. We are women of many vibrations and many forms. This book is an example of what can happen when women allow their consciousness' to expand, dare to defy traditional boundaries, and come together across planes of existence.

Majai provided seed Dream, and to that the rest was added. None of us is more important or more correct than any other. Our perspectives exist simultaneously and compatibly, in diversity to complement your ranges of consciousness.

Ellen is our connection to the physical plane (the earth). She is the link between vibrations. She is a medium. She is able to communicate with entities in other forms by changing her vibration to harmonize with theirs. She does not "channel," nor does she do "trance mediumship," but remains fully conscious during all communication. Her range of operation and degree of expansion include all the places the rest of us exist.

It was important to the value of this project that Ellen's experience include firsthand knowledge of all that has been presented. We feel it would be a disservice to you were we to present any information that was beyond our experience or development. So we can say to you that we do indeed own the contents of these words, and have spoken only from the depths of our beings. Everything written on these pages is the truth as we know it, and none of the characters (entities) or stories is fictional.

Too often success is seen as a function of the accumulation of knowledge (with associated degrees and letters), the amassment of wealth, the attainment of power over others, or the arrival into positions of authority. Such measures of accomplishment are then glued to a person to serve as indicators for credibility and expertise, often in inapplicable areas.

Our position is that who we really are, what our vibrations are, is independent of chosen roles or accumulated knowledge. As you will come to see, we disagree with a lot of things, and identify alternative approaches throughout the book. And so, concerning the matter of the introduction of the participants in this book, we face the issue of criteria for accomplishment and credibility. And when we escape the one-lifetime mentality, where does such a list of identifiers and credifiers begin?

The most important factor regarding any of us is individual vibrational state (which equals evolutionary level). And that you must evaluate for yourself, using your own criteria for quality. Nothing we tell you will change our vibrations. Nor should any facts convince you one way or another to believe what we say. As you read you will come to understand better who we are, where we live, and what our terminology really means. In actual fact, the vibration that comes with these words is far more important than any of the words or the individual speakers.

Majai (pronounced ma zhay, as with a French j), Inyani (in yah' nee), Amna (ahm' nah), Kioka (key oh' kah), Gyta (guy' tah), Dytoianta (die' toy ahn' tah), Anja (ahn jah), and Grace (formerly Grace Walking Stick) are entities who are not incarnated on any planet, although their places (vibrations) of residence vary. When a word is spoken or thought, it emits a vibration of both sound and color. Repetition of that word has a cumulative effect upon all who come within that vibration. Therefore, in our choosing of names, the consideration was the impact of the word on you. These chosen words are void of meaning. No longer do any of us actually have names. Where we exist we are known by our concentration of yin or female energy. "Grace" and "Ellen" are names associated with particular incarnations, and have been deliberately used because of their familiarity and respective associations.

It was hard for us to find a starting point for the presentation of this material; no matter what we decided to say, something should have been said first. Comprehension of some of the concepts may best be achieved by reading the book through a second tme. Then the concepts will have opportunities to go full circle in your mind. Understanding, however, will only come from your ability and willingness to feel what lives behind the words.

Our wish has been to simplify cumbersome and unnecessarily complicated philosophy in order to promote your understanding of yourself in the universe. Ultimately, we want to help make these concepts useful to you in your daily life. In order to to do this, however, we felt it was important to establish a foundation of theory prior to undertaking lighter discussion and stories. Therefore, the reading should become easier as you proceed.

Please enjoy your journey through *Beyond the Eagle*. Many entities from other vibrations will be with you as you journey, and will help you in whatever ways you need, ultimately to go from your present state deeper into the yin. Our love.

MAJAI

For too long the women in this universe have been afraid to speak up about their spirituality. It has not been time. It has been a warranted silence. Until recently it has been too dangerous for women to speak their experience, to live their experience, to be from their sense of knowing. The scales of female/male balance had been weighted on the male side. However, the imbalance reached its absolute state and the universal energies have reversed. Momentum is building and the yin (female) energies once again have reached sufficient caliber for women everywhere, *all women* to feel their connectedness to this universal surge. The force of the universe is unquestionably behind us, so now we must risk speaking, once again of *our* spirituality, of *our* path through the universe. We have support from every aspect of the cosmos; it is infused with the force we know of as *ours*. As the yin increases, so does the potential for every woman to remember her connectedness to the earth, to the solar system, to the universal cycles, to the ebbs and flows of the cosmos.

Women have always owned a sense of knowing. We do not doubt this. Yet we have not trusted our knowing enough to make it the basis for our spiritual growth. We have for centuries looked elsewhere, always outside of ourselves for answers and direction. The more we have failed to trust ourselves, the more we have lost touch with our own spirituality. Some of us have held onto our roots in spite of the difficulties; some of us have found them after they were temporarily lost. They are available to any woman who so desires to have them back.

We are deeply aware that something is wrong, that something has been wrong for a long, long time. We feel the tension inside and outside, a tension that results when self-determination has dissolved. Others who do not know us are making decisions that only we have the capacity, right, and knowledge to make. Thus we live in a perpetual state of tension. We are tossed to and fro on the universal ocean, all the time saying, "but if I did this. . . .if only it were like this. . . .it doesn't look like that to me. . . .I have a different idea. . . .let's try my way. . . .*listen* to *me*." We have not spoken loudly enough or with true conviction. We have not believed that our positions and views were valid. We utter meek objections or offer alternatives. They are ignored or criticized. We have not known how to proceed in the face of rejection.

We can be afraid of the consequences if we dare to differ. We can be afraid of striking out on our own. For too long we have done both, and where has it gotten us? On the ocean trip "to and fro." As long

1

as we wait for change to come to us, eternally we will sit in this state of tension, of dis-ease, of dis-harmony, of dis-satisfaction. No longer can we wait. Now is the time to take our individual and collective spiritual paths into our *own* hands. It is high time we said, "Enough, it's my turn. I have a better way. Now this is the way it is *going* to be. I know what *I* need and feel and want. I know that I know. I want it and I want it now." We can go forward with the energetic wave that is transforming this universe. It is our choice: to go with it, to make it ours, to come into our power which is to know the power of the universe, or, to let the opportunity pass us by.

I have come to say to you: take your spiritual power. I cannot guide you. I cannot tell you what to do. I can only help you recognize what is already yours. I can offer you a feeling of the universal collective consciousness of woman, and the security in knowing finally that you are not alone. Your voice can now be heard, heard by all of us, if you are willing to speak. You can now be known by your sisters if you are willing to be woman. And you can know *all that is* if you are willing to seek it.

MAJAI

Each of us is responsible for her own progress on her spiritual journey. No one can travel our path for us. No one can rightfully decide for us what our path will be. We need to accept full responsibility for our choices, our actions, our thoughts, and our inactions. We are *voluntary* participants on these journeys; we need to remember this.

There are numerous entities (physical or otherwise) available to guide us, to offer us suggestions, but any final decision is ours alone. No longer can we afford to abdicate to an unknown, vaguely defined, higher authority. At any given moment we are the sum of our experience and no more. If we listen to others who are more evolved than ourselves, we are valid only to the extent that we own what they offer. *We cannot be more than we are simply by listening to or following the advice of a more developed entity.* If we choose to act or believe based on what someone else tells us, we are responsible as if it is ours, because we have made it ours.

This is not to say that others do not exist who are more universally and developmentally traveled, or that others do not have experiences that can help us with ours. Most certainly we can and must learn from others. Their offerings, however, are only valuable if we can recognize their experiences as our own. Essentially in our daily life, each of us is the highest authority. To look beyond ourselves for validation, approval or direction amounts to giving away our self-determination. To defer to another because we have concluded that the other is more learned or knowledgeable when the contents of other's experience do not belong to us is precisely a giving away of our own power.

As we walk on our journeys as women, it is important to think of *female* experience as our guide. Who else except other women can shine a light on the territory that awaits us? We are operating in a female context whether we choose to acknowledge it or not. Women and men have different routes through the universe; they are routes 180 degrees from one another. We follow either a female or a male path. Our dharma is to follow the *correct* path. We need to do so sincerely and properly, expediently and courageously, regardless of where the path leads, where we need to exist or incarnate, or what form we need to hold. (We may at one time or another incarnate as the opposite sex, however, the chosen gender identity remains constant.)

There is a natural energetic polarity in the universe which we have come to identify as female/male or yin/yang. The significance in the polarity rests in the vibrational difference between the two poles. The vibration associated with the female is relative (to the male) high rate and high frequency, while that associated with the male is low rate and low frequency. A correspondent high pitch and acute, crisp light goes with the female, and a low pitch and soft diffuse light with the male. A value judgment cannot be placed on these characteristics. There is merely a difference. And it is important only that we recognize the difference in order that we proceed on our respective paths appropriately. As we do so, attunement with the vibrational progression of our path will follow.

To get consumed by an intellectual analysis of (what we define as) the physics of the situation is missing the point. *Our goal now is to recognize that a difference exists between female and male paths, in order that we follow the correct one: a female path.* Education and intellectual understanding are not prerequisites to spiritual development. Our aim is alignment of our individual vibrations with the vibration of our path, our respective universal vibration.

How do we do this? As women we go inside and feel. We feel from the depths of our being. We recognize compatible and harmonious vibrations, and equally recognize discordant notes, those which feel wrong deep inside. This is not complicated. In fact, it is very simple. Each of us is able to do this to some extent even today. It is something we have always known how to do, an ability we brought with us.

3

Problems enter the picture when we try to ignore, to suppress, to negate, or to deny these internal messages. If we do it for long enough or frequently enough, we come to live in a state of dis-ease, dis-harmony, and tension. And we lose touch with all that is greater than ourselves.

Women have for centuries attempted to fit themselves to a male spiritual path. This is discordant, and the result has been an absence of progress and a feeling of uneasiness. Synchronized and simultaneous vibrations are the key to spiritual progress and health. Easiness is the result of compatibility. Compatibility involves a merging of energies, a oneness, an effortless flow. (It is not a state of compromise until meshing is achieved.) When woman attunes to the yin rather than attempts to attune to the yang, easiness will envelop her.

As woman finds the courage to trust her own experience with harmonious and disharmonious vibrations, she will come to know her spiritual path once again. Both the individual and the collective serve to benefit from this refound knowledge. As the energies of individual women attune to the same universal energy, individually and collectively we will feel the resultant escalation in intensity and quantity. It will literally speed us all on our ways, as the individual and the collective/universal merge. That is woman coming into her power and power coming into woman. It is really rather simple.

(Note: We have chosen to use the word "yin" to identify and speak of that energy which is fundamental and essential to women, because it is the most accurate word in the English language. However, we do *not* agree with traditional concepts of yin and yang. Our understanding is that these are *only two* of the essential energies in a pool of many in this universe. As a microcosm of the universe, each entity contains the entire range of essential energies, with a preponderance of one's primary energy. For women, that primary energy is yin. For men, it is yang. Therefore, *the main difference between our understanding and traditional philosophy lies in our refusal to see yin in a relationship of exclusivity to yang [male].*

To undertake a detailed philosophical examination of our understanding is not particularly relevant to our purposes in writing this book. More important to present at this time on the earth are tools to aid individual transformations. We feel the emphasis to date on heady dissertations has detracted from women's spiritual progress. A woman's understanding of the principles of electricity, for example, does not make her better able to flip a light switch to illuminate a room. With identification of the function of the switch and simple knowledge of its operation, she can flip the switch to light the room in order to go about her business. Likewise, with spirituality, she does not have practical use for the intricacies of the universe. With elaborate understanding, we are not better equipped to travel our paths.

Further, for too long women have become so bogged down by the intricacies and speculations of philosophy that we have been distracted from forward motion. Thus purposely in this book, we avoid focus upon remotely relevant understandings, choosing instead to emphasize the identification and application of basic principles.)

KIOKA

A requirement of logical explanation in order to deem something valid will kill anything that belongs to realms other than the physical plane. Elaborate philosophies are nothing more than pacifiers to legitimize the existence of what does not fit physical reality.

I sit quietly next to another woman. I begin thinking that I am hungry. And she says, "There is food on the table if you are hungry." People try to explain this type of occurrence by identifying possible external stimuli which would cause both women to have similar thought patterns. They would add that the actual words spoken were very common phrases, typical of such a situation. And then as a blanket statement, chalk it all up to coincidence.

Is it not possible for two women to be harmonized with each other to an extent that each is known in her completeness to the other? Today society does not have a place for such a possibility. This is why we say the feeling self has been denied. This is why we say women have been forced into male operational ways. This is why we say that women discard the legitimacy of their own feeling and knowing, in deference to a system foreign and unnatural to their growth.

Do you know there have existed entire societies, *on the earth*, which functioned as completely as yours does today, where verbalization was absent? The absence of the written or spoken word does not equal lack of accomplished growth, as many of your anthropologists and biologists have chosen to believe. In fact, in many ways, these societies and the individuals in them were far more advanced than what is considered progressive on the earth at the present time. You can be sure these societies were not societies dominated by men. And you can be sure the ability to feel was the basis for the effectiveness of these systems.

5

MAJAI

Life can be simple. Life is simple. But we have learned to devalue simplicity and to venerate technological, philosophical, and intellectual complexity or sophistication. In fact the word "simple" carries with it undesirable connotations and definitions. One would never want to be seen as simple in any size, shape, or form. Furthermore, we shun that which simplifies.

The material I wish to present, on the one hand, is very, very simple and basic. So simple, in fact, it should be obvious to everyone. On the other hand, in its simplicity it is too difficult to grasp for the minds of those who have come to adapt to a world of complexity.

Daily I see women reject "the obvious" in favor of the compounded, the entangled, the convoluted, the irreducible, and the undecipherable. Something that is not understood is valued as if greater than the self. It is seen to be worthy of empowerment because it cannot be mastered, or controlled, or comprehended. It is not the complicated or unintelligible qualities which make something valuable. Your desire for expansion, to grow to encompass the scope of the object, and your inability to do so, *should make you strive for expansion rather than cause you to give way to empower the object.* Think of the times you have been accepting of a simple idea if the packaging smelled of complexity or sophistication. (This is how advertising works, by the way.)

What all of us have come to say is very basic and simple and ordinary. It is so simple, in fact, that it would be embarrassing were it not the case that we value simplicity. Not only do we value it, we cherish it. For we travel with less and less, our methods becoming increasingly uncomplicated as we go.

We are tired of splash and extravagance. We want to get to the basics. We are not telling of great adventures with airs of paradox, tales with bewildering outcomes, or labyrinthine stories. We want you to understand your basic nature, your own abilities, and your own path. We want to help you make sense out of this great adventure. So as you read our stories, feel them, understand them, and take the little messages from them. We are not here to confuse you or to glorify anything or anybody. While we may travel in different vibrations, our essence is the same. To solicit or entice or inspire veneration or awe would be counterproductive. We want you to return to simplicity.

There are vast implications inherent in the material I have come to present. My intent is to lay a foundation from which magnific changes can be built. The risks are many for all of us as you shall come to appreciate as you continue into this material. The state of affairs on this planet necessitates such a forthright and direct approach, due to time factors as well as the severity of the situation. A place for compromise can no longer exist.

The work that must be done can only be done courageously and from deep conviction. *I have come to offer guidance to those who already see the need and the way. My job is not to convince or convert, to persuade or argue.* Many of us already see, not only the incredible mess we face, but the need for total reformation of society. Many of us are beginning to see the ways we must go to move beyond the mess, but we have been isolated in our despair, in our drive to move forward, in our frustration in making changes, and in our tenacity in holding onto a Dream we know is possible and real. What we lack are role models and established systems to help show us how to do what needs to be done and to warn us when we threaten to fall back into the known but ineffective ways. It is a female system we must create, on completely different principles and methods from what we now live. The way we interact personally, the way we function collectively, the value systems and the goals must all undergo major adjustments.

Deep within us we know the ways. Nothing I have to say is new to any woman on this planet. I am here for those of you who recognize what I say as your own, and for those of you who are bursting at the seams with dissatisfaction with the status quo. Nevertheless, some of what will be said will be hard to hear. Some of it goes against what we have been socialized to accept, believe, and even on occasion, cherish. Some of it will scare you because of the far-reaching consequences if such ideas are put into practice.

Listen with your heart, not with your intellect, for that is the premise we shall always return to as a center. It is the basis for the female method. Remember this. Do not bother to read any further if you cannot do so from your heart. Only by experiencing life with your heart at the center, will you be able to find your place in the societies that are forming. Only in this way will you know what your right action must be. Only by doing this will you have the ultimate protection from any and all assailants. It will enable you to rise above *all* your fears. And this, my sisters, is the only way to love.

What I am giving you is practical, workable advice. No more can we live in our heads, planning and theorizing. It is time to act, and actions begin and end with the individual. Our responsibility is to our *own* spiritual growth. As we better ourselves, the collective too benefits. And when we better ourselves *in order to* benefit the collective, we then know how the individual and the collective dance together. When we recognize that an individual living in a vacuum serves absolutely no purpose, we move into the realm of true selflessness. And there we are infused with the light and the love, the peace and the harmony that we all crave so desperately.

I am honored to work with you again and my wish is that many of us have the courage and the desire to do what it takes to send us all home. My love to you.

KIOKA

The whens and wheres of incarnation are a choice. Believe it or not, women actually chose to incarnate on the earth in the midst of this madness. Why do you suppose? Must be a reason. Must be something for woman to learn.

Since the prevailing wind on this planet is disharmony and abuse of Natural Law, I don't think women are here to learn conformity with that. They are here to learn finally (I hope) to stand up for what they feel and know to be right. The extremes of imbalance are very clear messages that choices are in order - choices to continue the destructive, ungrowthful trend, or choices to say, "This is so bad, there's no way I'm going to be part of it."

Every woman incarnated on the earth at this time has in the past failed to take her own power in the face of resistance. Every woman here now has abdicated to men repeatedly prior to this incarnation. And every woman here on the earth has not learned to trust and value her own spiritual progress.

Each has arrived at the spot of her own powerlessness and immobility via different experiences. But collectively, all women share common lessons. Each has a need to once again move in love rather than in fear, to become her potential without imposing conditionality on the scope of that potential, and to trust *her* rather than his spiritual path as good and right for her.

Obviously where each woman stands amidst these lessons varies, some being at the beginning, some in the middle, and others at the end. The time is running out with conditions on this planet deteriorating rapidly.

8

And too many women are complacently going along with the degeneration.

Others, however at the limits of exertion and faith, have done all that is possible to effect their own redirection. That is when intervention by spirit is appropriate. Upon exhaustion of one's resources and failure of vision, assistance will come, for that is the Law.

We come in response to need. And we come in response to agonizing requests. We come to let you know that you do indeed see a future and can make that future yours. We come to give you commendation for your struggles, to give you encouragement to continue, to give you support as you do, and to give you glimpses of our experiences to help you direct your efforts. The vibration we show you can make you aware of the power of a solid connection to the universe. The information we have found to be useful in our travels might also be helpful to you.

As you will soon see, a woman's spiritual journey is not a free ride. You will have to keep working as hard as you have been, but perhaps with our suggestions you can be a bit more effective and efficient in your labors. We want you to move at least as much as you wish to do so. That is why we are here. Much, much love.

ELLEN

Running around in my head for months have been fears in all shapes and sizes of the consequences of presenting this material. As we began putting it on paper, the chill in my feet intensified. But also did my conviction that it must be done. All of us feel a tremendous drive to go forward. It just plain isn't an option to sit where we are. To go or not to go is not the question. Yet there is a scariness that comes from charting untraveled waters.

Majai told me that she too is very afraid, afraid of the consequences of being as direct and as blunt as she has decided she needs to be. Were we not to find the courage to bare what churns in our depths, its value would be lost to others.

ELLEN

In my most lucid moments, when suddenly consumed by the complete flavor of our words, panic prevails. Calmly my friends say, "what's the big deal?"

The big deal is that I have always been the kid dissatisfied, the kid tantrumming for the rest of the family, the kid people wished would just shut up. And now, big mouth open, in the company of a bunch of disembodied ladies talking without mouths, the *real* feelings pour forth. The ones I *knew* I had to sit on back then.

Back then is gone and now has arrived, and I've *got* to stand up.

ANJA

Women on the earth are afraid to change in the direction of furthering their connection with the universe, because they are afraid to take their own power. Certainly this is the case, because they have forgotten how. Meager efforts are the best they can muster. And even for such meager attempts, they have been persecuted, maimed and tortured, psychologically and physically brutalized, all of which are the ultimate messages of negative reinforcement for daring to venture into oneself.

Our fear lives. It is real. But to change we must once again love, love the future rather than fear the past. Dreams and change, growth and development are made in love. Dare to give up your fears. Dare to step in love.

AMNA

Fear is incompatible with love. Fear is defensive. Love is active pursuit. Fear is contracted. Love is expansive. Fear does not allow growth. Love encourages it. So it makes sense to travel where you are going for the love of it, rather than to run from what you fear. Maybe knowing that you are not alone will help you relax into a posture of loving pursuit of the universe.

AMNA

Primarily our focus needs to be on our individual growth. To do that it is necessary to identify our feelings and knowings, and then to respect such as valid and essential. By making our actions true to these feelings and knowings, woman will travel.

Because we do not live absent of context, however, individual choices impact upon other individuals, upon men as well as women, and upon social creations. What we as women need to do to grow is very simple. *To find the courage to act is another story.* And to see these actions in terms of their social, political, and economic impacts, is quite an extensive undertaking. Negligent it would be to deny the ramifications of our changes. But if we get bogged down by focus upon impact or by fears of reaction to our choices, we will necessarily avoid our own growth.

Pay attention to what feels correct to you internally and trust that actions in support of these feelings may cause waves, but will be for the good of everyone including yourself. There is synchronicity in all life. You have lost your connection to it. By relearning to feel, you will return to know that connection. Then you will see that *if you can keep yourself in alignment and harmony, you will benefit the collective, not detract from it*.

ELLEN

Majai and another spirit woman dreamed me: The three of us were transporting a valuable package, bundled and wrapped like a medicine bundle. We drove in an "armored" vehicle. Majai and the other woman were dressed in guards' uniforms, I as a plainclotheswoman. Our only "weapons" were ourselves, our own power, and the power of woman behind us. There was a feeling of security as we traveled along, *until* it was time to traverse a public place to take a public elevator to go into a crowd of people. At which point I began to fear and became nervous. The elevator arrived. I stepped on. A man followed me on. I panicked but managed to step off and push the button. The doors closed. He screamed in anger as he rode to his destination alone. The three of us got on the next car.

AMNA

The format that has been chosen for the presentation of this material is purposely varied. We exist on many levels even within our respective vibrations, and our approaches to the universe perpetually change accordingly. In fact, fluidity of approach is essential to development. Even without a moment's notice, we need to be able to change direction, to adapt to fluctuant internal and external conditions, and to receive love and teaching from whence it comes.

It is not the words alone that will interact with you as you read. The images we create, the vibrations we bring, our caring and concern, our desire to free you of your stuckness, and the hard and piercing quality of our stories are all designed to wake you up. Allow them to exist for you in the many ways you exist.

KIOKA

Why are we bothering to write this book? Because you are worth it. Because we care. We care that so many women on the earth are trapped in needless suffering and circuitous journeys because of lost vision. Lost vision of purpose. Lost vision of possibilities. Forgotten even are the differences between harmony and disharmony. Hidden is woman's connection to the universe.

Many have tried to get free, but without large enough perspective have succeeded only in traveling to new locations amidst the chaos. We are not magic. We tell an old tale. The effectiveness of the telling can only be measured by woman's consequent movement beyond her present.

Our intervention in your process is based on a glimmer of faith. Faith in Natural Law. Faith in your memory of your connection. To most these words will be nothing more than meaningless chatter. To some, too large a threat to take seriously. But to a handful, we hope, the piece of the puzzle you have been missing.

MAJAI

We can learn something by observing the behavior of cows. They are habitual animals arriving, departing, gathering, eating because they did so yesterday. They take shelter in the barn at the same time every day. One day the barn roof begins to leak. It leaks more and more until it offers little or no shelter. The cows continue to gather in the barn.

Our social structure has many leaks, and fails to shelter adequately many of its members. The leaks have grown, but we continue to try to collect under the same structure. Why do we do this? Why? I ask you to think hard. Because it exists? Is it easier than building a new system? I think so. What we must begin to question is the design of society (the barn). Is there only one way, the way with which we are familiar to build a social structure? Why is it leaking? From poor maintenance? Yes, partially. But I think primarily it stems originally from poor design.

We are aware of the imbalances and injustices in the racial, class, economic, and gender structures. We spend hours and hours and billions of dollars studying and commenting on the breakdowns, the shortcomings, the hierarchies of society, but what has changed in the last several hundred years? Nothing. Oppression still exists. War still exists. Decadent wealth and poverty live side by side in the same cities. Inequality under the law prevails. Why?

Because quite simply there is a struggle for power. We have come to believe that if we don't win we will lose, that we have only two groups to choose from: the oppressed and the oppressors. No one likes to admit that as "wealth" increases for one group, poverty increases for the other. We are either controlled or controllers in every aspect of our lives. It is a system of competition and survival of the fittest.

Never does anyone question the advisability of supporting the competitive system. Always one thinks that if only they were able to play the game better, or were given the right opportunity to enter the game (after all, it's a fair market, isn't it?), then surely they too would succeed at the game. So some are kept from playing, others taught to play impeccably.

I don't believe that a prerequisite to happiness or peace (isn't that what we fight for?) is a power struggle. Why must we continue to see progress as control over or power over another individual or group? Are we afraid to step off the game board and say I don't want to play this game at all? Even if personally we are winning or know we can? What if we did that? There was a slogan in the '60s: What if they gave a war and nobody came?

To come into our power we attune to the universal energy. As we connect with that, we have access to it and it has access to us. We merge and are one. (It doesn't matter what anyone else is doing, except that every time another individual merges with the universal, the total energy increases for all of us.) Power over another is an absurdity because it is irrelevant to our individual connection. It is a dead end street. In fact, it takes us away from what we so desperately seek by being a distraction to the formation of our own connection. More and more control over others will get us what? Absolutely nothing, and certainly nowhere.

We have also forgotten the idea of the collective. We are entities *in* society, the individual and the collective mutually dependent. As one develops so does the other. As one backslides or stagnates, so does the other. To oppress another individual oppresses us all. And energy spent oppressing and controlling is energy tied up and not being used to make our own connection.

Consequently, what seriously needs to be addressed and questioned is the issue of our quest for power. This is the barn that won't keep out the rain and won't support the cows fighting to find a place - the best place - inside. The barn is falling. This is no longer a disputable point. This is "the purification." It must go. The wheels are in motion and there is no stopping it, nor is it desirable to do so. The ineffective and the spoiled must continue on the downward spiral. This is Natural Law. Likewise, what is sound and good and moral, i.e. that which is in harmony with Natural Law, will spiral forward, gathering strength as it develops. Many of us are clinging tenaciously to the status quo, this collapsing structure. Why? It doesn't work. Why even think of rebuilding it? *What is long overdue is a system that just plain does not include power struggles and control hierarchies.*

Because the old is dying is not reason to opt for a new system. To grab at a new plan in fear of being left out in the cold is missing the point also. We support a new system *because* it is our ticket home. It is an active, conscious step because it has purpose, because it gives us what we want.

Why even fight battles of oppression? Step out of that system altogether. Join forces with your sisters and create a vehicle that insures that each one of us will get home. Our power is as big as our collective effort. I am not waiting. I am going regardless of who else goes with me. You can step out of the power struggles; all you do is refuse to play the game. Think about it.

Think about your attempts to manipulate, convince, control, direct, all of which amount to a quest for power over someone, to get them to do it *your* way. What difference does it make to your spiritual development what their choices are? What are the consequences if they continue to play the competition game? Are you going to wait just because someone else chooses to keep trying to get into the barn? Suit yourself. You must wear the clothes in which you dress yourself.

INYANI

I rather like the buildings in which large fish like dolphins live. While they have social structure and clear methods of communication, there is fluidity to their lifestyle and territory, ever changing, repetitive as appropriate, but based on genuine need. Rigid boundaries are absent and free flowing adaptation to the constantly changing environment transpires naturally.

KIOKA

Here we have woman with an innate sense of knowing herself and the universe, with visions of possibilities of living in love (rather than fear). And here we have societies which tell her to follow a path that is foreign to her knowing, a path incongruous to her growth. And here we have psychological and physical punishment built into the life around her to force her compliance and to force suppression of her power.

This is not a nice story.

Growth is difficult. It naturally brings with it doubts and insecurities, the need to be recognized by others. Woman is vulnerable in the face of change. To change she needs to admit to herself all that she is from her past, all that she experiences in the moment, and all the aspirations and dreams she has for tomorrow.

Her expertise comes from the application of her knowing. She is rusty. Her confidence comes from survival of her attempts to act in ways truthful to herself. She has been taught that she doesn't have a self worthy of trust. Her understanding comes from her expansion beyond the limits of the now. She has been defined into an existence of contraction.

It is woman herself who can change the story. She can do so alone and in group. It is time for her to live her story, her spiritual story.

ELLEN

For a time I lived high on a hill in a house with a wrap-around porch. The sides of the house were mostly glass, which afforded a southwesterly view of a large saltwater pond and the ocean in the distance beyond. Frequently birds happened by to play on the wind and to feast on the beach plums.

One fall morning a lone flicker (a woodpecker) stopped on the porch. Moments later, it flew full speed into the glass, breaking its neck. As I stepped onto the porch to assess the situation, I was greeted by an eerie silence. Squatting next to the fallen bird, I determined that she was in fact dead rather than stunned. I stood up, with the knowledge clearly in mind. And then, coming from the bushes, began a chorus of hundreds of birds.

I returned to the house, planning to attend to the flicker a bit later. Morning work awaited me, and I needed a little time to think about what to do with the bird. An hour or so passed. I walked into my bedroom, one of the rooms bordering the porch, to make my bed. A female cardinal sat perched on the porch railing not two feet from the glass. When she saw me, she flew to the window, and frantically airborne, pecked several times on the glass. When she could no longer sustain

15

her position, momentarily returned to the railing. And then again, repeated the performance.

It was definitely time to get on with the funeral. (Out of the intellect and into the feeling self! Thank you cardinal.) So back onto the porch I went, to find the chorus still in melodious session. (Those birds were *waiting*, and I was determined to *make my bed*. Needless to say, I did not, at that moment, feel good about myself.)

As I picked up the dead bird, instantaneous silence filled the air. Carefully cradling her in my hands, I walked around the yard. A little healing to help her transition, although certainly her friends were doing quite a magnificent job. Should I bury her? Should I put her on the ground? Nothing seemed quite right until I neared a scrub oak. And then I simply knew she needed to go back into a tree. So gently I placed her in a vee. Slowly bird noises resumed, but not the chorus as before. The birds did stay in the bushes for a few more hours, conversing in their usual tones, eventually flying away in dribs and drabs.

An occurrence such as this does not easily lend itself to an intellectual or rational explanation. Yet it was quite real. My response based upon an intellectual interpretation would have been highly inappropriate. In fact, to the extent that my prioritizing placed morning activities above the presenting situation, I *did* operate from the head rather than from the heart. Had the birds not had a different agenda, and had I failed to honor the cardinal's message, I would have been unable to appreciate my role in the greater scheme of the morning.

Woman's feeling self has been silenced by the intellect. Women have always acted as I did with the flicker, yet have done so quietly, secretly, and too often after an attempted repression by "rational" thought. Never do we admit to such "craziness" without at least a giggle of apology. But the *elimination* of what lives in places beyond the range of the intellect is not easily accomplished. In fact, it is ultimately impossible to achieve.

MAJAI

Women came into this earthwalk with an innate knowledge. There has always existed in us a feeling of "just knowing." We have recognized too that all other women are aware of it. It goes without saying, yet it is a fact we are enough comfortable with that we do speak of, we joke of its absence in men, and we take for granted. A quality of secretiveness surrounds this subject. We identify the existence of "knowing," yet it remains specifically undefined and not well articulated.

It is something that belongs to a world of generalizations.

We know that we know. Yet frighteningly we also know that we don't know, that there is something more to know than what we do know and it escapes us. We dare not speak even to ourselves of what we miss. It is a devastating lack. By admitting the lack, does it make it more real? Does it make it bigger? This lack brought to consciousness has a rather unsettling effect upon us. It becomes an annoyance like an itch, and after a time grows in size until its resolution becomes a necessity.

What am I talking about? I am talking about woman returning to her roots, to the place where she has total knowledge of herself as part of the universe. The "knowing" I speak of is but a glimpse of this connectedness. We see that a connection exists between ourselves and something greater, that it is common to all women, and even that it somehow connects us *to* all other women. This is correct.

We fear facing the connectedness we lack. If we do, it instantly becomes a longing, an obsession that cannot be distracted. How many times have you asked yourself something, and found the answer to be "I don't know?" And how many times have you felt with the "I don't know" answer a vague (or not so vague) feeling of failure at not knowing? And worse, that you know it is possible to have the answers to all questions? The intellect says, "I can't possibly know everything." The heart says, "Of course I can. It's free for the taking. I have forgotten how to enter into that place of knowledge, and I do not particularly like myself for being in this spot of forgetfulness."

The path of woman is one of going *inside* to meet the vastness of the universe. There exists the all. We go inside to merge with what is greater. Visually it is an impossibility. Intellectually we cannot find a place for something that is greater than we are, yet is inside of us; it is a contradiction. Do you have a problem with this? Or does your intellect have a problem with what I say? Feel as you go into your depths the limitlessness of this space and of the possibilities. It is a place to which you have unconditional access. No one can stop you from going there. The only limits are your own denial of the existence of this place, your own choice not to go there, and your inability to feel.

This is not a mind-game. This is part of the Dream. The Dreams are born of this place, come through us and live external to us. Yet where they live can be accessed by going inside. Some Dreams have been dreamt. They await fruition. The Dream of the oneness of the female energy has been created. It is there to be joined with. *The reason you feel the connectedness between your sisters in the "knowing" is due to the reality of the Dream; we experience a common reality, the Dream. Because we all go to a common place, we share common experience;*

17

this allows for the knowledge that all women "know" as I know.

Do you understand? I want you to understand. To understand you must come from your heart and feel. When you do you will own the reality of my words. All love.

ELLEN

We are striving to make feeling the basis from which we operate. Upon that, we as women add intellect. The two will come into balance with feeling predominating. However, what we face today is a state of affairs where scientific thought and the intellect have exclusive rights to our experience.

In this world it is only allowable to intellectualize and rationalize a compartment within which feeling can exist. Experience is valid only to the extent that it can hold its own in the intellectual arena. The free flow of feelings is *certainly* weak and dangerous and unsound!

This *must* change for our growth is suffocating.

MAJAI

When people have lost their connection to their universal energy, be it yin or yang, they live in a state of fear. It is fear of not being able to swim. They exist in the ocean of the universal energy but remain separate from it. Because of the separation, one minute they will find that they are in harmony, and the next that they are not. The interaction between person and universe is random. Possibly they happen to be in a position to ride the waves, or possibly to be crashed by them. No wonder they fear. They lack understanding of what is greater than themselves as well as self-determination.

It is difficult for such a person of disconnection to see others in a state of connectedness. They fear their own lost connection, and no longer are they able to rationalize that it is the way of all people to be disconnected.

Our power and our self control stem from the existence of the connection. The link with the universe enables us to understand and know the waves, to know when to ride, when to swim, when to surrender, and when to push on. The only way anyone can have power over us is by keeping us from feeling our link. *If we don't know ourselves in the universal context we are powerless. This is our only enemy: failure to know who we are and what our path is.* If we have even a glimpse of "knowing that we know," anyone will be hard pressed to keep us down. Increased awareness of the existence of our knowing fosters its growth. A foot in the door easily becomes a leg in the door. Once we start moving, there is no stopping us.

Silence and isolation from each other are dangerous. They are the instruments of our oppressors to prevent our self-empowerment. Remember this. It is why we must risk speaking out loudly and clearly. Awareness cannot be dispossessed. Knowledge cannot be taken away. Once we have seen, we cannot forget.

Very importantly we need to recognize that no one except ourselves is going to encourage us forward on our spiritual paths. There are many who, for one reason or another, don't want us to travel. It is not realistic to wait for one's oppressors to voluntarily and joyfully open the gates to our freedom. There are many women as well as men who are heavily invested in maintaining and promoting our disconnection, as are the established systems and hierarchies. Do not wait for the approval and permission of those who get mileage from our ignorance. They will never give it, you can be sure.

MAJAI

So far our journeys have seemed to have been solitary journeys. Although we believe there are other women traveling as we are, we rarely if ever have direct contact with them. The situation is beginning to change. And as more and more of us are willing to speak up, all of us will come to see that there is much support for our efforts and our work.

By traveling unrecognized, each of us has gained strength to continue despite difficulties, and has increased her conviction about the correctness of her path. It was a necessary part of our development, individually and collectively, to learn to build stamina, courage, and conviction while thinking we were alone. Each of us has come to own her path. And now we know we must travel our own path even if no one else travels hers. The strength that is now possible as we do come into union with other women is great because each of us grew individually and separately.

There is no more benefit to be gained from remaining separate. In fact some of our sisters have fallen or have started to fall away from lack of group support. This too was a necessary step and part of the purification. We had to learn our capabilities as individuals as well as to face our weaknesses. Those of us who are moving forward know it, and are better equipped to assess strengths and deficiencies because of this process. It is no longer necessary to travel alone. And now, because of the support we will increasingly feel, the journey will become easier. Trust this.

ANJA

It is important to know we exist in group. The support of women who understand our goals and thus our struggles to attain those goals can give us courage, even in the face of opposition. The opposition is our own resistance to taking our power. And it is the resistance of others to us: women as well as men. All resistance stems from fear. Acknowledge this fact. But endless analysis of it will keep you too occupied to go beyond it. Use the knowledge that other women think as you do, travel as you do, fear and love as you do, to find the courage to surpass your boundaries.

You do not need her standing physically next to you to make this connection. That connection is quite real even beyond the mental confines of the physical plane. Perhaps this book is nothing more than a little announcement: We are here and we know you! Won't you please recognize us, and take our support?

MAJAI

There are several "layers" of vibration surrounding (and infusing) this planet, this solar system, and other planetary systems. The vibration of each "layer" becomes progressively finer as the physical distance from the center increases. The density of physical matter decreases as the rate and frequency of vibration increases. Eventually the density reaches a point where "physical" existence can no longer be sustained. This is what I call the "non-physical." It is quite possible for entities such as yourselves to progress to exist beyond the physical.

Some entities in "spirit" form (as we call it) have physical qualities, although their physicalness varies in density depending upon evolutionary development. Entities who have not completed planetary (such as earthplane) incarnations, when in spirit form, have physical characteristics very much like those they held while on earth. When these spirit entities present to incarnated entities, they show form.

An entity who has evolved beyond the need to incarnate drops certain of these forms, but still has a density that holds much physicalness, although more subtle than previously. At the end of the physical spectrum, entities exist as color and sound.

The communication and guidance from spirit people with which most of you are familiar, occurs with entities existing in these physical layers. While they may be in spirit form, they are quite physical and identify with much the same vibration you do.

Until the spring of 1987, non-physical entities had not entered into the proximity of the earth. The intensity of the yin energy reached a height that allowed the first "layer" of non-physical entities to ride in to exist simultaneously with the physical. These entities are not of the same time and space familiar to those of you on the earth, nevertheless, in your terms, have moved in to join you. They actually came because they are part of the vibration that is infusing the universe. They are here by definition of the rate and frequency of their vibration. They are everywhere this vibration is. They existed prior to this time, but not in your space, as their concentration of yin was too great to move them into the territory of the physical.

These entities are instrumental in guiding the purification. They are female. They are the yin vibration. They are one with the universal energy of woman, yet they are still self-willed beings. Remember that they are non-physical entities. They are free of both sound and color. They exist as varying intensity of the yin energy, in its pure form.

The second "layer" of non-physical is where I exist. It is the outermost "layer" of non-physical vibration that has the capacity to interact directly with the physical. While I am no longer physical, I am still capable of decreasing the rate and frequency of my vibration to temporarily include color and sound.

Communication has recently begun with those beyond where I am. It is possible only via those incarnated *women* who can transcend the physical, move into the non-physical "layers," and then ride out on the yin vibration to meet them. This is the same as going inside of yourself to get outside, to go far enough to meet the vastness of the universe by internalization.

The purification we are experiencing will culminate when the earth becomes so infused with the yin vibration that it moves into the next "layer" toward the non-physical. The earth's density will decrease to one of sound and color. It will cease to be "incarnate," will cease to be in the physical form we now experience. To ride with it beyond its current density, we too must become the vibration of the next state.

The physical bodies of those who have yet to finish physical incarnations will die as previously, and the entities will move to other places to continue the incarnation process. Those who have finished the need to incarnate will cease to exist in their present densities and forms; this will be a gradual process as they come to live more and more beyond the earth's current density. As the purification progresses and in the years to follow the major earth changes, the earth's density will decrease even more to continue to harmonize with the accumulating yin. And eventually the planet will transform into the non-physical.

And so, my sisters, we have much material to cover to familiarize you with the tools to aid your transformation, a transformation which will parallel that of the earth. You are yin, the earth is yin, and so it is a matter of raising your vibration as the universal vibration of women (yin) intensifies. The earth can be your focal point during the process.

AMNA

I can see that some of you have already thrown yourselves into panic at the idea of leaving your physical forms. It didn't take long did it? One of the reasons this book is being written by women in spirit (plus Ellen of course) is to show you how ordinary growth beyond your present state really is. All of us have been exactly where you are, and amazingly have lived to tell of our transformations! Here we are, whole and functioning, writing a book! But more importantly, we are still just regular women, developing as usual. So do not be afraid.

INYANI with ANJA and KIOKA

With development vibration quickens, and this in turn affects the manifestation and interaction possibilities for an entity. At each level there is a typical range of operation, a distance into slower vibrations the entity can travel. It is not possible to extend into faster vibrations than your own, so communication with more evolved entities requires their visitation of you. The following is a basic outline of the continuum of vibration relevant to our present purposes.

People on the earth with physical bodies
I   Those whose need to incarnate is yet incomplete. Subsequent return/s to the earth or comparable environments will follow the present incarnation. These entities are in physical form because they are of a vibration which readily manifests in this density. They have the ability to change their vibration to A^1 or A^2 for communication purposes. (See below.)

II   Those at the end of their incarnation need. All prior aspects of these entities will unify before their exit from the current body, and the individual will then go to A^2 or B. For communication purposes, they have the ability to change their vibration to the vibration of A^1, A^2 or B.

III (Exception) In this case, the person's vibration is variable. The body was taken for the good of the collective, but can only be existent in conjunction or cooperation with an entity of the B vibration. These entities have the ability to change vibration to the vibration of their natural residence (the place the entity originated). The range of operation is variable depending upon purpose, work and simultaneous forms. (Grace Walking Stick and Ellen fit this category.)

Spirit

Physical Form exists but of lesser density and of faster vibration than people incarnated on the earth. They can communicate directly with incarnated entities independent of the incarnated person's participation.

A^1 The need for subsequent incarnations remains.

A^2 No further need to incarnate exists.

B   Physical form has decreased its density to sound and color. (This simultaneously with III, was the location of Grace Walking Stick. "Grace" will hold part of herself in this vibration as long as is necessary to allow Ellen to be incarnated.)

Non-physical Form is known only in terms of the concentration of yin of the entity. The density has decreased and the vibration increased relative to spirit holding physical form.

C^1 This is a transition state between physical and non-physical. The entity is still attached psychologically to the physical and hasn't yet made the full transition in terms of consciousness. Here exists the ability to communicate directly with A^1, A^2, B, and with I or II if I or II is able to change to the A^2 vibration. (Dytoianta is here.)

C^2 Identification with non-physical is well established, but the entity can still communicate directly with physical spirit entities (A^1, A^2, and B) and with physical people if the person can change to B (sound and color). (Majai exists here.)

D   The entity can communicate with B if B is receptive. And with B's cooperation, can then communicate with A^1, A^2 and other Bs. (Gyta is here.)

E   Communication can happen directly with C^2 and D only. (Inyani resides here.)

F   Here exists the ability to communicate directly with E only.

23

G Communication can happen directly only with entities in F. (Amna's place of residence.)

Beyond G a new category should rightfully be made. Entities henceforth are not able to communicate directly with anyone of slower vibration than their own, as doing so would involve a contradiction of their own forward motion. To intentionally slow amounts to the same thing as resistance. To go "backward" at all delays progress. (Anja is here, as is Kioka. Kioka is a bit farther along than Anja.)

KIOKA

There are a few apparent discrepancies in our outline upon which I would like to comment. We have said that it is not possible to extend into, thus communicate with, a vibration that is faster than your own. We have said that spirit people have faster vibrations than do incarnated people, but that incarnated people can communicate with spirit. We also have said that a category I can communicate with an A^2. Rather than being true contradictions, we have situations which are difficult to explain in earthplane terms.

Because a spirit person does not have a physical body of earthplane density, s/he is able to vibrate slightly faster than an entity of comparable developmental level who is on the earth. Were s/he to take a body, the vibrations of the two entities and levels would become essentially equal.

The developmental levels of people in I and II are not tremendously different. Likewise, entities in A^1 and A^2 do not differ greatly. The A^1 and A^2 categories can be seen as the spirit counterparts to I and II, all four really being of the same territory.

A category I normally is confined to communication with an A^1, and a II to an A^2. However, there are times when a I can communicate with an A^2, or a II with a B. At the conclusion of a certain level, one ceases to be the former vibration and begins to become the vibration of the new level. So upon approach to a new level, it is possible to begin communication with entities of that new level. This is only possible at the transition points; an entity in the middle of a vibratory category does not have such an option, however.

Sometimes travel via growth from one category to the next happens very quickly. It is not the case that a particular amount of time necessarily needs to be spent at any one stage. All of us can move as fast as we are willing. Many women are moving very quickly now, thus transitions between two places will *seem* to be miles apart from one another.

AMNA

It is not possible to describe characteristics associated with any of the non-physical vibrations, for characteristics understood to physical entities do not exist in the non-physical. So it is easiest to simply be aware of the range of operation of entities in each vibrational state.

How does communication happen then with entities from my location, for instance? It can happen only when the incarnated entity can change her vibration to meet the vibration of these entities. Since an entity cannot extend beyond her own degree of expansion, necessarily a level III incarnated entity is required to make such a connection.

It is important to mention briefly here (more will be given later) that communication found in "channeling" and "trance mediumship" involves spirit people of the A^1, A^2, and B levels *only*. In these cases the spirit entity changes his or her vibration to synchronize with the vibration of the incarnated entity. So it is possible for a spirit person to communicate regardless of developmental level, physical condition (health), or participatory consciousness of the incarnated entity (levels I or II). The spirit person could be of higher or lower vibration than the incarnated.

Communication, although less well known at the present time, is also possible when the incarnated (I or II) changes her vibration to meet an A^1 or A^2. This we will talk about later.

ELLEN

Developmental level and functional range is largely determined by the presence and amount of resistance to spiritual pathward motion. Our inabilities reflect our existing resistance, and our abilities our forward or pathward motion. None of us actually passes through stages or into categories, as we would through a gate. At any given moment progress is therefore a bit fluctuant, even while we may "average" at a certain vibration.

Further, expansion is not linear. To me we are like pulsating globs of energy, refining to grow and to travel into increasingly less dense living quarters. Just as we are alive, so is our expansion. It breathes, molds, and fits environments through which we pass.

KIOKA

The "levels" we speak of are not levels of achievement. They are degrees of refinement, of individual purification and of simplification. I think it would be advantageous to refrain from viewing your growth process as one of accomplishment, achievement or status to which pride could be applied. These are all concepts of competitive systems.

Rather, see your growth process as one of relinquishment of excess to uncover your essence. That essence is of comparable value to everyone else's essence. Each of us is innately equal with identical core purity of essence. We carry material extraneous to that purity, thus our process is one of simplification or reduction in order to increase our awareness of our sameness, not of specialness. Thus we actually become less accomplished, less proud, less extraneous. We aim to settle quietly into the pureness at our centers, which will turn out to be incredibly vast.

When we said that I was actually a bit farther along than Anja, it is that I have realized my sameness a bit more than Anja has realized hers. Because this means I am less extraneous, in one sense I am actually smaller and less fancy. And, I might add, would likely go more easily unnoticed in a crowd than would Anja.

ELLEN

You may wonder how, given the limitations of communication between vibrations and the ranges all of us include, this book was written. Majai began by communicating with me. Once the thoughts became manifest (put on paper), they were made available to the others by my retention of them as I traveled into the others' vibrations. If I read the written words as I traveled into the other vibrations, the words became available to anyone in that vibration.

The book was actually written in layers, with each spirit woman contributing based upon her own assessment of need relative to what had previously been written. Each woman communicated with me, as well as with any of the other women within her range.

Given the presence of my physical body, I have reached the limit of my range. Were I to extend beyond Kioka's vibration (which equals my current vibration), I could not stay in my body. A woman's range of operation is dependent upon her individual vibration (her essential energy plus the baggage or impurities she carries); with expansion that range increases. At any given moment, her span is fixed.

Her range extends from herself in one direction into slower vibrations and in the other, into faster vibrations. An addition to either end requires a subtraction from the other end. Disharmonious surroundings add to the slower end, or extend her range into slower vibration. The presence of an entity of faster vibration than her own, for example, adds to the faster end of the continuum.

Given the conditions contrary to Natural Law on the earth, the only way I can maintain balance while spanning the distance from the physical plane into Kioka's vibration, is to carefully control my environment. This is an attempt to keep the slower end of the continuum constant; I accommodate the faster vibration by eliminating as much disharmony as possible. Nevertheless, my body is awfully quick to reflect disharmony but equally responsive to its rectification. Necessarily I am a constantly fluctuant state of being.

By standing in the middle of New York City, I add to the slower end of my capacity. Were I to insist upon communicating with Kioka in New York City, something would have to give at the other end, and that something would be my body. Thus while in New York City, Kioka would be blessed with a vacation from my questions.

These principles apply to all women, regardless of range or what vibrations that range includes. The growing woman is continually expanding her range. The growing woman in disharmonious surroundings limits her expansion capabilities by keeping weights on the slower end of the continuum. Thus, by choosing your environment and your interactions, you can maximize your potential for growth. (We have more to say on these subjects later on.)

ELLEN

At a certain point (according to need) in an entity's development, she divides into several parts, usually four. Each part is thereby free to incarnate independently of the others and without conscious knowledge of the others, enabling her to learn diverse or contradictory lessons. Since we do not only learn in body or on this planet, the parts are thus able to exist simultaneously and overlap in terms of time, space and form. *All parts are developmentally equal* regardless of form or location.

Balance and alignment as well as decreased resistance to development occur with growth. Prior to the time the entity becomes sound and color (or moves into B), the four parts must once again merge. Oneness of a sort is regained. The illusion of separation dissolves, and awareness of all the forms (perhaps greater than 100) grows. This means all forms taken in all previous lifetimes and times in spirit cease their individual and separate identities. All forms realign to allow the entity to exist as a unified whole, rather than as an entity of disjointed parts.

Entities who incarnate voluntarily often divide similarly to maximally utilize their abilities, and to partially diffuse the total intensity of their energy (access to the universal). They take form as determined primarily by the need of the collective.

My experiences with Grace Walking Stick are with the entity of which Grace Walking Stick was a part. A piece of her entity incarnated voluntarily as Grace Walking Stick to do certain work. The rest of her entity remained elsewhere. Because of her developmental level she was able to be who she needed to be at any given moment or in any given place. Her work still requires that she hold onto her physical forms, but soon these too will go and she will exist completely in her vibration in the non-physical.

It is not accurate to call her Grace Walking Stick now, since she relinquished that body a few years ago. She can best be known as just Grace. To me she has always been the entity of Grace, as I did not even know the physical aspect of her Grace Walking Stick form. In other words, she and I never met in our bodily forms.

To me her form is ever changing according to what situations or moods require. She and I have been the best of friends for a long, long time. Our connection has evolved through various planetary and spirit walks of many forms. Our friendship has been tested and tried, sabotaged and nurtured under quantities of conditions. We have been in many roles relative to one another, at times working together from places of different form, and at others from places of same form. Certainly we have our favorite arrangements!

Some of our experiences are offered in this book with hope that you will be able to grow from them. We have a commitment to each other's spiritual progress unlike either of us has experienced with another entity. We have our hard times, of course, and we occasionally come up against the limits of our courage. (Occasionally, I wish!) We have needed help from other women. We have needed time to flail around, weep and scream and holler. But always we have trusted in the honesty and sincerity with which we pursue a common goal. We have come to trust in Natural Law, and in our ever growing knowledge that if we act from our hearts and are truthful to our feelings and to each other, it is possible to do anything or to go anywhere. Our friendship has weathered incredible storms, and some of these we will tell you about.

MAJAI

Friendships such as that of Grace and Ellen are rare. Normally entities do not interact for such extended time periods or over so many changes of form. But the two of them keep getting themselves in deeper and deeper, and one thing leads to another! Not always are they making messes. Much of their work is an extension of their previous work. There is no reason to cut off a good thing. So, as long as they are able to grow and move forward independently of one another, their interaction can continue. At times it has been necessary for them to separate. At others each is precisely what the other needs to move ahead. Usually they make the equation that gets results.

ANJA

As Grace Walking Stick, Grace operationally was not at all confined to her body. Her roles, functions, and presentations were nearly as diverse and as numerous as the people who knew her, ranging from her position as head seeress for an intertribal medicine society to her work for social change. The majority of her work was with circles of women unbound to the earthplane, yet whose purposes were key to the preparations for the currently unfolding earth changes as part of the larger universal transformation.

Her intervibrational experience is vast. Her facility of movement between vibrations is exceptional. But of greatest value to us at this stage in the transformation, is her understanding of and experience with the struggles of women as they journey spiritually. We face extraordinarily difficult situations in our attempts to expand as women, and Grace's appreciation of the intervibrational scope of these difficulties offers us unique help in facilitating our progress.

GRACE

I was Grace Walking Stick. Now I am Grace. I want to tell you about some of my experiences in that form and in others. My time as Grace Walking Stick does not appear to be altogether pleasant or fortunate, however, this was *absolutely* my last opportunity to incarnate on the Mother, and I needed to make good use of the time and the body.

I chose to incarnate voluntarily, so I could work and so I could clean up some old imbalances I had created. There were other ways to do this but I chose another earthwalk for several reasons. The earth is in need of all the help it can get. I have many ties to this planet from my many journeys here, but more significantly I know the earth and how it lives, as if it is part of me.

All the forms I had previously taken as an entity had merged before I came. I was thus able to have abilities allowed by embodied form as well as abilities allowed by spirit form. I was not confined by the limitations of the body, was able to experience physical suffering, function on the earth as Grace Walking Stick, and function as if an entity in spirit. I was a Dreamer, as long as I held to physicalness, and this was another reason I chose an earthwalk to do my work at this time.

My work centered around organization and consolidation of the yin. I held many positions or roles, but they are not important except for the fact that they all were to consolidate yin, on this plane and others. I feel I was not as strong or as forceful in advocating my positions as I could have been. I compromised too easily and so still feel a need to continue my work for women on this earth. That is why you find me in this book! I never thought I'd see the day, as books are not much my style!

I like to tell stories, though. My stories are true stories. Stories need to take different forms, to match the different sides and colors of our lives. This first one is a serious story about something I am learning. I wish I could tell it in the past, but this one lives in the present and the future too. It is something I have been working on for a long time, too long it seems sometimes, but really just as long as it takes for me to get it.

Looking backward I see clearly that I did much to avoid tension and to maintain harmony. Any change of direction needs tension for it to come to pass. Even the seasons are full of tension. You see it in big ways when the tides are high or the moon is full. When the energies are very, very full or very, very empty, sometimes we see. But in smaller ways, you do not usually see, I think. Does the dry leaf always fall to the ground in autumn? Sometimes the spring growth needs to encourage the old leaf to let go. Is this not true? Tension is not bad, and it is not the opposite of harmony, I have learned.

For hundreds of years, and in many circles, all of us have been working to get our feet firmly planted in the yin. It has been difficult with all those yangs running around! But this is just an excuse, and one of my old time favorites! I did a lot for the cause of accommodating the yangs. They were never satisfied because I still didn't play their yang games. And the yins were planted too shallowly, because my energy was split between the yins and the yangs. I saw these mistakes as they progressed, but failed to have the courage to take action to correct some of them.

Perhaps I was afraid to make waves. I was afraid to act in ways that might seem disharmonious. I thought I was acting in ways that would avoid the creation of more tension. Really I was trying to avoid facing tension that already existed.

Now I walk in different circles of women. And now my step is sure and strong. We are running out of time and I see now that it is all or none. No longer can I compromise on the importance of sowing my seeds to the proper depth in the proper fields. No longer can I waste energy placating the yangs. No longer can I be afraid of feeling the tension from the imbalances that have been created, especially by men.

I speak my mind. I do not apologize for my positions. I am ready, finally, to move without hesitation, and just as I no longer have patience with my own avoidance, I no longer have patience with yours. I push and I push hard. I am glad I am finally able to do this.

I am a separatist. My path has taken me farther and farther from men. This is inevitable. I am female energy. This too I will not apologize for. To do so is an attempt to appease the yangs or to deny the imbalances. Have the courage to be who you are, to own your path as a woman. Lots of women will not want to hear this, nor hear it from me.

Are we so much defined by male ways, male lifestyle, male thinking, male supremacy, that we must accommodate them by compromising our spirituality? Does your fear of rejection by men become your reason to deny your essential nature? Are you afraid to stand in your own nature? I was. And in my circles of women I was. I had the option of taking stronger stands for women many times. I did not take them, out of fear of male reaction. But now I stand stronger and deeper as a woman myself. I am learning. The story will continue for some time yet. But now I walk in a new chapter. And this chapter is "for women only."

Don't wait for the group of women to get strong enough to carry you. It doesn't work that way. It carries only those who carry themselves. You have two feet. Use them to join me on my walk. Love.

MAJAI

We go external to ourselves to create. Accumulation results from continual creation. It is a process of adding more. This is the male way. In this system worth is measured by the ability to externalize the self in order that increased quantity result. The self becomes greater in size by the process of externalization. This is "bigger is better" thinking.

Women have learned to externalize, and some of us are quite adept at doing so. The natural process for women, however, is internalization. As I mentioned previously, to go to increasing depths to merge with the universal energy is the process of internalization. It is not that we are not capable of externalizing, rather that the path of least resistance for women is internalization.

The result of internalization is the opposite of accumulation and increasing quantity. As we develop we need less and less, and eventually we come to not need even the physical. We find that we need fewer objects external to us. We are even comfortable decreasing the density of our bodies. As we come to actually live in the depths of ourselves, what is external loses its value and importance. This is the direction we must move in order to develop spiritually, in order to find harmony with the yin.

It is not an obligation or a duty. It is what comes most easily and naturally to us. There is no problem or effort in relinquishing that which we no longer need or have use for. And this process for individual women will parallel the process of change the earth is undergoing. Not only is the earth changing in this way, but the entire universe.

What will happen to men? It is time for them to learn their yin natures, the part of themselves that is yin, just as women have learned their yang, external capabilities. Change is the nature of the universe. Flexibility and pliability are how we enable ourselves to exist in change. Rigidity and resistance to change make us brittle and set us at odds with the prevailing universal forces. Men will need to back down from their externalizing mode in order to be flexible enough to avoid a head-on collision with the yin. It is a posture of humility and respect. Just as women are capable of externalizing, men are capable of internalizing. We have learned respect for the yang, but now, with this knowledge and respect, must travel the path that is ours.

How men choose to see and deal with the energetic changes is their business. We have no responsibility to their process or to the fact of their participation in their process. To focus on their path and their growth potential is irrelevant to our growth as women. It is not our job to see that they find a way to cope with the increasing yin. Our obligation is to take care that we do justice to our own spiritual growth. That is our business. Their business is to attend to their spiritual growth.

The men and women who cling to the mode of externalization will have great difficulty, and increasingly great difficulty as time goes on. They will find themselves consumed by a state of resistance, tension, and exhaustion. Physical illness and mental deterioration will be prevalent.

We must remember that our obligation is to make sure we are doing our work. Reactions to our doing so will at times be very ugly. Fear will be rampant: fear of woman harmonizing, fear of women harmonizing, fear of being lost, fear from the increased physical and mental tension, fear of just about everything.

We must stay tuned to the yin, that we not get distracted by the further degradation and deterioration we will see around us. The opposite of fear is love and as we become more and more at home in the yin, and come to know our sisters who live there with us, the love will be breathtaking. We *will live* in peace and harmony despite the chaos around us, despite the disharmonious choices of others. What I say here is critically important: learn where your center is, and how to be in it every minute, while functioning amidst the chaos. You are the yin. Know yourself. Feel.

MAJAI

Many of us are accustomed to seeking advice, opinions, approval, guidance, information, and direction from other people. Not only do we seek it, we use it as a basis for our decisions and actions. We have come to empower "the other" rather than ourselves. Even if we make an independent decision, too frequently it is contingent upon evaluation by another.

And many times the other is a male. Some of female and male experience does indeed overlap, but most of it does not. (Today we do not appreciate the differences between the sexes as positive. Any move toward unisex is ultimately not possible, and requires a negation of the natural evolutionary processes of both women and men.)

Although my concern is women's spiritual development, it is not possible to separate it from women's perspective and orientation to all earthplane (and other plane) experience. Spiritual development necessarily includes all actions and thoughts as well as approaches to and perspectives on every aspect of a woman's life. When a person's spiritual development is her primary goal and purpose, *all* else either contributes to or detracts from that aim. And so when I speak of the importance of coming to appreciate the differences between women and men, my reason is to enable us to better direct our efforts to our individual spiritual growth.

It is obvious that men hold most positions of authority: political, social, and economic. I do not underestimate the actual roles of women for one moment, but practically speaking men have the decision making power and the final say in just about every aspect of life today. The situa-

33

tion has begun to change in certain areas and this is good. There are many strong women who are no longer willing to give away their own power, especially to men. Slow to change however, are spiritual and religious matters. The absence of role models for women has contributed. (And why is there an absence of visible women saints and leaders?) The religious institutions worldwide are deeply and firmly established in the social structures, politics, and economics of all countries. It is here that men have their stronghold. So it follows that men too control the religious and spiritual arenas.

Fighting the male institutions and systems is an absurdity. But more importantly, to fight invests energy, even if it is contrary and disruptive in application, in the existing systems. We fuel what we oppose by our resistance. This is an important principle to understand and remember. Again, we must find solutions that do not participate in or interact with the status quo in any way. Again, the answer is to step aside, not ahead or behind, and create what we feel is desirable and necessary. This too will cause tension and reaction, but far less than an attempt to change the existing male institutions and hierarchies. *The idea is not to have a battle to prove winners and losers, it is to find ways to foster our own development.*

Most important for women to realize is the crucial need to create vehicles, for ourselves as individuals as well as for the collective, that facilitate and promote our spiritual development. We will continue to lose sight of *our* business if we continue to empower "the other," and especially if we continue to empower men. We *must* take charge of our own spirituality. Default on this responsibility has hurt our progress dearly. It must stop.

The male saints, religious leaders, and masters have done little for women's spiritual progress other than to re-identify certain principles of morality. To some extent women have been able to use these teachings, but only the teachings that pertained to both female and male development. *Perhaps* these men have been successful at illuminating the way for men, beyond the teachings on morality. They have definitely not done so for women, nor can they be expected to have done so. Men do not have access to the knowledge and understanding that we need, so are unable to impart it.

But the teachings of the men are all we have had to work with, short of going inside ourselves for the answers. Some women have done just that, because of frustration, because of longing, because of not being heard in the existing systems, because of aching memories of another way. But many have been afraid even to entertain *an idea* of going beyond the popular teachings, never mind to take action to do so.

34

Built into all these systems, philosophies and institutions are threats of dire consequences from questioning the systems, questioning or doubting the master, or venturing forth on one's own. This is a time worn tactic to oppress, yet we still fall for it. Such thinking devalues our innate senses and capabilities. It keeps us herded and organized and functioning in unison. And it may or may not foster our spiritual growth, depending upon our state of evolution. Independence, self-determination, and autonomous thought are contrary to these social/religious institutions. Is the truth so fragile that it cannot stand up to rigorous questioning and doubt? Is it impossible for an entity to grow beyond the developmental level of such an institution or a particular teacher? Many of us have entered this earthwalk at levels far beyond the levels of these concretized structures.

In male systems, men ride on top of the hierarchies. Is it not the case that women are *not allowed* to hold positions of spiritual authority in these religious institutions? (Who is it who is in the positions to allow or disallow?) Gender is the primary qualifying factor, rather than spiritual consciousness and development, for such positions. In a system of mutual respect and acknowledgement, fights and struggles are non-existent. Women would not have to fight for these positions if an inherent discrepancy in value and worth of women and men did not exist. If men hold the positions, do they not then control the content of the information disseminated?

I need not continue in this vein. The point is that women as developing spiritual entities have not been and are not represented in the current religious structures in the world today. Not only do we lack representation, more importantly, we are not basic to the framework of these institutions. The result is that neither do we control our own development, nor do we have autonomy anywhere within the systems. Oppression of women as well as ignorance of women's spiritual path is blatantly obvious, yet many of us continue to invest in and depend upon just these systems to carry us along our paths. This is ridiculous.

It is time to step away from the male institutions. No need to hate or disparage these institutions, but there is a sore need to acknowledge their inappropriateness to women's growth. And then, to find methods and ways that do work for us. *It is high time we empowered ourselves, rather than male religious institutions and male role models.*

As we make choices for ourselves, especially in the beginning, we will make mistakes, but we will also achieve what we intend. And the act of making our own choices, in and of itself, takes us further along our path. Long overdue is reinforcement for these efforts regardless of their outcomes. Long overdue is the valuation of self-determination, self-reliance, and independent, creative thought. And long overdue is the appreciation that the collective will *benefit* rather than suffer for such an approach.

ELLEN

There are many things women have been taught or have chosen to believe that are good for male development, but that are either not good for female development or inapplicable. It is unfair to put the blame entirely on men, for we must be held accountable and responsible for our own choices, be they to comply, to accept, to refuse, to ignore anything that might be presented. A few simple examples of different growth requirements might help illustrate.

The placement of a body during sleep in terms of compass direction is important. Generally it is said that the head should best be to the north, the feet to the south, to maximize receptivity and clarity. I have found many spirit people in concurrence with this view, male and female.

Magnetic north causes a dispersive effect while magnetic south causes accumulation. (The north pole of a magnet placed on pain or swelling will decrease the congestion, while the south pole will add to it. Conversely, the south face of a magnet placed on an area of deficiency or obstructed energy flow will draw energy to that area, whereas the north face placed on the same spot would increase the existing shortage.) The North Pole of the earth is actually the magnetic south, and the South Pole, the magnetic north.

To place the head to the north (pole) therefore will draw energy, whereas to place the head of the body to the south (pole) will allow its release or dispersion. Were the growth processes for women ones of accumulation, a position with the head to the north would make sense. But it is not. We grow by decreasing our size. I have found far greater clarity and receptivity in my sleep states with my head to the south and my feet to the north. (And there are quite a good number of spirit women, by the way, that I have found who appreciate the benefit of this positioning.)

Gardens are commonly arranged in straight lines, parallel rows. We all learned in algebra that straight lines extend infinitely in their two directions, away from the central point. Energy traveling in a circle feeds itself, and naturally accommodates centering processes. (Counterclockwise movement, by the way, results in the gathering of energy centrally, and clockwise movement causes the energy to gather at the periphery of the circle.) The power (universal connection) I feel simply from being in my circular garden does not remotely touch my previous experiences in gardens arranged in linear patterns. Were I to wish to externalize any energy I access, rows would make sense. But I do not wish to do that. My process of growth involves internalization and centering.

Many Native peoples came to understand long ago that the workings of the earth were circular. When the aim is to harmonize with the earth (in order to harmonize with the universe), circular shapes can be conducive to the process. My father once responded when I said I wanted to live in a round house, "Furniture doesn't fit in a round house." It comes down to a question of goal.

Contradictions are logical incongruities or opposites. Contradictions simply exist. I have never found a problem with that, or felt pressed to reconcile contradictions. They simply live simultaneously in the context of their appropriate relativities. How can something be both hot and cold? It can be. It can be hot relative to something that is cooler, and cool relative to something that is hotter. And it can be so simultaneously. It does not seem necessary to me to place it into a fixed categorization, or to define it next to one "most important" relativity. My experience of the universe is fluid. It is void of clinging to find definition. It is here that contradictions are not problematic. This is female experience, not male experience.

I could probably continue for pages with similar examples. The deal is that much of what women have come to accept and believe does not fit their growth processes. And the only way we will find ways that do promote our development is to have the courage to feel, to test our assumptions, and to make changes that fit our needs. No matter how basic or fundamental a method or way seems to be, do not be afraid to question it or to examine it relative to your own spiritual process.

INYANI

Are you afraid to see the quantity of your anger at the fences that surround you and limit your mobility? Think about the long accumulated tension from being so entrapped. Anger *is* an appropriate response. Feel it and transmute it by stepping over, under, around, or through the fences. (No need to waste your energy tearing the fences down as you pass them by.) They stand in open fields in the clear air. The space is vast. Even the deer leap them at a moment's provocation. Your choice to stay is all that can keep you inside.

I want to speak a little about respect in terms of group. Respect is not the same as obedience, allegiance, duty, correct and orderly behavior, or blind deference. Commonly people are *told* to respect their elders, their boss, their parents, the group leader, a church, whatever. Respect does not result from directives.

Respect is feeling coupled with opinion, that grows in response to desirable actions or behavior. It is not possible to feel respect without consciousness of a behavior, without evaluation of an action, or without a conclusion that there was wisdom behind an effort. The recipient of your respectful feelings may never do another quality thing again, or may repeatedly become respected. But because of one such gesture, automatic respect for subsequent actions is without basis. We must constantly be accountable to perform in quality ways (which of course requires continued growth on our part). To ride on our previous accomplishments is not permissible.

Respect can and must certainly go in many directions, not just up a ladder. People appreciated in context can easily be seen to do what *for them* is very high quality work. And such an approach is so important to process in a viable group.

Dissatisfaction with male methods or the results stemming from male priorities has motivated the formation of a variety of groups of women. Yet the woman on the threshold of operating in group in the presence of only women, lacks models to follow other than male creations, some of which are the very ones she is trying to eliminate by the formation of her group. Her learning has happened within male systems, and her experience gained has been through participation in the existing hierarchial structures.

When our purposes are new, or our goals different from male goals, the old methods will not work. Method must be appropriate to goal. Method must be consistent with goal. We are in process, thus the means to an end is at least as important as the end.

So many groups, even with good intentions, sincere and dedicated efforts, and traditional competence, are falling short in terms of effectiveness and viability. Many, many dissolve after a few years in frustration, confusion, exhaustion, or exasperation, frequently following an unresolvable power struggle.

There was a group of spirit women working as overseers of health on the earth. The job of the group was to confer with women on the earth and elsewhere, in order to identify need in terms of human, animal, plant and earth health, and then to direct the efforts of other spirit women effectively to the identified need. These women were having many difficulties, among them problems with communication between planes.

Grace and Ellen have been working to clean up existing methods of intervibrational communication, and to find methods compatible with women's spiritual needs. Since each of them has extensive knowledge of healing, the group was reasonable to request their involvement. (Ellen is currently an acupuncturist and a Physician Associate/Assistant. She has been trained in crisis counseling, and works in a number of healing capacities on the earth and elsewhere.)

So they entered the group, quickly to see a rigid hierarchy within the group itself. Directives were given often without the participation of the concerned parties. Thus work, while advantageous to the group goal, did not always benefit the worker. Implementation of directives was expected without question of the women in authority.

All members were quite capable, and all had the best interest of the goal in mind, so competence or unity were not the problems. Rather, there existed problems with method. How could open, honest, bilateral communication occur intervibrationally if it was not a method within the group? If the group functioned internally in a hierarchial manner, it could not then expand to more mutual methods as it interacted elsewhere. Nor could it reasonably expect to dictate to women in other planes who were struggling to refine their own methods away from control and power oriented ways.

Glaringly absent from this group was respect for the positions of all the group members, and appreciation for each woman in a context greater than her particular jobs. We all exist in process, as does a group. The group may have a goal, and each member quite aligned with it, yet each member is simultaneously developing and growing and learning as part of the group and separate from it. Allowance for her individual process has to be made, for it is impossible to separate her from her work. She is who works. A view of the individual woman in her totality, is necessary before respect for her work could possibly occur. The idea is not to build in a place for incompetence, rather to allow each woman to continue her spiritual journey *while* she works in group.

A few adjustments rapidly occurred in this group, with the elimination of the hierarchial system altogether. Those in power do not welcome such rearrangements, nevertheless, the control of others is counterproductive to our goal as women. We cannot develop as women if we get caught in methods that are not our own, that do not foster our growth. Just as female methods are necessary to our individual progress, they are essential to collective progress. Women in group are extensions of women alone. Trust and respect of each other as well as of Natural Law are fundamental to everyone's growth, collectively and individually.

ELLEN

As women, the motivation for the formation of many of our groups has been the need for correction of the unnatural choices of men. The war games with the nuclear toys, for instance, are obviously contradictory to Natural Law. It is not wrong to seek to make balance where imbalance predominates. Certainly it is an improvement over the imbalance, whatever we do.

But this is a responsive mentality. It amounts to traveling around with a broom to clean up indiscretions or bad choices already made by someone else. Then our role exists solely in terms of the other.

By leaving control in the hands of these obviously incapable people and by trying to make good of their messes, we give away power. It is time to see that it *is* possible to act rather than to respond. We can initiate that which is compatible with our hearts. From the beginning we can create the correct and the harmonious.

What we face on the earth is an enormous garbage heap, the accumulation of defiances of Natural Law. Conditions on the earth are so bad, the broomstick routine doesn't even make a scratch in the heap. While that is not my point, it does demonstrate the absurdity of responsive behavior as the ultimate solution. My point is that when we stay within the framework of the other's choice against Natural Law by spending our efforts in rectification, we still exist as a subset of those who initiated the original action. Without the compliance of the original actor, potential for the rebalance necessarily stays under 100%. With self-initiation, potential is without limit.

Our groups can easily be motivated by our knowings and feelings, thus the application of group purpose can be outside of the context of the choices of others. This, I think, is what is going to be necessary if we intend to effect our spiritual progress as women, *especially* if we intend to effect it to our potential.

GRACE

Quite often women aim somewhere way below eye level. Do we think we will receive credit for not asking or seeking much? (Whom, by the way, might be the donor of all this unsought after credit?) If you only lift your arm 5 inches, you can't reach what's on the top shelf. Of course, you might be too short, but at least you'll know you stretched that arm as far as it would go.

Ellen has been known to plead in absolute frustration, "Why? Why can't I know?" Others have said to her, "You can't know everything, my dear, so why don't you make life easier on yourself and just give it up?" She won't. Of course she drives us all crazy seeking and seeking. But she does get, sooner or later, answers to those questions, and you can be sure, we all then want what she's got.

Whether you are in group or alone, don't sell the possibilities short. Across the board, women could do well by aiming much higher. The accomplishment of amazing things can easily happen when woman's power is allowed to collect individually or when she is part of a group. I want very much for you to aim for every last one of your dreams. And don't stop until you get them all.

KIOKA

There is a difference between being realistic and limiting the scope of our growth. We need to be realistic with what is impossible or unlikely amenable to change. We always need to keep open the possibilities for our expansion. So, what has not been realized, what has not been made real, is void of boundaries, and what has been must be faced squarely so that new aspirations can proceed from there. Without realism about the givens, our goals lack starting points.

MAJAI

For some time the surface of the earth has been reflecting the abuses it has received. The integrity and the stability of its crust is greatly compromised. No longer is the condition reversible. Nevertheless, some people are neither ready to admit the severity of the damage done nor face the consequences of the abuse. The earth is so unbalanced that it must die in its present form to be reborn on another plane.

It is painful to accept that each of us is part of the process, that we cannot detach or separate from the inevitable consequences. The transformation of the earth will parallel our individual transformations in order that both the earth and we once again come into alignment with the universal energies.

We must admit that each of us by the fact of our involvement with and participation in the existing diseased systems (be it consciously or unconsciously, voluntarily or involuntarily) are part of the cause. We cannot change the course of events or the physical conditions on this planet. And it is inappropriate to bemoan the situation, using limited time and resources to lick the/our wounds.

The solution is the very progression of the natural consequences as per Natural Law. We can participate in the solution by becoming synchronized with the events and by eliminating our resistance (physically and mentally) to its unfoldment. This includes the removal of all thoughts and actions that contradict the unfoldment.

Thoughts of denial of the state of affairs contribute resistance and fear. Concern for the individual at the expense of the collective or the larger processes forces attention and energy away from the solution. Fears of pain, injury, or death keep identification on the physical body. Relinquishment of responsibility or blame of others are diversionary tactics. *To see the physical events as necessary and positive is essential to harmonizing with the process.*

We can also become more clearly aware of the events as they do unfold. We can learn to feel the changes firsthand and deeply. This will help us psychologically and physically to be prepared, as our aim is to be able to maintain our center as the changes progress. To do this we necessarily must attune to the earth itself, to feel the yin energy as it pulses through the earth.

To feel another (be it a person, someone in spirit, a stone, a plant, the earth, whatever) we need to let go of our own program (our vibration) long enough to become the other, in order to experience the other. We change our vibration to match the vibration of what we wish to read or feel.

Once we do let go, we must have a way to experience the object of perception. And women have two ways of doing this: by feeling either the sound or the color of the other. Very early in our evolutionary process we found an affinity for either sound or color, and began developing our skills of perception accordingly. It is narrow thinking to limit the perception of color to seeing or sound to hearing. To perceive we momentarily become the other and we do this with our whole being. So I say we must develop our ability to *feel* color or to *feel* sound.

My concern now is your ability to feel the earth and thus the changes that are occurring within it. As you walk on the ground, fly above its surface, visit another part of the earth (near or far), you need to begin to observe, to make comparisons, and to come to reliably interpret *for yourself* what you experience. And then come to have confidence in your interpretations enough to take action based upon them. Important to pay attention to are differences in density and clarity, presence or absence of harmony and ease, quantity of light and energy flow (in and out) at any given location. Each quality can be processed through your particular orientation be it color or sound. This skill will enable you to guide yourself on the physical plane, and help you maintain your center throughout the changes.

MAJAI

While the earth changes represent a significant transformation for the individual, the collective, the earth, and the universe, focusing on the earth changes is a mistake. It is too small. Our focus always needs to be on our spiritual development, and in this light, the earth changes represent a marker along the way. It is a major corner we will have the opportunity to turn, but please remember to see it only as one event in a vast number of events during your total development.

Perception of the earth as it transforms is important. But the extension of our ability to perceive increasingly vast arenas is progress on our spiritual paths. The act of perceiving another amounts to the same thing as the act of going into our depths to tune to what is greater than ourselves. Color and sound are still the interpretative mechanisms, as long as the object of perception has physicalness.

As we come to include larger spaces, times, and energies in our everyday lives, the opportunity for communicating with entities who exist in these vibrations presents. And so, appropriate to our discussion of internal expansion and spiritual development is information on communication with entities in other forms. The nature of the communication can vary, but some basic principles apply regardless of the type of communication, the vehicle for the communication, or the spiritual development of all parties involved.

So if you choose to communicate, two things need to be asked and answered: how and with whom?

The situation we have before us is (A) you, with a given vibration, and (B) the entity to be communicated with of a possibly differing vibration. For (A) and (B) to meet, one or the other or both must change her or his vibration. I am interested in having you remain 100% self-controlled, self-determined, self-reliant, and learn to feel your environment and those in it for yourself. You need to be capable of maintaining

43

the integrity of your being in order to control yourself. To do so you need to choose who and what enters your operational and vibrational fields.

If (B) changes to meet (A), (B) sits in the determining role, and (A) can work only in terms of (B), at (B)'s choices and actions. If (A) and (B) meet in the middle, each is both self-determined and other-determined. If (A) changes to meet (B), (A) holds the reins. And this latter case is the only situation I find satisfactory to (A)'s, to your spiritual growth.

First you need to have the ability to come and go at will *to* the vibration of another. Then you will be in a position of choosing to form a mutually satisfactory relationship with the other entity. Clarity of purpose and self-determination are the prerequisites to entering into *any* relationship. Go deep inside and feel, and you can learn to meet the vibration of any other, be she on this plane or another. (The other may or may not choose to participate with you, but you can learn to go to her limits.)

A balanced, bilateral arrangement in which both you and she control each of your participations and choices can foster your growth as well as hers. It should be a relationship of mutual respect and mutual understanding of the material given. It is important to remember that you should always control fully the extent of your participation in the relationship. You need to clearly set your limits, intentions, and commitment. If the entity is willing to meet those terms, the next step is to consider her limits, intentions, and commitment. There should be no need for compromise by either of you. She controls her involvement, you control yours, and if the two of you can come together to benefit the collective, all is well. If not, you will find that there are plenty of other entities you can consider working with. Or perhaps it means you need to find another way to work, as you continue to promote your own development.

In answer to the question of how, as far as we are concerned, there is no place for "trance mediumship," in which case (B) changes to meet (A), or "channeling," in which case a specific (B) changes to meet (A). When you are in control, you can communicate with anyone who is out there (within the limits of your vibration). It is not a matter so much of development (although certainly without it you cannot communicate), but of who maintains control of your systems. If the other entity does all the work, what does that really say about your abilities?

With whom the communication is, has to be left up to your discretion. But I will give my opinions, nevertheless. Always you should ask: what is the benefit to my growth and development from such an arrangement? Seriously and rightfully ask this question.

Downgrading your vibration, changing your vibration to one that is slower or more dense than yours can be dangerous to your development. To allow an entity of slower vibration free access to you can be even more detrimental. In almost all cases, for a woman to allow a male entity to communicate through her is serving the interests of that male entity, but not her developmental interests. (Remember, all entities have gender identification. An entity may present to you in any form or as either gender, but vibrationally is either female or male. Failure to disclose gender or claims of genderlessness is unacceptable.)

An individual's teachers and guides normally do not work with an incarnated entity in the capacity of giving information or advice to others. Since karmically their role is one of indebtedness or gratitude to you, they would not likely ask that you serve them, or be likely to participate in an arrangement that did so. They are present for your spiritual development. Your lessons and your work are two different matters. You learn by participation in what is new to you, but your work involves passing on what you have already learned to others. Your guides' primary concern is with what you need to learn, not with what you have come to give to others.

When dealing with physical realms, there is no reason for entities of higher vibration to communicate with entities of lower vibration. So even if a spirit person claims to be more advanced, he or she is of comparable vibration to your own.

Because of the earth's transformation, there *is* need for more advanced entities to help incarnated people. However, unless the incarnated is of level III, information does not come from higher than the B level. Help from higher than B level could only be given indirectly via a person's guides.

A need does not exist for vibrationally unbalanced relationships between incarnated and other entities. Part of taking our own power and always maintaining self-control and self-determination, involves learning to do so beyond the scope of the earthplane. We must not permit ourselves to be used by those in other vibrational states any more than we should by others on the earth plane.

There is a glamor (that, by the way, is especially popular at times of desperation and disaster) that is attached to communication with entities on other planes. Such communication needs to be demystified and placed once again in the realm and perspective of ordinary life. It is just not a big deal. So do not think of it as inherently special and be taken in by the spectacular. It is made possible by the expansion of the self, and is a resource that must be kept and used in perspective.

Important to remember is that entities in other forms differ only *in form* from you. There exists a wider range of developmental levels than is experienced on the earth, but within that range are still very human characteristics, the same as you experience everyday on earth. There are liars and cheaters, deceptive, fearful and self-serving immoralists of all kinds. And there are loving, competent, evolving, selfless entities of the highest quality.

So if you agree to work with or to communicate in any way with someone on this or another plane, know with whom you deal, and maintain your self-determination. Implicit in any relationship are changes as you develop. Be clear about your purpose for interaction so you can stay on your path and keep moving.

GRACE

Concurrent with the influx to the earth of entities from higher and higher vibrational states, many women have begun to realize their own natures and abilities to expand. Because of the large number of entities in the proximity of the earth, only a little bit of expansion of a woman is needed for her to become aware of the presence of another entity. This is especially true if the spirit entity crosses over into her space.

Unfortunately, many, many women have allowed the use of their systems by a now readily perceptible entity. With expansion, awareness of others is a given. A decision to interact is quite another matter. Just because she *can* do it, doesn't mean it is in her best interest *to* do it. Discrimination is a most important part of one's spiritual development. Please remember this. Just because something is for sale, do you always buy it?

"Channeling" and "trance mediumship" have become quite faddish. Initially the woman expanded and it is her change which was responsible for her gain of awareness of the other entity. However, beyond this first tiny expansion, the spirit entity is the actor. The woman is what is acted upon.

Some women have the wherewithal to set limits as to time, duration, or methods of "channeling" or "trance mediumship" and for this they should be commended. However, as Majai explained, it is a situation where the woman lacks control and places herself at the mercy, the discretion or lack of discretion of the spirit person. This is bad business, very bad business.

Furthermore, a disproportionate number of such communicating entities are male. Think about this very seriously. Think about control by others, control of women by men, the desire of a woman to be controlled by a man. And most importantly, think about the arrested expansion/development of the woman that has resulted from the participation as a "trance medium" or a "channeler." I cannot think of one case in all my years where it has been progressive for a woman to "channel" or to go into trance. For a time an illusion of progress may be present, but it soon falls away. The information given by spirit is likely not very special. Think of the quality of vibration of an entity who would need to use such a method of communication.

I shy away from being the newspaper that brings unpopular news. But again, I have learned to value my ability to discriminate. Hundreds of years, literally, of experience on both sides of mediumship work, as the spirit and as the incarnated, has taught me to easily and rapidly discard poor quality. So with love I say to you that you can have far more by doing the necessary work to change your vibration, than you can have by giving yourself away as a "channel" or as a "trance medium." The choice you are in essence making is a choice between your development and hers/his. *Never* should you need to lose consciousness of yourself on the earthplane during any communication with any entity from another vibration.

ELLEN

Just because a spirit person tells you something, it doesn't make it so. The fact of her existence in spirit form doesn't automatically indicate authority, correctness, or perfection. Her opinion is based on a perspective different from yours, but remains only her opinion. If you cannot know what she tells you firsthand, how can you know her quality or accuracy?

On occasion you disagree with things your best friend tells you, even as you understand her perspective, her way of thinking, her sources, etc. How would you feel about living your life based completely upon the decisions of another person? And what if you didn't even know the morals, the ability, the carefulness or concern of that person for you or the life within which you were placed?

To know and have access to the place (vibration) the spirit person resides gives you context for understanding her choices and opinions. Why not figure out how to know what she knows? Then you can work together, each from your divergent perspective on common experience or knowledge?

This is why we want so much to encourage you to take your own power, to live only to your abilities, and to be in control of all that happens to you. It is only a little bit harder than the shortcuts, and can last an eternity.

ELLEN

The evening's culinary adventures had begun, as usual with a variety of exciting events happening simultaneously. At which point Grace does her identifying routine, letting me know she has something important to talk about. "Forget it, Gracie. The dinner's gonna burn anyway and I don't need you to help me do it. I'll talk to you as soon as I can."

Forty-five minutes later the dinnertime disasters have subsided. The honor of dishwashing is unequivocally mine. With soap up to my elbows, I tell Grace I'm finally ready for her. She says she was sorry to have bothered me then, but Flying Horse is about to call, and she felt we needed to discuss her situation first. It was important for Grace to let me know something was up, *and* important for her to do so a reasonable distance ahead of the crisis point so that the rest of my life could continue and I could make time for the communication with her.

"Flying Horse is confused about an interaction with a friend of hers," Grace tells me. "And I think we need to talk about it a little bit before she calls." She explains briefly the situation, just enough to expedite my process. After looking at the present I realize it is not as simple as just this lifetime. So I look in all the places I need to. With my assessment in hand, I do the pros and cons routine from my perspective, and Grace does the same from hers. In the nick of time, as usual, we arrive at a mutually agreeable approach. (Each of us works at times with Flying Horse without input from the other, so sometimes renewed synchronicity is important.)

The phone rings. It's Flying Horse. She tells me her difficulties. I relay parts of my discussion with Grace, and we move through the confusion. Grace interjects occasionally, making for a few "Wait a minute's, it's Grace's turn." Clearly we have a three-way conversation going, Flying Horse at one end of the country, I at the other, and Grace wherever.

MAJAI

Because of the magnitude of the transformation—remember that what is happening on the earth is only a tiny incident in universal terms— many entities from other planets, other vibrations, and states of being are very curious. The earth is a model example of imbalance carried to its conclusion, and others wish to learn from this situation. They have come to watch, and occasionally to interact with people on the earth. UFO visits, for example, are on the increase.

Many people are enthralled by the vibration and energy these other worldly entities bring. Remember they are here primarily for their own purposes. Their motivation for all interaction is for their benefit. They come from other *physical* vibrations, have perspectives comparable to earthplane perspective, and are not worthy of your time or energy. Oftentimes they will tell you they are here to help, but this is how they get their feet in the door. By and large, they merely add to the chaos and confusion and ultimately distract many of us from our purposes. So please do not be distracted or tempted by the unfamiliarity or novelty of their lifestyles. Keep your focus on your development.

GRACE

When you come to travel easily in other vibrations, you will find that the earthplane loses its appeal. There is nothing wrong with having or acknowledging these feelings. Accept any feelings you have about the earth as valid. The earth isn't exactly paradise and the other vibrations will be a relief when you find them.

As long as you have work to do on the earth, it is necessary to continue to invest energy on the earthplane. There will come a point of balance for you. You will be able to grow in other vibrations and also be able to continue your progress on earth.

If you develop smoothly and travel where it is appropriate for you to go, you should never experience vibrational readjustment problems. With a balanced and centered system of bodies, and appropriate behavior, you should be able to change great vibrational distances in a split second. When some other entity is in control (rather than yourself) the transition can be both rough and difficult on your bodies. This would be an example of inappropriate change in vibration.

When you are in harmony with Natural Law, transitions are smooth, health and balance are maintained and feelings of easiness and correctness prevail. Keep your center so your growth can be steady, sure and lasting. Trust your knowing to guide you only into quality endeavors. And then you can soar beyond even the eagles.

Without the strength and stability of your physical bodies, you will be unable to effectively transform, as Majai has spoken about. Always I am drawn to individual health concerns, for the integrity of the individual woman is fundamental to the integrity of the group. And too, unless your system is functioning maximally at its current state, it is not ready to make a progression.

With each jump in developmental level precise, exact, unambiguous and carefully directed thoughts, words, and actions become more and more essential. *Our physical forms must maintain alignment with our mental and spiritual aspects. All three must progress simultaneously for advancement to occur.*

You are living in an extremely toxic world. It is therefore crucially important to emphasize your efforts to maintain healthy bodies. Whatever you can do to move in the direction of building clean and strong physical (which includes mental) bodies will be of great advantage.

You literally are what you interact with, with whom you exchange, what you breathe, and what you eat. All that is in your environment contributes to your system either advantageously or detrimentally. There is an energy exchange between you and your environment, and each party is affected and altered on an ongoing basis. Interaction happens with all vibratory levels (densities) of your physical body, thus I use the term "bodies" for each of you. Interaction is continual and long lasting. See your system as an ecosystem, in a constant condition of change. *Any and all input alters this system, never to be the same again.*

The maintenance of health is the maintenance of harmony, harmony within our bodies and between our bodies and other environments. It is really a common sense matter. Our systems should be maintained such that they are capable of adapting easily and quickly to the changes around us. Bodies that are so fragile that symptomatology arises at the drop of a hat are not healthy systems. A woman's body, from the most dense to the most subtle parts, can be healthy simultaneously. Each body density has different requirements but *none is contradictory.* We are innately harmonious, a package deal. Our job is to maintain that harmony, a difficult job indeed in our existing environments.

We aim to foster the individual's synchronicity with universal flows. As such, change and flexibility are key to the preservation of individual balance and health. We must be adaptable. If we cannot accommodate increased toxins, external energetic surges and irregularities, and variations in availability, quality, and quantity of food, we will literally not be able to keep our physical bodies alive.

Those of us who have strong immunologic systems, intact and functioning endocrine, cardiovascular, musculoskeletal, respiratory, dermatologic, hematologic, digestive, excretory and purification systems have the *minimum* requirements for meeting the changes we face. The integrity of all of our bodies, the clean and efficient functioning of all the biologic systems, give us the potential for expansion into more subtle realms. Without strong physical bodies, we will not be able to accommodate the vibrational changes that will affect the planet. As Majai said, the non-physical will come to exist with the physical. The physical must be able to maintain balance while accommodating the ever increasing yin.

And this is why my words are strong and direct. There is no time for fooling around. Many of you have much healing work to do *even before* you can begin building a strong system of bodies. Unhealthy bodies are the norm today. The growing lists of aches and pains, ailments both severe and mild, are indicators of far more extensive imbalance than either ourselves or our medical systems wish to acknowledge. Health is a real and attainable possibility. Take my words seriously because as time passes, the yin grows, and the earth transforms, you will increasingly feel the strain of your disharmonies and will find that your work has compounded exponentially.

The main reason we need bodies of integrity is to provide us with vehicles from which to expand. The bodies are the home base, and from there we develop. They can be seen as a center, as the earth is a center. Growth must proceed from somewhere or from something. We need our bodies. No use going into other realms if our bodies are not strong enough to sustain us as we journey. Our growth will be limited by disharmonious bodies. Endurance and stamina will be absent. The cleanliness of our system affects the clarity of our minds. The clarity of our minds affects our ability to be one-pointed, directed toward our goals. Our systems must be tight and efficient if we have designs on expanding to higher vibrational states. Always our goal is internal expansion, spiritual development farther into the yin.

To keep yourself in a state of health you have to feel, and trust what you feel. Be it dietary or energetic requirements, only you can know from the inside your harmony or disharmony. *Never let anyone tell you that you are too insensitive to feel for yourself.*

Necessary is working knowledge of your bodies' basic requirements from nutritional, vibrational, constitutional (heredity), and existing health (physical and mental) standpoints. Lifestyle, age, and past experience also contribute. There are a wealth of nutritional, dietary, and energetic systems that exist that you can use to your benefit. Add pieces of these systems to your sense of knowing and your ability to feel. Do not give away your power to any one of these systems. See them as information sources, resources. Take what you need, leave the rest, and process what you take through your feeling and knowing. Learn everything you can from wherever you can.

Food has three basic functions: the cleansing, maintaining, and building of body systems. All food has effects on the physical, mental and spiritual aspects of the bodies, with individual foods causing specific effects on each. Again, there are many philosophies and systems that address both function and effect of food. Compare what you learn from these different schools of thought, and then process the information through your knowing.

Remember the importance of flexibility and adaptability. Time, place, and person must be considered at any given moment. Fit your food to your spiritual growth requirements. As your work changes, as your emphasis changes, (be it on physical, mental or spiritual matters), as the environmental and energetic conditions change, as your reactions and your balance/imbalance fluctuate, adapt your food intake.

The most important questions to ask when considering diet and food are: What is the food capable of doing? What do I need food to do for me at this point in time?

The only "incorrect" food is food that fails to serve your purpose, thus your development. (As such toxic or devalued food contradicts your aim.) Figure out what you need to accomplish with food, why a specific food is beneficial or detrimental to you, and what and how you need to eat.

Eat food as close to its natural form as possible. Use care during preparation to avoid depletion of minerals, vitamins, and other nutrients. Eat whole grains, unprocessed, unbleached, fresh foods without added or subtracted nutrients. Your nutritional requirements should be met by eating food rather than food supplements.

Eat clean, non-toxic food. Avoid pesticides, colorings, preservatives, radiation or chemically treated food, medicated or hormone filled food, and foods exposed to roadside poisons. Any type of adulteration compromises food value and usually adds toxins.

Eat a variety of foods in balanced quantities at *every* meal. Make sure that nutritional requirements are met by eating foods containing ample vitamins, minerals, protein (in usable combinations), fats, carbohydrates, fiber, etc. Attention should be paid to the inclusion of beans, legumes, grains, sea vegetables, nuts, fruits, vegetables, seeds and animal products (fish, poultry, meat, eggs, or milk). It is also important for food type to be balanced, so eat roots, stems, flowers, leaves and fruit. A simple way of ensuring that you are eating a diet balanced in minerals and trace elements is to use a color system; include orange, green, red, purple, white, beige, black, blue, brown and yellow foods.

One of the most important substances eaten with food is life force or vital energy. Processing and many popular cooking methods rob food of this essence. So it should be common sense that microwave cooking or synthetic food should be avoided. Think of food as living substance and remember that life force leaches over time.

There are also energetic requirements for health. Energy exchanges occur simultaneously in all the body densities. A balance between the in-flow and the out-flow of energy must exist. Workload must balance the amount of input (food, sleep, etc.). Obviously a woman can't do more than she has the energy for, but how many times do we nevertheless try to do just that? Imbalance and stagnation are sure to result if we allow energy to enter, and then fail to give out an equal amount. Likewise, uninterrupted and even flow within the systems is essential.

There are many sources from which we can receive energy: from people in all types of relationships including work, student/teacher, love, friendship, and sexual, from plants, animals, minerals, the earth, other parts of the solar system and universe, and from entities in other vibrational states.

Work and activity on the physical plane must balance mental or emotional activities, and these must balance happenings and interaction with happenings in other vibrations. Times of stimulation and activity are as important as times of rest and sleep. Different states of consciousness allow for different input from various vibrations.

GYTA

While our primary energetic quality is the female vibration, we exist as a microcosm of the universe, thus contain all of the universal energetic polarities. So within us exists yang and all the other essential energies in varying amounts. It is important to remember that the essential energies are relativities, and exist only in relationship to each other. Without one, another simply is. As long as we exist in the physical, we need a system of comparisons. However, once we move into the non-physical, such concepts become useless. So for now we need to allow all of them to exist simultaneously in a state of balance within our systems. When we can do so, we will progress as yin entities.

See your being as a rotating, bobbing, amoebic disc on an axis. You wobble when you are off center. When to the disc is added something that you cannot readily accommodate, wobble occurs. For every item that enters the environment of your disc, a complement must be added elsewhere to retain the steadiness and evenness of rotation. You need to course ahead on your spiritual journeys like a top spinning through internal space. If you lose your center, if wobble sets in, your progress is slowed and your direction is altered. For health, you as a microcosm of the universe, with all its energies, must be in balance.

I too am honored to make contact again. It is good to see you again and believe me, I do see each of you! My best to you and love.

ELLEN

Toxins and impurities in the physical body create impediments to the flow of energies, both into and out of the system and within the system itself. It is as if dams were built haphazardly throughout a river system. In some places the flow is stopped completely, in others it is diverted. Uniformity of flow is lost, resulting in areas of backup and trickles.

When a woman is exposed to a surge of energy external to herself, or suddenly enters into the proximity of an entity of higher vibration than she is accustomed to, that energy courses through all her bodies, in new concentrations or in newly accessed locations. Exaggeration of the pre-existing imbalances occurs. With the increased energy, there results increased divergence, backup or surging. The irregularities or disharmonies become blatantly obvious.

Sometimes the woman will experience physical pain, odd sensations, jerking or jolting movements, or actual pathology. Too frequently I have seen women who have developed quite rapidly in mental and spiritual areas, but who have failed to make comparable refinements of the physical body. *The physical, mental, and spiritual must always maintain alignment. We grow as a unit, not as disjointed parts.*

An example: There was a woman whose system existed in a state of moderate balance. Over a period of a few years, she became involved in workshops and seminars dealing with metaphysical subjects. She grew many miles relatively quickly in terms of mental outlook and spiritual expansion.

When she sat in meditation, she occasionally experienced jolts of energy up her spine with associated involuntary twitching of an arm or leg. Fatigue had become commonplace. Lunch was standard restaurant fare, followed by a snack of diet soda. A typical dinner was grocery store meat, one vegetable, white rice, and a glass of wine. Her winter had included several head colds with chest congestion.

No longer was her body able to accommodate the mental and spiritual expansion (subtling of vibration) as well as the ingested substances. Much of what she was feeding her system was denatured, synthetic, and processed, all void of life force. If she was to continue expanding, more usable and less toxic substances would be needed for fuel.

This is a very typical case. Many women eat far cleaner diets than this woman, yet they too will have times when their mental and spiritual growth outdistances their physical development. The presenting picture, at times of such misalignment, is one of fatigue and toxicity. Decreased clarity of mental function is a common development, especially in women who do mediumship work. Keep in mind that a diet, or living environment could well have been acceptable prior to the time of increased growth.

If a woman changes her diet or living conditions radically from worse to better, she will soon find a need to make comparable reforms in mental or spiritual areas of her life. Perhaps the people she associates with or the environment she works in will have to be modified. Things ordinarily acceptable she may find now to be rather unpleasant. Keep changing as the need arises, and be glad you are moving!

Diet can be a facilitator of spiritual development, but it is not the determining factor of an entity's vibration. Total evolution holds far more weight than diet during a particular incarnation. Too much focus on diet or food can distract us from our larger purposes. Yet diet certainly has an impact on spiritual potential. If I were to drink alcohol, for example, it would just not be possible to maneuver in the non-physical. I prefer to see all that I interact with, including people and food, as either potentiators of or detractors from my growth.

Red meat, poultry, fish, eggs and milk products are the sources of animal protein. Many schools of thought disparage meat consumption, often for good reason. I feel that *some* form of animal protein is necessary to build and repair the physical body. With increased requirements - physical activity, pregnancy, the growth of children, or severe injury - more materials capable of building are needed. Once growth is achieved, by and large maintenance is the primary focus.

Toxicity is a major concern, and will become an even greater one in the next few years. Toxins accumulate over time, and can become burdensome when doing spiritual work. Vegetable proteins do quite well in terms of providing clean fuel with little toxic waste, and are adequate for most maintenance and minor repair needs. Even so, it would pay to be mindful of eating clean vegetable products. Commercial sources for the above mentioned animal proteins are full of hormones, antibiotics, chemically treated feed residue, and environmental pollutants. Clean sources are difficult to find, but serious thought should be given to the consumption of such contaminated foods. Sometimes cleanliness should take precedence over food type.

Different foods have different vibrations. You are what you eat. If you desire to raise your vibration, it is logical to eat substances of lesser rather than greater density. Think of the difference between a cow and a hummingbird, and then between a hummingbird and nasturtium flower, and perhaps you can get a sense of the vibrational continuum. While you may desire to raise your vibration, nasturtium flowers will do little to help you repair a broken leg, so keep in mind that it is always a balancing act.

As with the rest of life, moderation and changes made in graduality are often the most effective and stable approaches to diet. Trust yourself, and consider what others have to say. Many health practitioners are men, and methods were developed by and for them. So remember that you as a woman may need a slightly different approach or modified system. And always the "correct" diet is person specific.

GRACE

Pretty often I hear people think or say, "If she can smoke cigarettes (eat meat or chocolate, drink coffee or alcohol, use drugs, or whatever) and do the quality work she does, then lifestyle must not really matter."

We are dealing with potentials. Lifestyle and specific choices can inhibit or aid the realization of that potential. A detracting behavior will compromise that potential. So even while the person may be capable of magnificent things from your perspective, from a perspective more expanded than hers, she is falling short of what she is capable of doing because of particular lifestyle choices.

The extraordinarily low standards on the earth at the present time, coupled with the acceptance and incorporation of daily abuses of Natural Law, have resulted in many, many people compromising their spiritual potentials on a constant basis.

Unfortunately for me, I too have chosen or been socialized to choose compromising behaviors in the past. In every group of people norms are developed. Lots of times those norms do not promote growth. To deviate from that "sacred" norm is a major undertaking. I know I have at times just not had the inclination to go against the accepted ways, even while knowing I would be better off if I did.

I feel badly now for the effect my laziness has had on others. They have concluded by watching me just the thinking I began this section with. "If Grace can do it, it must be OK." I am very sorry that my example could not have been seen for what it was: laziness and compromised potential, rather than legitimization.

ELLEN

The entire nervous system is used to allow a woman's awareness of incoming energies from realms beyond the earth. She translates her experience in other realms through her body, and the nervous system is the predominant route. Primarily the afferent or sensory system is used, involving certain cranial nerves: Olfactory, Optic, Trigeminal, Vestibulocochlear, and Glossopharyngeal, and less frequently, the spinal nerves, especially those leading to the limbs. Pressure sense and touch discrimination are the most important. The autonomic nervous system (parasympathetic and sympathetic) is used in varying combinations of predominance throughout daily activity. With added stress or load, the autonomic nervous system becomes more active.

Interpretation of all stimuli transpires via the nervous system. The same is true when a woman interacts in vibrations or with entities in realms different from the earth. Interpretation of her experiences (especially in physical spirit realms) requires neurological mechanisms. The stimuli is of faster rate and frequency and involves a steady influx of new information.

In my case, for example, I am aware of the presence of both Grace and Kioka on an almost constant basis. They reside in different vibrations, so this means input comes from two sources simultaneously. Our patterns of exchange vary, yet nearly 24 hours per day my nervous system is geared to those two vibrations. Those realms impact on me, just as does everything in my environment on the earth.

With expansion, acclimation and tolerance of the new vibration are necessary. At first, perhaps one's nervous system can only accommodate the new vibration for a few moments. Eventually the moments will grow to become an hour or more. So typically we see limit setting by people who do spiritual work, in order to maintain balance and to avoid depletion (or in the extreme, exhaustion). With gradual and appropriate development, exposure does not compromise a woman's center. Feelings of fatigue and exhaustion would not be present. Nevertheless, additional fuel will be needed to maintain expansion. Nutritional requirements increase, yin connection becomes more important, and absence of compromising lifestyle choices are essential.

I would like to speculate a bit on the reasons for some of the typically witnessed lifestyle choices among spiritualists. It has become relatively common knowledge among women who do mediumship work that additional potassium is required in order to maintain health or balance. It seems to me that there is in fact a physiological basis for the greater potassium need.

Briefly, with stimulation of a nerve, the intracellular/extracellular sodium-potassium balance is altered. For the nerve to return to its resting state (for repolarization to occur), potassium is used. Nerve stimulation and return to rest happens in milliseconds. With steady stimulation for 30 seconds, this process would occur many, many times. And potassium would be used at each repolarization. If for any reason constant or long-term nervous system stimulation were to occur, it seems logical that the body's requirement for potassium would also increase. With constant or regular exposure to vibrations beyond the earthplane, nervous system stimulation *is* increased.

The symptoms of hypokalemia (decreased potassium), as recognized by the medical community, show *extreme* imbalance in my opinion. Subclinically low potassium also indicates imbalance, but not of the nature that would land a woman in the emergency room. At times I am strongly drawn to potassium rich foods,especially when my work level has exceeded the usual. (In *no* way am I recommending that *anyone* take potassium supplements. Supplements, especially potassium supplements, can be *very* dangerous. If you have need, it is not difficult to find foods high in potassium and to eat them *in moderation*.)

Many mediums smoke cigarettes. In fact, so many, that, as Grace said, people are not alarmed when they see someone doing spiritual work and smoking. The same is true for caffeine.

In the autonomic nervous system, when a nerve is stimulated it releases a substance called a neurotransmitter, which in turn impacts on a second nerve. One such neurotransmitter is acetylcholine, and another, norepinephrine. There are receptors on the second nerve which are sensitive and responsive to specific neurotransmitters. In situations of sudden influx of stressors, acetylcholine is released, stimulating the body to rise to the occasion with quickened responses.

Receptors sensitive to acetylcholine are equally receptive to nicotine. And those responsive to norepinephrine are sensitive to caffeine. These are only two examples of substances which mimic or alter normal neurologic function. There are many others found and consumed daily in ordinary herbs, plants, foods and drugs.

My understanding is that when there has been prolonged use of a woman's body by spirit people, or extended inappropriate exposure to realms beyond the earth, imbalances are bound to result. Likewise, when less than desirable lifestyle choices have been made, especially for extended time periods, imbalances ensue. The imbalances, perhaps subclinical at the moment, may compromise not only the ability to travel into other realms, but may permanently weaken the neurological system. Sooner or later, subclinical will become clinical. Eventually we are sure to witness extreme exhaustion or other pathology. Inaccurate perception or inability to perceive are too commonly seen today, and are partially examples of compromised function. In fact, with mediumship, accuracy percentage under 100% is not only accepted but *expected*. Perhaps what we are seeing is the accommondation of subclinical imbalance? Therefore, both lifestyle and method of contact with other realms are very important and consequential. For the woman whose systems are particularly strong, at best, potential growth suffer, as well as the quality of work performed.

When an imbalance has been created, compensation will be sought. Not always is compensation true rectification of the imbalance. Sometimes, it amounts to adding a second imbalance to the already present imbalance. I believe the smokers, the coffee drinkers, or the chocolate eaters, for examples, are doing just that. An illusion of balance or stamina can temporarily be created, mostly owing to the neurological impact of these substances as mimickers or meddlers, but the stress on the system is only being masked by such usage.

GRACE

I am sure I will receive much reaction to what I am about to say. Nevertheless, I wish to say it, as I hope it will ultimately lead all of us into more complete balance.

Native societies in every corner of the earth have maintained (relatively) easy contact with other realms. Worlds of spirit have been routinely incorporated into daily life for centuries. Some of the methods used by members of these societies have been of the nature we have described as less than desirable: various states of trance, altered states of consciousness such that awareness of the body has been lost, manipulation by spirit, etc. Consequently, imbalances in the body resulted.

Tobacco use in traditional Native American societies, I believe to be originally based in a need to rebalance where balance was lost. Because of extensive contact with other realms, compensation had to come from somewhere. Tobacco was not the only substance to fit this category.

Herbs and other plants have produced similar effects. Such use and their incorporation into rituals and ceremonies have long been encouraged by medicine women and men, who themselves had particular need for rebalancing.

Very respectfully I say now, that we did our best to maintain balance. (Perhaps these *were* the most harmonious ways to keep balance at the time.) However, some of our ways look to me now to be less than perfect. Were our methods of communication with other realms more balanced, perhaps some of our ways of rectification would not have grown to become sacred in and of themselves.

The application of the ways of the past to the present does not always work. Time, place and person must always be considered. And I will add, that just because the Native people, or any other people, did something, doesn't mean it is desirable or right, and doesn't necessarily mean it is desirable or harmonious for you.

I don't believe it is worthwhile to hoard practices or knowledge. That is elitist thought. But I also don't believe that the ways of one person, or one group of people are necessarily good for another. Sharing helps us all, but discrimination is important to achieve appropriate application of what has been shared. If any of us was perfect, we would not be here. So here we are, looking to eliminate as much contradiction to Natural Law as we can. We can't afford to cling to a contradiction under an illusion that it is sacred because someone in the past was able to use it to grow.

ANJA

There are many people who consider themselves to be great spiritualists, yet their affairs in physical and emotional areas are perpetually in disarray. Without respect enough for levels of physical existence to value attention to earthly detail, efforts in other vibrations, inevitably deemed loftier, are *worthless*.

If a gap exists in functional ability between planes of existence, emphasis on "spiritual pursuits" will only serve to widen the gap. Instead of focus on activity distal to the earthplane, better to temporarily emphasize growth of the deficient aspects. Catch up in areas of lack so you can once again move in unison.

People like to do what they are good at, or what comes easily for them. And they tend to avoid the problematic spots. Be cognizant of the "holy one" who can't get her dishes washed, or those too spacey to arrive promptly for appointments, the woman who works with crystals and uses drugs, or the workaholic who can't produce without coffee. In such cases, there are big gaps in development.

None of us is perfectly balanced, but there is a reasonable alignment of all of our functions that can be expected. The gaps are beginning to become more visible, in others and in ourselves. Spend whatever time and energy you need to catch up. Keep quality as your priority, not speed or distance. And be careful in your interactions with those who are "too important" to use care in every aspect of their lives. Recognize the gaps around you, so ultimately you can keep your own quality high.

MAJAI

The energy drainer. Usually unknowingly, but occasionally knowingly, these people being of low physical or mental vitality, are drawn to stronger people. The energy they siphon is not yin, but the denser energies gotten from food, water, air, the current and prenatal environments. Literally they take part of your supply to pump up theirs.

As the earth's activities push us to our limits, people will feel acutely their own lacks. They will seek the presence of those with stamina and strong energies. When you encounter such a person, physically keep your distance, try not to touch or be touched, tighten up and pull in your bodies to make the boundaries sharper and more compact, avoid direct eye contact (instead look at the space between their eyes), and do not continue to think about this person when the encounter is over. Remain loving. Ideally your aim is to continue the flow of yin, but to stop the draining of your other energies.

If someone does succeed in depleting you, perhaps even without your awareness, eat (something other than sweets), take a rest or a nap, and if possible sit with your back to a hardwood tree trunk. These measures should help replenish you.

MAJAI

When women act independently of men they begin to access their power. They grow in strength and ability. They find quickly that they are quite capable of doing wonderful things. A mental attitude of strength follows. The power is not only experienced internally, but pervades the woman's total environment. It is an energy that cannot be contained in the individual woman. It is too big and surges through her from areas of greater to areas of lesser concentration. Once a pathway is open, the energy pours through. You are a conduit for the energy, but the energy *is you*.

Perceptions of and reactions to the presence of the yin vary. You need to stand prepared for the effects the yin can have on others. Your awareness of the yin and your cooperation with the flows allow for increased concentration of the yin in your energy fields. Consequently, you will most certainly be recognized in your power. Depending upon the developmental level of the observer and her or his willingness to move forward spiritually, reactions can cover a wide range: nervousness, feelings of being unsettled or disrupted, anger or hostility, combativeness, fear and avoidance of you/the energy, strong attraction to you/the energy (which often is translated into sexual attraction), or desire to possess or own you.

It is necessary for you to learn to read people's responses in a new light as you come into your power. So important it is to discriminate between reactions to the energy (which is you) and reactions to your behavior or personality. Also important is to learn to evaluate the other person's ability to handle and process the increasing yin. You can save yourself much personal heartache, many confrontations, and uncomfortable situations if you expand to accurately read another's vibration. It is possible to learn appropriate and smooth ways of standing firmly in your power, yet interacting with others.

At times you will need to side step, to let the reaction go by. Sometimes to allow the other to wrestle with the situation, in order that she may grow, is the best way. A conversation about perceptions and feelings may be in order. Or it could be the worst thing you could do. Often for you to have an attitude of detachment *and* love will serve everyone well. You will come to know your strengths and weaknesses in dealing with your power in the context of society. It will take time. But I say to you, *do not conclude that it is wrong to take your power because of reactions or another person's inability to process and harmonize with the yin*. That is their problem.

If you are particularly vulnerable at any stage in your process, rather than back down from your power, avoid putting yourself in a potentially difficult or hostile situation. Protect yourself and see yourself as tender even as you come into tremendous power. This will be necessary at many different stages in your development, no matter how far you progress.

What you can do is to avoid creating a situation of resistance and confrontation. To attack or to be attacked is a power struggle. Remember that you are not trying to win or lose. You want to go about your business in the easiest, most flowing way possible, and at the same time know that any interaction others have with you is for the good of all.

MAJAI

The yin is a primary energetic force that drives the universe. The scope of the yin is immense relative to a woman's energetic size and current expansion capabilities. The yin is moving into a dominant position in the universe (as we know it), and will become the largest force in the realm we evolve through. In our terms, there are other spaces where different energies dominate. However, until we evolve to become the yin, and then with the yin grow to its absolute state, and then transform to become the next energetic force type—and this is long, long time away—the other energetic forces are irrelevant. We have experience with the yang because we have existed at the point where the yang reached its absolute and changed to yin. (And this occurred a long, long time ago, linearly speaking, yet still during part of our evolutionary process).

Our opportunity to merge with the yin has arrived. It is fortunate for us as women to live in the time and space of the yin, for it provides us an opportunity and a potential to realign with ourselves, in a way and to an extent that would not be possible if the dominant universal energy were anything other than yin.

By being strongly connected to the yin, you are guaranteed stability and centeredness. In one's daily life it is sometimes convenient to think smaller than universal. So shrink your thinking to consider just the earth. (This makes matters a little easier, I think.) The earth is yin, so think in terms of becoming one with the earth.

I spoke before of the importance of sensing the earth's changes. Underneath the level of the changes is a stability. Do not confuse stability with rigidity or lack of change. The earth is in constant flux, nevertheless has a center. "To be grounded" is synonymous with being connected to the earth's center or stability. The yin of the earth can be experienced strongly far into the solar system. We are so close that often we take the energy for granted, have come to co-exist blindly and unconsciously with the yin. Better to know it consciously and never lose touch.

Walk barefoot and feel the energy come up through the bottoms of your feet to fill your bodies. Put your palms to the ground and feel the yin. Put the front of your body on the ground and again feel the energy enter. Because you too are yin, the energy can enter and leave at any point. You can literally pulsate with the earth.

(There are many energies that enter and leave your bodies. Do not limit your thinking to the pathways of energetic systems with which you may be familiar. The yin is more subtle, more pervasive, more fundamental to your bodies than any of these other energies. There are points such as those I have mentioned where the flow is concentrated, but know that it enters and leaves everywhere on a constant basis.)

At times of depletion, loss of center, or increased chaos external to you, go to the earth. Touch it. Reconnect by placing your bodies on the ground. Sleep on the ground. You will experience in moments the replenishing and empowering. Anywhere on the earth will do. It's all the same. Connect at times of depletion, and at times of strength. One day you will find that you will remain connected effortlessly, day and night, even as you go about your business, sleep, or travel in other vibrations. I promise.

ANJA

Each entity is a microcosm of the universe. Therefore all the possibilities of the universe exist within each of us. Familiar are the concepts of yin and yang, but other such energies also exist. None really has a name, but each has its own vibration. Within each of us exists them all. Which of these universal component energies we choose to emphasize or allow to predominate within us, determines our alignment or identification preference.

That the yin is coming into predominance universally merely means that there is easier potential for individuals to align with yin rather than with a different energy. Alignment with anything else would be a struggle. A little easier to have the universe behind you than at odds with you, I think.

Such identification with a specific energy type does not negate the existence of the rest within you. What is happening is a change in percentage of component parts. And with expansion, it does *not* become necessary to eliminate any others. You are just able to include *more* of the predominant energy.

One part is not inherently more valuable than another. However, for women the predominance of the yin component provides us with an opportunity to connect in kind with the macrocosmic yin. And this opportunity for women is a pretty valuable one!

Really, the microcosm and the macrocosm seek parallelism. It does not exist presently between the earth and the universe, or between the entities on the earth and their essential energies. This is the imbalance, thus the need for transformation (or purification) to rebalance. One way or another, the parallel will reform. If we consciously and willingly align, the ultimate potential for growth is simply greater.

And for those entities of different than yin essential energy, there is nothing to lose from alignment. They will come to know the yin component part of themselves. And at such time as the predominant energy once again becomes theirs, the same opportunity that women now have will be theirs also.

ELLEN

There is a lot of talk about honoring "the male within us." Yang, or the essential energy identified with male persons, is *not* male behavior, male spirituality, male choice or male method. It is an energy in pure form. It is a particular vibration. Yang is relevant to us in its pureness, but yang, as has come to be associated with current male lifestyle and method, is irrelevant to us as women.

My understanding is that we exist from many perspectives simultaneously. From one angle we are microcosms of the universe; the component parts of the universe are represented in us. It is a construct of earthplane thought (dare I say male construct?) that in order to grow or develop, we must increase the size of these component parts. And since only two basic parts, yin and yang, have been acknowledged, it has followed that in order for women to be whole, their yang parts need full expression.

This entire premise is not at all my understanding of either the workings of the universe or of our process as women. From another angle, each component part exists as a complete unit. When the units are then placed with other units (or those of different essential energy), the macrocosm results, representing again, all possibilities.

In this light, I see that women are trying to eliminate all elements other than pure yin, or extraneous to pure yin. Once that yin comes to exist in its pure or absolute state, it is in a position to realize its relevance to all other essential energies, and then to transform into another energetic type.

For now, it is too early for any of us to focus on anything other than becoming ourselves. We need to have a clean, well-defined self to contribute to the whole. Those pure selves are the only pieces refined sufficiently to fit the big puzzle. Rather than trying to fit the universe into us, we are trying to find our place in the universe. The process of perfection is for the purpose of fitting precisely into that place. In

65

fact, I don't believe our focus will ever be on anything other than becoming ourselves.

Therefore, I think it is a sidetrack to focus on "accommodating" other essential energies. Too many of us bend over backwards (thus breaking our focus on what is in front of us) to make room for yang *instead* of making room for the growing yin. "Accommodation" of other essential energies does not equal acknowledgement of or respect for them. Every time I hear a woman utter the phrase, "the male within me," I cringe. That very woman is the woman who occupies herself seeking ways to maintain a bond with men, when it is high time she sought to find her bond with herself.

We *have* to acknowledge the importance of the *yin*. To grow, we *have* to be willing to take our power. We feed ourselves by aligning with ourselves as good and valid and complete. *We do not need other essential energies to complement us in order to make us total beings.* We are real and we are complete all by ourselves.

ELLEN

There is absolute chaos on this planet. Identification and alignment can be either with chaos or with our center - either/or. (Being a little centered is akin to being a little pregnant.)

Frenetic behavior and incessant activity belong to chaos. It is a choice, a statement of priority to stay so busy that you don't have time to feel: feel what is inside, feel what is outside. "I am too busy to meditate (*every* day)" equals "I am choosing to align with chaos."

Feeling is not something that can happen in seven and a half minutes between dinner and running to the meeting. It requires time and space. It needs to breathe and live for it is the perception of life. It exists in fluidity. (Feeling and thinking are entirely different animals. Thinking can be forced into time frames. Thinking is factual, and exists in finite realms.)

To maintain *my* center on this planet I need three things: room to feel, consistency of lifestyle, and a strong bond with the earth. Meditation time is the structured time to feel, to open and to promote receptivity. (Prayer is asking, wanting, thanking and is busy, mental activity. It is quite different from meditation.) Meditation happens 365 days per year *because* its absence is felt sharply and acutely. We *miss* being separated from ourselves. One hour at a sitting allows enough time to quiet the body and the mind so it is even possible to begin to feel.

Cleanliness and order in the immediate environment keep the center from being compromised once it is found. Regularity in sleep-wake patterns in harmony with the seasons is essential and has a profound effect on our systems. Balanced, scheduled meals eaten at a comfortable pace and in easy company also will not detract from the hard won center. And a daily direct connection to the earth is the physical counterpart to the meditation process.

We are here to contribute to the collective growth and to our individual growth. The body exists to be used maximally to accomplish this growth. We feel so we can apply ourselves effectively in the context of the universe. (Too much time in meditation is not effective.) What we gain through our growing receptivity must be given away. That is the application of our connectedness, the process of *living* in harmony. It is the give-back to keep the connection fluid.

KIOKA

We have tried to emphasize the importance of feeling and experiencing life for yourself. We want you to trust that that which feels right, *is* right for you. We are trying to give you specific guidelines in general ways, in order that your feeling not be limited by our preferences. We do not wish to set up conditions or boundaries which could further curtail your efforts.

Meditation is a state of receptivity and feeling. How you do that needs to be up to you. If you are encumbered by thoughts and emotions that you have been unable to express or release, you will find when you sit to meditate that all those thoughts and feelings will avalanche into consciousness. This is not anything you should try to prevent from happening. When they finish falling down the mountain, stillness will prevail. If you manage your ongoing thoughts and feelings in ways that allow suppression of truthfulness, desires to please others instead of yourself, or denial of your experience, the avalanche will continue. It has to because then you continue to add more that needs to be eliminated before the quiet can come.

Many techniques for "the correct" way to meditate exist. All these techniques serve specific purposes and are not wrong or bad. (Most however will come to you with statements that all others are inferior.) *Ultimately you are going to have to find your own way*, the way that serves your purposes.

My suggestion is that you learn from the inside rather than from the outside. Trust yourself for a change. Make adjustments based upon *your* experiences. And allow your meditation time to be whatever it needs to be in the moment.

There should never be a need to compare it with another's experiences. Yours and hers are mutually exclusive, and you do not need external validation to legitimize your choices. Because you choose is ample legitimization. Your development of your ability to feel is the best you can offer yourself. Anything that leads to this goal is an excellent technique. Do not assume others have anything better than that.

All of us writing this book have made the progress we have because we have dared to trust ourselves.

AMNA

Your work is ongoing. Learn to feel to find your center and yourself in the universal context. Protect that center and your need to feel. See that they don't get compromised by lifestyle or negligence. Stay open to continue to feel, so your center is free to expand. This is your work. It is the work of all of us.

The condition in which you keep your body and the environments in which you function and interact, reflect the respect you have for your spiritual growth. When you value it as number one, what we suggest will seem very logical and essential. It is only when your priorities lie elsewhere that your spiritual progress looks burdensome.

If you find that you are reacting to our words on the care, feeding and nurturing of yourself, please take a peek at your priorities. You will lack energy to invest in your growth if it is not important to you to grow.

KIOKA

Because we do not write to convince, but to illuminate our travels for those who need to know that their processes do have a place in the greater scheme of the universe, our words are sometimes quite straightforward. We have found conditions (outlook, emotions, blocks, etc.) which directly affect our travels.

Each of us journeys a unique route. Development varies and resistance varies. We wish for you to begin to think about concepts new to you, to run with the bits of information you have been lacking and wanting, and to leave what is not useful. The material is not intended to meet you in your completeness, only to give you jumping off points where you have need for them, and to give you ways to travel without need of constant assistance.

MAJAI

As we open we allow more and more to enter our consciousness. It is not possible to selectively open, as the process of opening implies the absence of conditionality. So we open to what is, and what is, often is rather unpleasant to experience. Sometimes it is very difficult to look at a larger picture, but always the more we see, and the more expanded we become, the more resources and information we have to draw upon. We are improved by our expansiveness, not impaired.

We are able to expand internally until we reach a point when our center is compromised, when wobble sets in. At that point the expansive process ceases and remains so until center is regained.

Courage is necessary to keep stepping forward to expand. We need to risk losing our centers, but if we get caught up in fearing what will happen next (or what we will see next), we resist the expansive process. Focus on gaining courage and as you do your hunger for answers to and information about *all* unknowns will surface and grow. Once you are sufficiently hungry, opening to expand becomes a gratifying undertaking.

AMNA

There are people who spend more time and energy telling of or showing their progress than making progress. Certain ways to act are in vogue to show how holy you really are: peaceful, slow, floating manners should accompany every action, even emergencies; sweet, smiling countenance should be maintained throughout every situation, especially during pain and tension; smooth emotions in the face of dramatic change are essential. Forget it. Be real.

Diversity, variety, and extremes naturally exist in this universe. And each will elicit an appropriate feeling. Respond to these feelings spontaneously. Do not worry if you get angry or feel hurt. Feel it and get on with it. With understanding and perspective many responses will cease to be relevant. But before that perspective becomes yours, do not fear what you feel naturally. If you censor your feelings, no matter how distasteful they may be, you break your connection to the universe. Be glad you have the capacity to live no matter what you feel.

ELLEN

Controls on your feelings preclude genuine experience of your environment. How is it possible to access the relevance of your place in any situation if you walk into it with conditions of acceptability? Feelings cannot be limited. They are not dangerous. They reflect your interaction with your environment. When that interaction is disharmonious, the feelings to follow are likely to contain equally disharmonious components.

Censoring is denying. The first step to growth is acceptance, not denial. When feelings show disharmony (anger, pain, tension, hatred, etc.) the solution is to change your interaction with the environment or to change the environment. It is not to suppress *the feelings*. Allow yourself the freedom to experience the universe as you naturally will, via your feeling self.

KIOKA

It is not only distasteful feelings that women censor, but attractive ones also. Draws to specific people, qualities, or environments are frequently disallowed. The most appalling censorship I find to be of other women, censorship of her abilities, her dreams, her natural beauty, her essential nature. Other women are commonly denied and depreciated for body type, competence, feelings, behavior, or social discontent.

Woman must accept and love other women in order to accept and love herself. If she cannot have positive feelings about other women in their totality, she cannot possibly allow her own growth from her present, for she cannot accept herself in that present. If she censors the feeling of the other woman, she censors her own feeling. Without feeling herself, she cannot know even where she stands.

ELLEN

Periodically throughout the book we mention woman in group. Group is important to woman and she is important to the group. But her own vibrational achievement is what she has to contribute to the group. Inadequately developed, she lacks quality offering to the group. Without development of her feeling self and respect for the feeling selves of the others, she is a subtraction rather than an addition to the group.

Her connection to the group can sustain her, but only if she can sustain herself. Therefore, individual development always comes first. With it she bonds to other women. Meanwhile individual development continues. And her bonds will change appropriate to her vibrational expansion.

DYTOIANTA

A transformation of consciousness must occur for woman to come into her power. By seeing woman as down-trodden and oppressed we entrap her and limit her. She cannot fly because she lacks power and energy to move from her lowly position. If we define her with clipped wings, she is helpless and pathetic. But this state of affairs is only one of the possibilities. We can see woman in any light we choose.

She is precisely the energy she chooses to be. She can be the light of the moon, or she can be the darkness of the moon. She can be whatever light comes her way, and she can turn this way and that to forever be the light.

I am here to talk about woman in group. Our awareness of group feeds our light. It is an energy we can use to sustain the individual. The magnitude of this power fuels us and boosts us into the cosmos. Only must we learn to acknowledge it and to tap it.

Learn from the eagle. She rides on the updrafts, effortlessly traveling hundreds of miles. The eagle has learned to use the natural forces to her advantage, minimizing the cost to the integrity of herself. One or two beats of the wings and she is off. The wind currents and the weather patterns are there. We can use them as she does.

There is no limit to where we can soar. The more we feel the yin in us, the farther we can expand. It is an energy that cannot be contained. It surges into us, we know it as ourselves, we are one with it, and we burst forth, going farther into ourselves. We ride with it because we arc it. We do not exist in separation from the yin unless we define ourselves as separate. Nor do we exist in separation from our sisters unless we define ourselves as separate.

It is so important to see our connectedness to and oneness with our sisters. We are the same. Yet we painstakingly keep our distance and fail to love one another. I must love myself to love my sister. If we are the same, I cannot love one (either myself or my sister) without loving the other. When I love my sister I contribute to her light. Is this threatening? Only in a competitive system. When I fuel her, we connect, and when we connect, we soar. I love her and in so doing our light merges. Her response or her consciousness does not matter. *I* know the connection and *I* draw upon it. If she too knows the connection, then it is even better.

The group of women exists; it is the updraft. All you have to do is plug into it and ride on into yourself. To make the connection with your sisters is to plug in. It is so simple to soar like the eagle.

GRACE

We are individuals and we are part of the collective of women. The two can come into balance, yet it is very, very difficult for this to happen while you live on the earth. It is just *barely* possible.

Do not despair in your seemingly ineffective attempts. One day you will know success. Keep going for that updraft. And keep working at the same time on your individual tasks. It will come together, it really will.

ELLEN

One of the most difficult parts of living on the earth at this time I find to be my lack of synchronicity with the values and behavior of the majority. Not only are my perspectives different, often contradictory to "the norm," but my goals vastly incongruous. And to the extent that I am true to myself, my actions and behaviors align with these views and goals. To this is sometimes added the efforts of others to counteract my work, to alter my direction, and to prevent my progress.

Women are labeled with permanent and "untreatable" psychosocial diagnoses for far less than such disparate views as these in the book. Countless women are medicated and/or institutionalized today for daring to differ and for struggling with these differences.

Of course we need to struggle and react and feel not only the extremes of our experience, but the meanings of those experiences in social context and in terms of our own growth, and then to process the reactions to us for owning these experiences: rejection, condemnation, withdrawal of that too conditional love, labeling, compartmentalization, and more.

We work, and we work hard. And so often we work hard in isolation and in untraveled territory. If we are truly expanding, by definition we venture into what for each of us is the unknown. Repeatedly we go beyond the beyond. At each step, peers, acquaintances, teachers, students who do not step with us fall away. We *feel real* pain.

Yet we know we must continue. And at each step as we regain our balance from the climbing of the previous step to stand tall again, we see the new view and we know we move with our heart. And again, feel *real* pain, as there become fewer and fewer to share the experience with. But the new view is good.

Long ago we as women grew beyond market value, in this marketplace known as earth. Every single woman incarnated on this planet is developmentally more advanced that the functional mentality of the systems and hierarchies we witness and live with daily. Yet we live here for the moment to clean up lessons and to help each other journey. Speak to your sisters of the important things. We all need each other so very much.

MAJAI

You are on an adventure. It is exciting to journey into the cosmos. The increasing expansion is the reward, the journey itself the gratification.

There are obstacles that hinder your travels, some because of the actions of others, some because of your own doing. There is little you can do about the choices and actions of others. At best you can work around these hindrances. How fruitless it is to worry about and invest energy in what others have done or are doing.

Most important to eliminate are self-created obstacles. Some are due to self-imposed limitations, some to attitude and expectation, but most are karmic: the result of your previous doings. For some of us this amounts to an enormous pile of baggage that must be toted around until a way can be found to release it. As long as we are encumbered by our past it is difficult to move forward. A ball and chain around the ankle make it very difficult to walk.

The first step in the removal of our unfinished business, the unripened karmic debt, is the *desire* to remove these obstacles. If we focus on our goal, which is spiritual expansion, we then seek to further the fulfill-ment of this purpose. The removal of obstacles becomes necessary and desirable. We *want* to clean away any debris on our path. We see that it is useless to step over it, to push it aside, to ignore it, to deny its existence. We simply cannot move forward as long as it is there. *Recognition of this fact that avoidance is not possible is essential.*

First is the commitment to your spiritual progress. Then is the search for obstacles. When you find them, look them squarely in the eyes, touch them, feel them, *own* them. And at that point you have taken your power back from them and returned it to yourself. You can then see them for what they are and know what to do to act appropriately to compensate for your previous actions, if compensation is necessary. You are then well on your way, a step further down your spiritual path.

How do you recognize the obstacles? They are exactly those things that you fear the most, that you avoid, and that make you squirm. Lights should flash when there is something you are afraid to say, do, think, or feel. And as soon as you recognize one of these, courageously chase after it. See it as an impediment to your journey. *It is not a battle, it is a reconciliation*. Relentlessly use whatever resources you have to get to it, while awake, while asleep, in your meditation. Ask for help from books, therapists, other people, women in spirit, your guides. Most of all pursue.

Each time an obstacle is cleared completely, you will feel relief, you will feel your progress, and you will be reminded that you *are* on an adventure.

ELLEN

To the extent that you have unfinished business or resistance, you will experience as disruptive the changes brought about by the non-physical joining the physical. As the non-physical enters the realm of the physical, it stirs up everything that isn't tied down. All that is part of your center remains intact and stable, while the rest is thrown hither and yon. "The rest" is anything that has not yet been harmonized with your center, or anything that is inherently disharmonious so it can't be.

Nevertheless, all the "stuff" is still your responsibility, so it is necessary for you to recollect it as it is tossed about. It can then be either added to your center or released to its proper place.

To conceptualize the process, physical matter (thus everything of the physical planes) can be seen as large particles in motion, and non-physical as smaller particles in faster motion. When they are thrown into the same pot, the non-physical is easily able to flow into the spaces between the physical particles. Because of the rapid motion, the non-physical is responsible for stirring up the entire mixture and dislodging the previously quiet physical matter.

So to the extent that anything in your life, be it of past, present or future, is not attached to your center, it will be forced into view. If you continue to add more of the non-physical vibration, the turmoil will only increase. And the subjective experience sooner or later will become overwhelming chaos, disorientation and disruption.

For you to stop to attend to collecting the loose ends is not backward motion. The temporary effort to realign is part of pathward motion. This is universal quality control at work. Those of you who would sooner forget the debris (the emotional issues, karmic baggage, old business, attachments to other than your path), will find that it becomes impossible to move ahead. The chaos and turmoil will impede your progress, for without the collection process you would be unable to function effectively in the new environment.

Many women are experiencing this situation already. They desire so much to move ahead, and are attracted to the new energy they are beginning to taste. The old baggage is looking pretty tiresome, a tedious proposition at best to keep digging around in the old lessons. Try as they might, the unpleasantness grows. Every contact had with the new energy (which would include entities of higher vibration) is simultaneously attractive and repulsive. Repulsive, because the contact serves only to stir up that which does not belong to the center. Attractive because it *is* progress.

Even in your anxiousness to move on, slow down to attend to all that would compromise the quality of the new experience in the new vibration. Don't wait until the debris reaches critical mass and forces your attention! Your progress is best when steady and even.

MAJAI

While the truth, the goodness, the light, the yin exists, we cannot always see it. Sometimes the debris has accumulated to an extent that it obscures the yin almost completely. (The yin is our "truth," by the way.)

Think of yourself as a wire screen. Upon it is thrown fine soil, but also rocks and stones and sticks and other foreign matter. The fine soil easily passes through the screen to join the pile accumulating behind it. Some of the soil is unable to pass because of the other debris. So you shake and wiggle and change your position, and eventually the soil will find a way to pass through and the stones will fall away. The more troublesome debris you may have to move out from under. Or it may be necessary to maneuver this way and that to be able to side step.

The universe, you can be sure, will keep tossing quantities of material at you. You need to sort and filter and screen all that comes your way, and all that you encounter on your journey. You need to take what is useful, the yin, and know how to let the remainder fall to exist where it will. Remove the obstacles that are self-created, that are yours. (They are stones too.)

The yin is yours for the taking.

ELLEN

A tremendous amount of what will come our way, simply because we live amidst such chaos on the earth, will not be to our liking, nor will it be harmonious with Natural Law. Nevertheless, it will come, along with willing participation of others. Sometimes it seems we are permanently oppressed and entrapped, rendered spiritually immobile, without a chance of escape. This is really not true, but our frustration and anger as we appear to stagnate can be momentous.

The choices are: to fight it, which so many of us have done for so long, with varying amounts of success; to go along with it, which unfortunately too many of us do; or, to move away from it, which some of us have done minimally with moderate success. The first two are not promising in terms of fostering our spiritual growth. Yet the last I believe can offer us much success if only we are willing to carry it to its full conclusion in terms of our spiritual work. As Majai has suggested, it amounts to side stepping in order to establish a space within which we can truly grow. With very little growth, many of us will find we have moved far beyond this chaos forever.

ANJA

We wish to emphasize the importance of avoiding confrontation. Confrontational behavior can kill our progress. It takes necessary energy from our goal. It invests in struggle. It invests in the opponent.

Yet equally important is to prevent anything or anyone from blocking our progress. To wimpily yield to something that stands in our way is not the same thing as avoidance of confrontation.

Please try to remember that your aim is to grow. Anything else is not forward motion. So it is necessary to make yourself a space within which you can grow. It involves the avoidance of participation in distracting pursuits.

And it involves carefulness. Carelessness can be as dangerous as confrontation. Care must be taken to avoid insulting Natural Law (thus causing the accumulation of karmic work). And care must be taken to ensure the integrity of your entity. Preserve the quality you have cared to build.

ELLEN

Confrontation is not limited to adverse situations. Frequently it is used as a game for avoidance of change. Seeking to make successful attack prevents another person's approach and entry into the vicinity of your realness, thereby eliminating all potential for change.

The play of confrontational behavior is not restricted to the earthplane. Unfortunately we are not graced with a shortage of women who take adverse positions with their guides. The competitive system has led to contest mentality where the avoidance of work or lessons means success for the incarnated and failure on the part of spirit. Game playing is without purpose in terms of spiritual development, and counteracts any possible benefit to be gained from honesty, straightforwardness and sincerity.

On a few too many occasions (any is too many), following a particularly "on target" albeit uncomfortable message from spirit, the woman resorts to avoidant behavior. It is hard to fight the written word or a tape recording. For a woman unable to perceive the vibration of the spirit person communicating, it is easy to question identity (or existence) of speaker or even the need for lesson learning.

She erroneously assumes that if she can prove that the speaker was not her guide, the content of the message is rendered inapplicable. Or if she can prove faulty character traits on the part of spirit, the message is thereby voided. In either case, she has beaten out attempts to alter her program; she has defied change.

When a woman is about the business of growing, she welcomes whatever from wherever or whomever. She carries an attitude of receptivity. It is when she seeks to hold back or to avoid change that she falls into *games* of proof, in which case, she carries an attitude of defiance.

From a technical standpoint, it matters not who delivers a message. If the words or the vibration make contact, the recipient then possesses a tool for growth. To refuse to hear the words unless spoken by a certain entity, or unless delivered in a particular format, amounts to avoidance. It is the seeking of an excuse.

On the other hand, it is advisable to require certain standards of performance including accuracy, with all people and entities encountered. Without consistency it is difficult to assess quality or accuracy. So it becomes very useful to know the speaker, the reasons for speaking, and the qualifications for speaking.

There are many, many problems and shortcomings glaringly obvious within spirit realms. Some we will mention. Discrimination is essential. Constant evaluation and ongoing choices cannot be avoided if quality work is to prevail. Nevertheless, contentious attitude or confrontational behavior will not promote your expansion. It will not allow legitimate evidence to show. It hinders the flowering of possibility. If you wish to grow, do not apply contentious attitude to your experience with spirit. Question fully, demand quality, and discriminate to the best of your ability. And do so with love and openness.

MAJAI

Previously mentioned was the continuum of development and the fact that entities existing on other planes are not necessarily more advanced than earthplane entities. The "levels" spoken about actually contain subsets, or form possibilities within each "level." Developmentally an entity in spirit form who has yet to finish, for example, earthplane incarnations, is at the same "level" as an entity still in the incarnation process and living on the earth.

Entities at certain stages of development, as Ellen mentioned earlier, can be divided into several parts (usually four or five) and are thus capable of existing simultaneously in different states. It is possible to have more than one simultaneous or overlapping earthplane incarnation, more than one in spirit form, or some of each (which is usually the case). *But regardless of the places of existence, the developmental stage of the entity is determined by the entity in her entirety,* as if undivided.

If you exist on the earth and also in a non-earth form, each of these states is developmentally parallel. I therefore take issue with the concept of "the higher self." How can a self be "higher" than itself?

Entities in divided states do not normally have access to their other forms. The purpose of the division system is to allow progress in differing areas of development (personalities, abilities, etc.) simultaneously and in a non-confusing way. The division is for the purpose of creating simplicity.

As one's spiritual development progresses, the division system terminates and the entity returns to being one. And all the forms taken in the divided state realign and merge. When the entity no longer has the need for earthplane (or other comparable) incarnations, the forms will finish the realignment process. This consolidation is necessary for the entity to move into the next "level," that of sound and color. At the point of consolidation, awareness of the process is common, although not necessary. Those of you who transform parallel to the earth's transformation into sound and color will undergo this final merging of the selves.

KIOKA

If a woman can be convinced that she is not capable of assessing her environment or her position as part of that environment, she is rendered immobile. Concepts which tell her that her conscious awareness is unreliable empower things or people other than the woman herself.

It is true that she exists in many aspects, some unfamiliar to her as she lives daily on the earth. But, as Majai said, these parts are neither greater nor smaller, more capable nor less capable than her waking consciousness of the earth.

In all the places through which I have evolved so far, concepts such as a higher self, a superconsciousness, a subconscious, etc. have never been created. Rather, in all these places have lived appreciations for the vastness, and sometimes inaccessibility of an entity's totality. (With expansion, awareness and accessibility do increase or change.) Appreciation of that totality does not belittle or disempower any part of that total entity. And therefore, there has been an avoidance of legitimization of excuses leading to the failure of an individual woman to take responsibility for her own decision-making, direction determination, or quality of choice.

I can see from my perspective that on the earth these concepts are perpetuated by those determined to keep men superior to women, as well as by women determined to avoid growth and action. Women who genuinely seek answers fall prey to these philosophies because they feel small in their lack of clarity and perspective. Remember, the first mistake you can make is to define yourself as small and inferior. With that kind of thinking it follows that you *will* receive (and welcome?) disempowering philosophies to substantiate that smallness. Once you accept that you are indeed quite able, astute, accurate and competent to discover your own answers through internalization, *and* you decide you are willing to take responsibility for your own progress or lack of progress, these concepts will be useless to you.

Because many of those in spirit form (including some of your guides) have yet to finish the incarnation process, developmentally they parallel entities on earth. Remember, many of these entities are no different from you. Many of the social problems as well as the lack of collective consciousness exist in this realm, just as they do on earth. One's vibration, thus place of existence, is determined in part by consciousness (selflessness and collective consciousness vs. self-perpetuating consciousness) and by amount of fear. Fear is often based in the self-perpetuating consciousness and a win-lose mentality. Spirit people are not free of the competitive system any more than are earthplane folks. Their behavior necessarily reflects their consciousness and fear levels.

The problems we face as women on the earth, also exist in the other realms. The needed changes in social structure and consciousness, the changes away from the competitive, individualistic system, are also necessary on other planes. As you can see, the situation is more extensive than you may have realized.

Many are working to change these conditions. Nevertheless, we are still faced with a difficult situation on the earth. Our facility in interacting with other realms is poor. We are adolescent in our ability to be self-determined. And it is necessary to be self-determined in our relationships with entities in other realms.

The major issue that needs to be addressed is the familiar one of control of others. Spirit women and our guides have specific work to do. They are there to guide, not to direct. Incarnated entities have come with certain work to do, certain lessons to learn, and a pre-decided, agreed upon general developmental plan for this earthwalk. The guides' job is to poke and prod and intervene as necessary to ensure adherence to the pre-decided plan. Each of us must make her own mistakes; to deprive us of that right does us a disservice in the long run. We are here to learn completely and well, not to slide by or squeak under the wire. We need to make our mistakes and our successes as they are true reflections of our development.

Those in spirit are in positions where control over the incarnated is certainly possible. Many do in fact see their roles as ones of autonomy and control. Control of the incarnated has become almost traditional, and has evolved to now be an unquestioned state of affairs. This is similar to the male institutions on the earth, I spoke about earlier. Again, the thinking is male, the priority being control over another rather than the fostering of self-control.

Unfortunately many spirit people commonly use deceit, trickery, and manipulation to get the incarnated into the desirable spot. It has literally become a game, a game with laughter, a game of laughing behind the consciousness of the incarnated. This information should come as no surprise. It is the common method of the earth, and each of us has spent time in spirit in these same roles.

I have come to identify this situation to you, but more importantly to help us all change it to create a mutually beneficial way of operating with the priority being the spiritual development of all concerned. There are those of us who know that the manipulative, control oriented way is neither necessary nor desirable. We have been functioning successfully in open, honest, unfearful relationships with incarnated women for a long time.

We know we have a job to do, and we trust that you know this too. Because we all have the same goal, each of us is trying sincerely to reach that goal. We trust your sincerity. We know that we can only do our part and it is not up to us to manipulate you to do yours. If you do yours due to our creation of false pretenses, the job is not done.

Your communication with spirit women can be direct, honest, open, and clear. Confusion serves no purpose. Nor does a feeling by the incarnated that she is not expanded or evolved enough to understand, or worthy enough to get truthful answers to her questions. Remember my sisters, *if you are able to sincerely ask a question, you are able to receive an answer you can understand, in a form that is clear.* Expect such quality in all your relationships, be they interplane or earthplane. Set an impeccable example of such quality by your thoughts, words, and actions. Only then do you have the right to expect reciprocation. My love to you.

INYANI

A tremendous amount of the present day way of acting needs to change. By writing this book we hope so much to give you the encouragement you need to try new and better ways.

Many, many women in spirit share your frustrations. They too are committed to establishing methods and systems based on female principles. They too want to create, for a change, in the best interest of women.

In spite of good intentions and strong motivations, some spirit women are finding the implementation very difficult - difficult because of old habits, difficult because of efforts to contradict their attempts, and difficult because some earthplane women are struggling in their own ways with the changes.

Not uncommon, we are finding, is it for a spirit woman to do her best to make changes toward openness and honesty, only to be met by resistance or rejection on the part of the earthplane woman. So many of us in all vibrations are afraid to trust a straightforward, sincere, unmanipulative approach. Always an ulterior motive is assumed or suspected.

It is wise neither to be naive nor suspecting. A stance someplace in the middle with trust is necessary to allow our attempts to succeed. Please try to remember that spirit women are taking chances on new trust just as you are. Both parties need to prove sincerity, commitment and honesty, and this has to take time.

ELLEN

Some years ago a spirit woman said to me that it would be advantageous if I would welcome her and make her feel wanted and necessary, "for we all need to feel wanted and necessary," she said. Our desire to be loved does not vanish when we change form, any more than our awareness or consciousness changes. There are many sources from which we all receive sustenance, but always this inflow must be plentiful regardless of our place of residence. Spirit needs to feel your love for them.

I wish to mention the importance of mutuality in our relationships with spirit women. In one way or another, we exist for each other, we need each other, no matter what our specific roles may be. Frequently we forget the person behind a role: her vulnerabilities, strengths, weaknesses, struggles, and needs. Each of us is able to function far better when we are known in a job, as our behavior has context and meaning.

She acknowledges my hurts and joys, my fears, my feelings and sensitivities, my efforts and courage in light of my abilities, but I also acknowledge hers. *It is not a sign of weakness to let yourself be known.* Rather, it is a mark of courage, an indication that you are willing to accept yourself in your totality, willing to risk acceptance or rejection by others, and capable of receiving the other in her totality. When we are accepted in our totality, we are then free to grow beyond it. The same holds true for spirit women.

We all seek perfection. To have perfection walk in the door is everyone's wish. This wish, however, can be quite a burdensome greeting. Do not receive spirit with an expectation of perfection. These women are fallible, and yet must also be held accountable in a realistic way for their actions and be expected to perform appropriate to their abilities. They are strong, capable, courageous women and need to be seen in such a light without the negation of their vulnerabilities and struggles to grow. They are working as hard as you are. They struggle and hurt at times, as you do. They are sensitive. They need to be treated with the same respect and care you require.

Unconditional love is what we have to offer one another. We may not like certain personality traits or certain behaviors of another person, and they may not like plenty about us. But we can continue to accept the person with love regardless of these distasteful characteristics. There is such freedom, joy, and relief to be had from the realization that spirit will love us no matter how badly we blow it, no matter how many times we fall on our faces in the same mud puddles. They hear our every thought, our deepest heartaches, our condemnations, our doubts, and our worst fears, and yet continue to stand by us and love us anyway. They may not like all that they see about you, or what they hear you think, but they see it anyway. You may not like all that you see about them, but it exists nevertheless. Mutual acknowledgement makes it much easier to deal with. Accord spirit the same unconditional love she accords you.

Give her feedback on her efforts. Thank her for her consideration and caring. Sincerely and respectfully tell her what you *don't* like, what she does that makes you uncomfortable, and ask her to tell you the same. Make amends as necessary and allow her equal opportunity to do so. The honesty and openness that is possible is magnificent. It affords us all opportunity for maximal growth. Be committed to the relationship. Forgive and repair that you may each grow and progress and change for the better. Eventually you will come to comfort in the total honesty and openness that you both create. Use it to grow, use it to love, and use it as a template for your earthplane relationships.

GRACE

You know, it's a hard job being a woman's guide. The guide is with her 24 hours per day, all year long, for 80, maybe 90 years. That's four or five times the commitment of motherhood!

The guide listens to every thought, ranting, sadness, joy and aspiration of the woman. She is the recipient of the slanderous attacks on the universe or goddess/god. It is her responsibility to promote the woman's growth, to heal her wounds, and to keep her moving, regardless of the woman's opinion of these efforts. And in most cases, she is an unknown presence, usually not even identified at the closure of the earthwalk. This can definitely be one of the most thankless tasks! I say this not to solicit sympathy (although a little wouldn't hurt), but to alert you to the complexity of your situation.

While you have guides (and spirit people with you other than just the two primary guides), you are the one who is responsible for your progress and your route through the universe. You decide with or without their help. You make use of the opportunities they provide or turn them down. You choose to learn your lessons or to avoid them. It is you who resists or moves forward. None of these things is your guides' responsibility.

Your lack of progress is your doing. While guides may fail to facilitate to the extent that they are able, they do not impede your progress. You can work with them or against them.

They too are in the role relative to you to grow. They are learning cooperation, consideration and group dynamics. They are growing as individuals separate from any growth they achieve from their roles as your guides. So they too will make mistakes. Some they can fix. Others are lost opportunities. Their choices *do* impact on you, just as yours impact on them and their progress. It is a group effort and all are affected by its process, not only you.

And so for any of you to seek to blame is not a good idea. Always it is important to return to the primary focus: your spiritual progress. Forgive and move on. Just because someone wronged you doesn't give you license to be legitimate in your stagnation. (And I say this for the benefit of both you and your guides, for all of you are capable of such thinking.)

Your business is your development. In addition to your lessons, you have come to work, to contribute to the collective. Your guides' business is their own development, and because of their role with you, their work is to facilitate your growth and your work. Do not be concerned with your guides beyond their work with you. See them as feeling women in those roles, but continue to focus on your own growth.

The extent of the relationship between you and your guides is dependent upon your developmental level, your specific lessons, your work, and both of your choices on how to interact.

GRACE

A long time ago, Ellen was a Tlingit woman who lived on the coast of Canada. As usual she was a medicine woman, and a medium. I was her main contact in spirit. (I really wasn't her guide, but that doesn't change the story.) I had a name for her which meant She Who Lives With White Eagle, which will mean more to you later in the book. I mention it now so you will know where the name originated.

She was responsible for making sure she accomplished the work she incarnated to do, and I to be an accurate communicator. We got pretty wrapped up in our friendship and were having quite a good time of it. And while we did the work that was intended, Ellen became sloppy about attention to detail in her village. One day on her way to trade in the marketplace, she managed to get herself killed, by walking unaware into the presence of an angered and emotionally unbalanced man.

She and I were shocked by the sudden interruption in our work and our relationship. The village suffered for the loss. Work was left undone. And believe me, we learned a very hard lesson in the importance of adhering to the goal.

We had taken for granted things we shouldn't have. I suppose we thought we would be taken care of if we did the work, and that somehow we were exempt from responsibility for the maintenance of our presence on the earth. We had a responsibility for carrying out the work, but also for making sure it *could* be carried out. Others were there to help us, but not to do for us what we should have done. And since we failed to do our part, we sabotaged the entire plan.

MAJAI

Women are guided by specific entities, usually in spirit form, while on the earth. There is a basic structure or format for this guidance (which differs from the format for men), that is followed until a woman's development precludes its usefulness. Women have two main guides who work together but who exist independently of each other.

One is in charge of insuring the woman's physical, mental, and spiritual well-being. She makes sure balance and health are maintained as development progresses and interaction with other spirit people occurs. Commonly she is known as the Healing Guide. The other entity is responsible for keeping the woman on the pre-decided path, in order that she learn the necessary lessons and accomplish the intended work. Additionally her role is one of protector, in a sense, as she controls access of other entities to the woman. She is known as the Path Keeper.

The Path Keeper usually stays with the woman throughout her incarnation, but the Healing Guide may change as major stages are reached in the woman's development. Requirements for health change with progress so it is logical that a woman might outgrow a healing guide's abilities and expertise. Depending upon vibrational status, lessons to be learned, and the karmic situation of the woman, she may have a male guide. If so, it is usually the Path Keeper who is male, rather than the Healing Guide. These two guides reflect the developmental level of the woman, the three entities being at comparable levels. This allows for functional compatibility.

Hierarchically beneath these two guides are various other entities, who function in a range of capacities and for varying amounts of time. They are directed by and are answerable to the two main guides. They usually choose to assist the woman because of common experience, gratitude, or particular expertise in an area relevant to the woman's journey. Most often messages from spirit are given by these adjunctive entities or guides.

The most important relationships a woman has with spirit are those with these two guides. They might not choose to communicate directly with a woman, or may do so in a number of ways. There are many possibilities for communication, so do not fall into limited thinking concerning this matter. It is the guides' decision as to the most beneficial means of communication, although certainly they hear and consider a woman's preferences. Allow them to do their job, and respect them in their perspective and thus their choices.

Structures exist for guides to get help in guiding a woman. Problems too difficult for the guide to manage, or relationship problems may arise, in which cases it is appropriate for the guide to seek assistance. A guide can also call upon entities of higher vibration to offer their expertise or guidance. This will become increasingly necessary as the transformation progresses, as many entities (incarnated and not) are moving into what for them is new territory.

ANJA

Confusion has arisen about the difference in function and quality between a woman's guides and other entities, especially message bearing entities. The role of the guide has been stated. Guides exist to facilitate your progress as you grow. Developmentally they are your equals. They have been chosen for this position because of a previous connection, an existing debt, or particular skills that could help you at this time. They are necessarily slightly less resistant to forward motion than you are, and slightly more skilled in specific areas relevant to your blocks.

Guides can be negligent but not detrimental. Because they do not work in isolation, much opportunity for scrutiny of their choices by others constantly exists. So do not worry that they would not work in your best interest. If problems did arise, they would be replaced or assisted until adequate resolution was achieved.

Other entities in spirit, such as those who speak through a woman when she is in trance, or channeled entities, are not guides. Usually these entities have something they wish to communicate and have sought out a vehicle in order to do it: the woman. The quality of such entities is variable, but at the present time reflective of male thought. Those who are capable of working using cooperative methods, do not seek vehicles.

So it is with these entities that your ability to discriminate becomes very important. Discrimination is equally important even with entities who communicate as we suggest, who use methods compatible with women's growth. So if you choose to listen to information or messages you must be alert to the identification of material that is not productive of your expansion. Yet there are those in spirit who can help you tremendously if you are willing to risk understanding and listening to their perspectives.

ELLEN

Entities of the A^1 and A^2 categories exist as collections of their previous forms, forms from all the planetary and spirit walks in various vibrations. The entity is then most accurately referred to as "they," being as yet a group consciousness. With the transition into sound and color (B), singularity must occur.

At the junction between physicalness and non-physicalness, the paths of women and men necessarily separate. (It can happen earlier, yet must occur before entrance into non-physical realms.) Regardless of diversity of gender in the collection of forms taken, gender identity is a given. Therefore, the "they" indicating group consciousness, is actually a plural form of "she" or "he."

KIOKA

Claims by an entity to be group consciousness are not inaccurate. However, her/his awareness of the fact of uncollected forms also means that it is quite time to return to singularity. This means that the relinquishment of many attachments is essential for her/his growth to proceed.

An entity who wishes to use an incarnated person to serve her/his own purposes (as in cases of trance mediumship) needs to keep the person willing to participate. Novel ideas or concepts foreign to usual earthplane consciousness, by virtue of their seeming incomprehensibility, can ensure the attention of the person quite effectively. Presentations as a group consciousness meet the criteria of sufficient novelty to warrant attention.

It is technically not inaccurate to show duality of gender. However, behind the apparent duality remains the ordinary and the usual: one sex or the other. As with singularity, this is not likely to be viewed as particularly special.

A presentation with the following announcement, while not very fancy, is actually more accurate than claims of genderlessness or group consciousness: "I am a male entity. (Or I am a female entity.) I still identify with all my disjointed and unaligned forms. But I want you to think I am special enough for you to allow me complete access to and expression through your bodies. I guess I am not ready to give up my attachments to physical form such as yours, so I seek continued participation in your territory."

MAJAI

As the purification and the transformation unfold, more and more incarnated women will open to spirit. The best system of quality control is your own knowing and feeling. You must sort what you hear from spirit just as you do information from other incarnated entities. Again, trust your feelings. And fine tune them to be reliable. Many messages are being given by very unconscious and minimally evolved beings. There is much erroneous information in circulation, much sensationalism, much manipulation and control of others being perpetuated by and via spirit entities.

It is possible for an entity to lower her vibration (to a point) to see what is developmentally (vibrationally) behind her. But it is not possible to raise it beyond her own level. Keep this in mind as you process the information that comes your way. You will often find indications of "contracted" (as opposed to expanded) thought in many messages from spirit you encounter. The vibration that comes with the messages can be very telling, as can the behavior and consciousness of the message bearer. *Be very wary of messages from male entities or via men in the days of the growing yin. We must face completely the ramifications of the changes*; as the yin increases and women raise their vibration, their view of the cosmos will be from heights never before experienced by incarnated entities. Trust the expansion as you watch it unfold.

ELLEN

All of us are subjected to the prevailing universal winds. All entities in every vibration, including respective guides, are undergoing changes comparable in magnitude to our changes on the earth. Each of us has free will in our approach to these universal winds, so just as we have an option of resistance and hesitation, spirit has the same.

It is likely that you will encounter entities in spirit, especially in the lower vibrations, but by no means limited to these vibrations, who resist change equal to the resistance prevalent on the earth. If you encounter such a person, do not let her/him stand in your way. Simply articulate your concerns and ask for assistance from a higher vibration. It will come.

There are many entities whose job it is to intervene in situations of difficulty. They may come at a guide's request, or because they spot a difficulty possibly unknown to you or your guide. Sometimes their intervention is with the cooperation of a guide. At others it is in order to allow you to surpass the scope of a guide.

Especially at this time, many of us can benefit greatly from more expanded perspectives than that of our place of residence. That is one reason for the existence of this book. Seek any help you need and do not be shy about doing so.

KIOKA

When you were two years old you were only tall enough to see the edge of the kitchen counter. By the time you were four, you had grown in size to be able to see the entire counter. Necessarily, you also had a view of everything on that counter, simply because it was there.

This is the same process of growth you are currently undergoing in terms of your spiritual expansion. As you drop your unnecessary baggage, your view of your surroundings will become clear. The visibility will increase and so will your accuracy in identifying what is before you.

All entities who exist in the space you are expanding to include - the space of essential energy minus the amount of baggage you too have released - will become known to you. Your ability to read spirit should not be criteria for accomplishment. Focus on feeling, opening and growing beyond your present ability. Trust that you will come to know the entire picture one day. All realms are available to you.

Throughout the book we talk about the elimination of baggage. Nevertheless, it is something you need to wish to do. When your desire to move forward reaches sufficient magnitude, you will release your clinging. And then you will know your progress. Right now, you are unaware of your surroundings to the extent possible simply because you carry too much baggage. That baggage includes expectations, fears, conditioning, karmic debt, and emotional turmoil. Behind it is your center. It is with that center that you experience your surroundings including the entities in it.

MAJAI

There are really only two directions an entity can travel, forward or backward. Forward and backward (thus progress and anti-progress) are relative terms. A place of stagnation or lack of motion cannot exist, as change is the nature of the universe. And relative to movement in one direction, stagnation amounts to movement in the opposite direction. So if you aren't going forward, you are going backward.

I mention all this because I want to talk briefly about what happens to the entities who do not follow their dharma. All of us are headed to merge with the universal energy of which we are formed. It will happen whether we go forward or backward, although the manner differs.

An entity has free will to resist the universal flows, and to refuse to be carried by them. There are those who have made a practice of resistance and at this point, know not how to reverse their courses. Some are, in fact, quite content in their state of resistance. There are even those who go so far as to actively resist, to fight the flow; they make it their work.

Resistance and counteractivity are easiest at times of major energy shifts, when momentum in a certain direction is at its weakest. Such a time of low momentum has just occurred with the shift from yang to yin. It afforded opportunities for stagnation, application of efforts simultaneously in contradictory directions, and indecision as to direction. As energy resumes a defined course, as is beginning to be the case with the yin, such directional chaos is rendered inoperative.

For a time, many of our efforts to expand into the yin were opposed, intentionally and unintentionally. Many of us have been involved in contentions of sorts. Our overall plan has been to not fight, but to hold our ground and defend our territory. A few women with particular qualifications have chosen to take specific forms in order to help us pass through such situations of adversity.

The universal winds (yin winds) have picked up to an extent that it is no longer necessary to stand our ground against attack to the degree that was previously necessary. The current situation for women is by no means free and easy sailing, but the extent of the contention has decreased.

And what happens to the contender, the entity who chooses to fight his or her dharma? Repeatedly they are given opportunities to make compensations for their destruction. In order to begin the process of the reversal of their efforts, to once again become universally harmonious, they need to face the full effects of their actions. Opportunities are given as long as Natural Law allows. And then the entity is absorbed into the universal, the collective, against his/her will.

As we expand our light becomes brighter. As we contract it dims. Energy flows from greater to lesser concentration. The dimness and the light seek to come into balance. There exists a critical point at which time it is impossible to stop the balancing of energies. The tension reaches a critical stage where return to balance *must* happen. The entity in his/her darkness gets swallowed by the light.

But in order for the absorption to occur, a dissociation of parts, past forms, and attachments is necessary. Just as with expansion, the parts cease to exist and, collectivity and ultimately oneness prevails. The dissolution of the individual occurs involuntarily for the adharmic entity, as opposed to voluntarily for the forward moving entity. Because of the entity's resistance to the process, the entity experiences much pain as the events unfold. (Resistance and tension equal pain.) The process is horrific to watch. It follows Natural Law. There is no punisher, no facilitator. It is simply what must happen, and is exactly the natural consequence of what the entity created him/herself.

KIOKA

Why do entities incarnate?

In every vibration a vehicle exists for the expression of an entity's imperfections, all that she carries other than pure yin. The physical spirit realms are governed largely by mental status and of course by vibration. Consequently, all thoughts manifest as form. There an entity does not act, but vibrates and conceptualizes her environment. The immediate environment mirrors the evolutionary and mental status very precisely, allowing her to watch the results of her thoughts, desires, and essence.

Incarnated physical form is of slightly greater density, requiring action to be taken to transform the mental process into manifestation. The mental status meanwhile manifests in other realms without the requirement of action. However, from the vantage point of the entity incarnated, awareness of these additional manifestations does not happen. This allows an illusion of time and space, within which decisions and choice of action can be made, and with it, an opportunity to alter the mental outlook prior to gross manifestation.

For the entity laden with impurities or imperfections, the instantaneous manifestation of mental status and vibration (as is found in physical spirit realms) can be overwhelming. A time in a body in a vibration a bit slower gives prospect of temporary relief. Time and space are created so that only select aspects of the entity receive manifestation. (Sequential and simultaneous incarnations allow many aspects to be addressed in climates of relative simplicity and order.)

During an incarnation, as the vibration refines and impurities are dropped, mental status and vibration creep into manifestation without action. (The entity is actually moving on from the earthplane vibration while she maintains her body, to function in more subtle vibrations.) With evolution, speedier results of actions and thoughts are presented. Contradictions to Natural Law become unmistakable. The capability of the mind to create the environment increases, and the illusion of time and space falls away. (She begins to function as if in physical spirit form.)

An earthwalk makes lesson learning (the elimination of impurities from the core of essential energy) easier. Yet with the opportunity afforded by time and space comes equal opportunity for avoidance. The need for lesson learning reflects the amount of impurity carried. Resistance to its relinquishment results from identification with the impurity rather than with the essential nature.

An earthwalk allows easy viewing of pieces of the total impurity. So it is by definition because of the impurity and resistance or clinging that an earthwalk is necessary. The physical body is the vehicle for the expression of imperfection. (No wonder such chaos reigns on the earth. The earth is a place *for* expression of chaos, disorder and disharmony. Of course, the idea is to view so that change in the direction of harmony can follow.) The physical spirit realms are in some ways even more chaotic, yet a bit more accurately reflective of vibration and mental status. There, fluctuations are also represented, whereas on the earth conditions tend to become fixed.

ELLEN

The condition in which the physical body is kept can hinder or promote expression of the imperfections. In the extreme, a disharmoniously functioning body can block altogether the expression. On the other hand, bodies in balance will provide a vehicle for precise and accurate reflection.

When the goal is growth, it becomes obvious that an entity would seek to present her true nature as well as the baggage she carries, for only after it has been displayed can it be adjusted. It is logical for those who prefer to block the developmental process to keep parallel dysfunction of the body.

MAJAI

A woman's body is her own. It is a tool which she can use to promote her spiritual progress. How she uses it, what condition she keeps it in, whom she shares it with, are her choices, and her choices alone. No one should have access to it or make decisions concerning it other than the woman herself.

Her body is an important instrument. Much effort contributed to its creation. Much energy is invested daily in its maintenance. It is not something an entity can afford to lose due to neglect, abuse, or control by another.

Current medical thought apparently values a physical body in and of itself. Longevity is esteemed, and drastic attempts are made to insure survival. Why? A body lacks use except as an instrument to spiritual growth. Perhaps more time on the earthplane would benefit an entity's spiritual progress. Perhaps it is the most efficient time for an entity to leave and change form.

Lessons can be learned via a body. The natural consequences of neglect, abuse, or control by another can be effective although harsh teachers. Certain limitations or conditions may be built into a body at the time of its formation. In such a way, an entity may be forced, or strongly encouraged to adhere to the prescribed path. An example could be a dyslexic child who necessarily has difficulty excelling in traditional intellectual pursuits (reading especially), and is thus forced to develop other abilities. In this case, the condition, the dyslexia, is not something to be eradicated. It is a vehicle to encourage development of specific abilities and sensitivities. And ultimately the child has, because of the dyslexia, an opportunity to move farther forward by developing these other sensitivities. Limitations and conditions can be gifts. Therefore, instead of a disabled or handicapped child, what exists is a gifted child. (All cases of dyslexia do not fit this category, by the way.)

A physical condition can facilitate the removal of karmic baggage. Perhaps an entity caused specific pain and suffering to another entity, and has yet to learn the ramifications and to understand fully the effects of those actions. A comparable congenital condition, or an injury resulting in a similar physical condition might be the most efficacious method to remove these karmic obstacles.

For a woman to give away control of her body to another serves no purpose. Another entity is not going to care for this body as she can to facilitate her spiritual growth. Does the other even know what her work or her path really is? The final assessment, regardless of skills and good intentions of the other, necessarily must be up to the woman herself. Information and suggestions can be gathered from others, but decisions must be her own. All health practitioners are tools, and nothing more. Do not lose sight of who owns the responsibility for a body, or who governs progress down the spiritual path.

Use your body consciously. Know what it is being used for and how. Make decisions regarding its care and feeding, health and sickness based on your spiritual needs and goals. Value it as a special instrument and give it the respect and care it requires to do the intended job.

When it is time to discard it, have the courage to do so. And try to make appropriate decisions about its care as it prepares to die, so that you as an entity will be ready and available to function in your next form. Remember that the environment your body lives in has a direct impact upon your mental functioning and consciousness. Your consciousness will move on even as you leave your body behind.

MAJAI

At certain junctions a metamorphosis of all the aspects and bodies of an entity occurs. The death of a body is merely a change of form. It has purpose. It lacks valuation as good or bad. It may be beneficial or not to the total growth of the entity.

The modern world has become fearful of the transformation known as death. The fear is due perhaps to the fact that understanding of an entity beyond the grossest physical level has been devalued, to the extent that an entity is no longer seen in a greater context of processes of transformation. Many entities are caught in a one-lifetime mentality, clinging to the "sacred body" for definition and purpose. But many who do understand the process of spiritual evolution and transformation, also see the death of a body as undesirable and to be avoided.

When the earthplane work is finished, it is time to move on. Death is a time of celebration, a birth into the place of the next adventure. To artificially prolong or terminate a body's life, goes against the universal flows. At best it amounts to a waste of energy, at worst to interference with the entity's spiritual growth.

One's attitude toward death has direct bearing on one's attitude toward life. If we live in a constant state of fear of death, and arrange our actions and purposes to accommodate this fear, our life takes on a far different quality than if we see death as a marker of the next phase of our journey. I ask you to think about your attitude toward your own death, and the death of others. What to you are acceptable deaths? Do you use words like "unfortunate," "sad," or "untimely" to describe an entity's passing? Do you find it sad for the survivors to learn the lessons that can be learned only in the absence of the entity? Such feelings are unproductive. It is important to expand the context in which you place death.

When you can release your attachments to death, you will find a freedom to live and grow. Motivation will be the possibilities for achievement and progress in terms of spiritual growth. You will cease to limit the scope of your goals and purposes to one lifetime. You will see that endeavors incomplete at the time of death can be continued at another time. You will let go of your attachments to other entities. (Remember control issues.) And you will be able to allow them to develop according to their need, in the most appropriate place and form. You will release energy tied to the pain and suffering of others (or yourself). The quality of your life will be much improved when you come to see death for what it is.

AMNA

The way a person dies is purposeful. Each death is specifically designed to teach the dying person and possibly those in relationship to that person. Usually the lessons are simple. The physical condition reflects how that body was used, respected, neglected and cared for. A death by "accident" or trauma tells us different things than does a death by consuming disease.

Awareness and consciousness can accompany *any* death, regardless of the way the physical body separates from the entity, or the abruptness of separation.

In some cases the presence of pain is karmically necessary. It is there to teach what can best be learned by physical suffering, and as such is not bad. In many cases, pain reflects resistance: resistance to forward motion spiritually, resistance to acceptance of the current situation, and resistance to facing feelings and emotions. Usually it is a combination of the three.

So to some extent pain is a choice, as is massive medication to cover up pain and to eliminate awareness of the experience. It seems easier for some people to opt for physical pain than to tend to that which exists behind it.

It is possible to transmute physical pain. With many people the emotional components of dying are denied or ignored. (The feelings that go with separations, the reactions of others, unfinished business, misjudgments or not so good choices, the subjective experience of dying: aloneness, isolation, fear of what is next, excitement, anticipation, and relief *should* be very real.) *Emotional unpleasantness unacknowledged quickly can become physical tension (pain). Spiritual resistance likewise can easily become emotional pain. And spiritual resistance is essentially an attempt to avoid change.* Change involves relinquishment of attachments to the present, and acceptance of something new.

(Failure to let go of what we like is difficult. But that doesn't mean we have to stop liking it or loving it. It means maybe we could move along better without toting it along. We can't possibly cling to everything that at one time was enjoyed. There isn't room to pack the whole universe into our suitcases. Easier to put ourselves into the universe! If we let go, whatever we love will not disappear. Our clinging is not what makes it real or valid.)

Dying is very visible change, a dramatic change in the state of the physical body. Those who have difficulty accepting change in any size, shape or form, have even more difficulty accepting death. As with any transformation, lack of resistance allows the process to unfold at its natural rate and in the most balanced manner.

All people are given forewarning of their own deaths. Most refuse to acknowledge the messages. Some do and they are then prepared to harmonize with the process.

An all too common misconception is that as soon as a person is off guard, s/he will be snatched out of her/his body. "Victim of death" thought is paranoia based in fear. Fear of an almighty god, fear of the universe as trickster, fear of punishment, fear of suffering for mistakes or misjudgments, and disrespect for the self are not the things growth and expansion are made of. These are products of contracted minds.

When a person lives in love, desires to grow, and seeks to restore balance where indiscretion has led to imbalance, a punisher cannot exist and fear of transformation and change (fear of death) have no place. In a climate where control over others, competition and ruthlessness to perpetuate the individual at the expense of the collective exist, it is no wonder such distortions of natural processes such as death occur.

ELLEN

Can you imagine a society that feared the birth of a baby as ours fears the death of that same person? The two are identical processes, separated only by a few years called life. Each is a change of form and a change of residence.

There are many babies who resist their own births, and there are others who are quite excited and even smile moments later. A willing and cooperative baby makes birthing so much easier for her/himself, the mother and others assisting on both exit and entrance sides, than the baby determined to go in the other direction.

ELLEN

A question was asked about suicide by a client of mine. Her Healing Guide, Anne, responded with the following comment. The succinctness of her words I found to be extraordinarily refreshing:

> It is a collective decision for an entity to incarnate. The person (entity) participates in that decision. The lessons to be learned are also collectively decided, as are ongoing modifications in that decision.
>
> Once the person has a body, it exists only as an opportunity to grow and to learn those lessons. As with other opportunities, it can be refused. If a person no longer wishes to continue with a particular body, that is her/his choice. Suicide can be a refusal of opportunity. Really, on this level, it is free of good or bad connotations. It could be a choice to do things in a different way.
>
> Usually suicide is done as a result of fear of dealing with issues or lessons, and amounts to resistance to forward motion spiritually. Even so, we are free to make a choice to avoid issues. There are not karmic consequences to suicide per se. There are karmic consequences to resistance to development. Suicide can be a very clear statement of resistance.
>
> It is also possible that the life anticipated (and agreed upon) prior

to the incarnation does not pan out as expected. If the collective agrees that it is not worthwhile for the person to continue with that body, death will occur with the help of the collective. However, if there is disagreement over the benefits to be gained from continuation in that body, or a complete change in game plan is necessary, it is reasonable for the person to say no. Without the cooperation of others, a death would not be arranged. In which case, suicide would be the solution.

Respect for the body and for the opportunity for the use of a body facilitates its functional capabilities. But it is not "sacred" as some people believe. And it is not the property of someone/s other than the entity who lives in it. It is hers/his alone.

ELLEN

A lot of work goes into the formation of a body. There are entities other than the body's owner who are constantly involved in its maintenance and purpose. Commitments have been made to the care and feeding of the body so that its owner can learn necessary lessons and perform agreed upon work. So a decision for suicide is a complex decision with many resultant effects.

In contrast to murder, however, which involves the theft of choices that do not belong to anyone other than the body owner, suicide is in an entirely different ballpark. The politics of death or a decision not to remain in earthly conditions certainly have contributed to the emotional intensity surrounding the subject of suicide. (What would happen to business and profits if all the laborers under a landowner killed themselves?) The extensive fear of death certainly reflects in the panic over a suicide choice.

KIOKA

Transformations involve the relinquishment of the old and the entertainment of the new. Death is the relinquishment half of the transformation process. People today have lost sight of the second half, the half which is the awakening to and movement into the new.

Transformations cannot be forced. They must unfold in their own time. If a feeling of being forced is present, a transformation loses its fluidity and brings with it fear from lost control.

A state of resistance unfortunately is the predicament of residents of the earth. Unwillingness to rebalance where balance has been compromised sets a person at odds with the universe. To some extent all incarnated entities are thus at least a little bit at odds with the universe. Transformations unfold as they will. Resistance does not stop the unfoldment, but contributes the "forced" quality. And with the feeling of being forced, of being out of control, of being at the "mercy" of the universe, fear results.

Therefore, when the subject of the death of the body arises, fear runs high. Resistance means clinging to the old and rejection of the new. Thus shortsightedness, or sightedness of only the first half of the transformation process is experienced. As long as people resist their transformation, fear of death is inevitable. To eliminate resistance, all one has to do is let go, so that opening to the new is even possible.

KIOKA

On the earth there is much speculation about what happens immediately after death. Plentiful are stories of "near misses," of those who have been pronounced dead, only to be resuscitated. These are not inaccurate reports by any means, however, are but pieces of the *beginning* of the transition process.

Because all those incarnated on the earth have experienced the birthing process as a movement from confined, dark quarters into the light, many also identify the death transition similarly. It *is* a change from greater density to lesser density, thus it is not infrequent for people to interpret the experience with images of tunnels, caves, or darkness to sunlight. The experience, however, is individual, dependent upon one's past experiences, fear levels, expectations and ideations. Each transition is individual; none is more correct than another.

As soon as one moves beyond the physical body, the environment is determined by the mind. Thus, the experience can be anything one wishes it to be, within the limits of karmic law and participation by other entities. The initial part of the transition is solitary. The time, in earthplane terms, is variable from moments to a few days (usually), and is dependent only upon the momentum (from the degree of tension created to sever the tie to the physical body) and the amount of self-resistance or self-encouragement to forward motion.

When a sufficient distance in terms of density is reached, other entities will slowly become participatory. Again, who these entities are, the forms they take, and the extent of the interaction are determined by karmic situation (lessons to be learned during the death process), expectation (including religious or spiritual beliefs), physical and mental condition at the time of death (awareness or lack of awareness that death has occurred, fear, medication, suddenness, preparedness, trauma), and decision-making on the part of all participating entities (how they feel this person can best be helped through the transition). Therefore, it is not inconsistent for one person to be greeted by previously deceased Aunt Tilly in her housedress, another by a guide, someone else by an angel, a fourth by Buddha, and another by a group of past women friends.

As the transition continues, the dead person will move through all the vibrations between the earthplane and her place of residence, as determined by her individual vibration (her essence plus all impurities attached to that essence). If she has made progress during her earthwalk, that new vibration may be very distant to the place from which she incarnated. If she made anti-progress, it will be not as far along vibrationally. Many people leaving the earth presently return to the same vibration they left, as they have made little or no progress in terms of lesson learning. (This is a waste of time and energy.)

When that destination is reached, the assessment and evaluation process begins. It is then that a detailed look at the earthplane experience is taken, *in order* to make better progress in the future. Entities having had interaction during the earth experience with the person are welcomed to participate in the evaluation process. This, of course, is dependent upon ability; since no one can travel out of her range of operation, or into vibrations more subtle than her own, direct participation by entities of denser vibration is prohibited. (This does not mean the completed interaction with these people is not considered, just not so via the person's direct participation.)

It is a means for the newly transitioned person to receive much teaching. The process can continue for many, many years, or be only moments long. It has been likened to going to school. It is time to learn, to get help with sticky lessons, and to share perspectives. Thus it is also a time for healing and renewed understanding.

The transition from the earth to the destination can be experienced in detail or with blind, disinterested eyes, just as individuals are free to experience and interact with the earth. The transition can be smooth or rough, fast or slow. With greater development, all around resistance decreases, thus all transitions become increasingly expedited and smooth flowing.

Once the assessment and evaluation process has been maximized, and plans made for learning in the place of the next adventure, regardless of plane, the entity will move on. Again, the timing necessarily varies according to opportunities presenting, difficulty or ease with understanding lessons and work, etc. If delays have been present due to availability of other entities, or conditions at the time of death, a new incarnation or a move to another plane can take a long, long time. Likewise, it can be very rapid.

ELLEN

When Grace left her Grace Walking Stick body, she and I were prepared for the transition well in advance. I was able to be with her (not in body) as she approached the death, during the tension building stage, as well as when it happened. To follow came the time when she needed to travel alone. It took her about 12 hours (my time) to return to her own vibration sufficiently to continue her interaction with me.

The intensive part of her assessment process happened in a few days. This was for the most part due to her willingness to keep moving. Immediately upon realizing the areas in need of improvement, she has sought to remedy them, or to find help in doing so. The process for all of us is really ongoing. Many opportunities still exist for her to improve and try again her methods and perfection process with me. Very efficiently she identifies many problems simultaneously, as she is not the least bit interested in holding onto her impurities.

There is no reason why anyone of us on the earth cannot pursue our individual purifications with as much efficiency and dedication as does Grace. There is no reason to wait until the death of the body, at which time the process becomes a necessity. It is the state of resistance and fear of a person that contributes to her avoidance of the issues until the last minute. In such a case it *is* necessary for others to initiate the evaluation process and to encourage plans for rectification. When you decide to be as ready and as willing as Grace, you will seek out areas of need rather than wait for others to push you to look.

MAJAI

We are constantly confronted by the limits of our courage. To grow we plunge beyond these limits. We must forever expand beyond ourselves, but never do we think we are ready or able to do so. Growth ceases when we resist, it slows when we hesitate, but continues when we dare to venture into the unknown.

The more evolved we become, the more readily our resistance becomes manifest in all of our bodies. It can show as physical pain or illness, mental uneasiness, agitation or imbalance, or spiritual confusion.

Regardless of the manifestation of the imbalance, the source is resistance to spiritual unfoldment.

Spiritual confusion is the disruption of smooth flow of our energies in the direction prescribed by our dharma. It is the alteration of our pathward motion. The path may no longer seem clear, the options increasing exponentially in direct proportion to our resistance. Think of energy surging forward in a focused beam. If a barrier is placed in the path of flow, flow does not stop but rather changes direction and is dispersed. It sprays in many directions, except the intended one. Clean, direct focus is lost. In the long run, resistance causes us tremendous work. And it is possible for an entity to become greatly distanced from her purpose.

One of the causes of physical and mental illness is resistance to forward motion. We get in our own way. While the origin is spiritual, the effect can be physical or mental. In such a case, treatment will be ineffective until the cause is appreciated and the resistance eliminated.

GRACE

It has been a long journey for me to learn courage to be forthright. I have spent many, many moons letting myself be intimidated by short-term pain and struggle, which resulted in even worse long-term difficulty. My fear of speaking exactly what I felt was often related to my fear of short-term pain for others. So one of the main messages I bring to you is: consider the larger picture of lessons and purpose before you intervene or get involved to alleviate pain or suffering. Struggle can be a great teacher and we must not fear it or necessarily seek to eliminate it.

GRACE

Flying Horse is a gentle and wonderful woman. But she goes soft right in her gut, whenever someone cries. Tears are no good for Flying Horse. She just melts into a puddle and scrambles to make tears go away.

Flying Horse's work is to help people die, to change form. She is good at this work, but she doesn't like to see anyone have difficulty when they change form. For any change of form to happen, there must be power behind it. And pain (tension) is a good way to give power. Nobody wants to stay in pain so they keep moving.

As you can guess, Flying Horse has a problem in her work, something for her to learn! An opportunity to see the good that can come from a little pain. Flying Horse, by the way doesn't always welcome these opportunities!

So, I dreamed her, and then took her with me into the dream. We went to a hospital where a mother and child had just given up their bodies during childbirth. The mother had a longing to put the baby to her breast, but she was smart enough to know there was good reason for this longing to go unsatisfied. Both mother and child knew they would be reunited later on, and when was not up to them to decide.

The mother had strong love for the child. Her lesson was to let go of her attachment and clinging to this child, her fear that their love for each other would not sustain the connection. The child died first. The pain of separation and the longing for the child caused the tension necessary to pull the mother out of her body and out of her form.

Now, poor Flying Horse! All she could hear was the mother's longing. Flying Horse asked her if she should go get the baby, but the mother told her no and that the others would decide when they could be together again. It was sweet of Flying Horse to feel so much for the mother. But I had to scramble to pull her out of there before she messed up the whole lesson! All that work growing a baby, going through the birth, and being almost finished, having learned the lesson well—and Flying Horse goes soft! Well, I got her out of there, in the nick of time—in fact so fast she couldn't wake up properly after the dream!

MAJAI

I would like to comment a bit on Grace's story about Flying Horse. The importance of understanding why it is incorrect to alleviate short-term pain at the expense of long-term learning cannot be overemphasized.

We are in training to perfect our sense of feeling. Increased sensitivity and perceptive abilities are desirable to our growth. This means we learn to include the total experience of another into our range of perception. But *we are not about the business of trying to control or change the experience of the other.*

Feeling can be painful or unpleasant. The discomfort is there for cause, and as such is not wrong. Resistance or tension exists in *all* cases of emotional pain. It is resistance to forward motion, to the universal flows. It is resistance to expansion. When we see the pain of another, we witness *her* resistance, *her* creation of tension, *her* hesitation or stagnation. If we do not wish to acknowledge the resistance, we seek to eliminate it. If we cannot bear to face the tension, we do what we can to

103

avoid it or to make it go away. Is not this an attempt to control? To control the other, the experience or the situation or the creation of the other? Is not this male thinking of "control over?"

There comes a time when the release of resistance occurs. In Grace's example, the mother was at such a stage. She consciously acknowledged her own tension (the longing and the fear of no reunion), but relinquished it and relaxed into trust and forward motion.

Sometimes at the point of relinquishment of resistance to expansion, assistance is needed from others. For instance, in the case of a physical condition, return to balance may require a medical treatment or procedure. In that case, the relinquishment sets the stage for the procedure to be effective.

Accidents or incidents can occur resulting in injury, followed by tension and contraction. In such a case, be it emotional or physical pain, if the incident was without necessity, intervention for the purpose of the elimination of pain or suffering can be appropriate. However, *regardless of the cause, the recipient of the pain must be ready to relinquish the tension and continue in the expansive direction*. As we all know, there are those of us who become very attached to pain and suffering and resistance, especially if caused unnecessarily, making us classic victims. We become heavily invested in preserving our state of contraction, and use it as an excuse to avoid forward motion.

Resistance to expansion is not a pleasant, harmonious, or flowing state of affairs. It is therefore not enjoyable to witness. But it exists. It is not to be avoided or denied or controlled, all of which amount to postures of resistance on our part. Then we have resistance compounding resistance. We need to open into the expanse, and this means opening to include all that is. It takes courage, courage to let go of our own resistance in the face of the other's tension and resistance.

Do know that with your expansion, understanding and knowing will come. And this is not void of feeling. *It is a state of total feeling*, which is able to allow tension to exist in its rightful perspective. As you grow to feel more completely, you will grow through the tension to feel tension in context. And this is what Grace was addressing with Flying Horse.

KIOKA

As Majai said, expansion leads to total feeling of ourselves and others as we exist within the universe. Complete acceptance of the givens in the moment allows access to the context in which these givens exist. It is then possible to understand and evaluate to subsequently act harmoniously with that context.

Fear leads to resistance. And with resistance we are sure to meddle with the universe to avoid our own pain, perhaps at the expense of all else. That is obviously not good. Total acceptance and total feeling actually free us of much of the discomfort we seek to avoid. Context affords meaning. And with meaning the tension from not knowing, from anticipation, or from dread falls away.

Regardless of how open you allow yourself to be, all actions contrary to Natural Law will cause dis-ease and dis-harmony. This is not pleasant to feel. Even that can be placed in context, however, such that events leading to the rectification of the imbalance become welcome. Short-term discomfort may be absolutely necessary, for it may be the only way to ultimately return to balance.

In all aspects of your life, it is important to strive for expansion, to strive to know context. Everything everyone does contributes to the whole. It is just so important that all contributions aid restoration and maintenance of balance. Without expansion, how can a person know the effects of a contribution?

ELLEN

Correct diagnosis is the first step to restoring balance or health. This is quite obvious, however, too frequently it is done incorrectly, in a limited way, or not done at all. Identification of the cause of imbalance is essential to its rectification, and can mean very rapid alleviation of difficulties, far more rapid than we have learned to expect (and far more rapid than those invested in the economics of disease would want us to know).

Many, many sources for imbalance can be identified: toxicity, injury, internal or external obstruction of life forces, lack of usable nourishment, disrupted connection to the environmental energies, emotional trauma or stress, difficult interaction with other earthplane or otherplane entities, resistance to one's spiritual path, unfinished karmic business, universal energetic interactions, and disharmony with flows greater than the individual including collective consciousness of the essential energy. Certainly skills, experience and knowledge play important roles in alerting you to possibilities and probabilities for diagnosis and treatment, but of utmost importance is your own ability to grow and to remain open. *The quality of your diagnosis parallels your ability to expand*. The more you are aware of, the more you have to draw upon for the benefit of your patient. So again, it all comes around to the fact that your primary work is on yourself.

The most reliable assessment stems from information you gather first-hand. Because you are the perceiver, you can interpret your findings in ways that make sense to you. You will own the diagnosis and can therefore own your treatment choices. If modifications become necessary, you will have access to your misjudgments.

It is possible and reasonable to read the vibrational fields (ranging from physical density outward) of a body, the mental state, the karmic situation, and spiritual developmental progress. Just as we organize scientific or medical data, we can systematize perceptions from more subtle vibrational locales. It is important to establish points of reference as well as guidelines for the interpretation of such data.

Next in line to firsthand knowledge, is information gotten from trustworthy secondhand sources. Nothing can be seen as you would see it, except by you. Nevertheless, there is an abundance of reliable data to be had from qualified sources. When gathering information secondhand, quality cannot be controlled completely, and to some extent you are at the mercy of your sources. So make sure you are in a position to evaluate the source as well as the opinion or facts given. Always process whatever you get through your knowing and feeling. And avoid the application of anything you don't understand. It is dangerous business to base any diagnosis or treatment on speculation or trust. Nothing will remove your responsibility for your choices.

I was asked to do an acupuncture treatment on a woman. I had a pretty good handle on her condition and was comfortable with my diagnosis. Her present situation stemmed directly from another lifetime, and again she was resistant to facing the issues. Treatment therefore needed to be directed to the facilitation of her opening and to the alleviation of her fear. Her Healing Guide came forward to contribute to point selection and location, which is a fairly ordinary occurrence. It quickly became apparent, however, that this entity (the guide) had scanty knowledge, at best, of the actions and effects of the points and was content to settle for sloppy needle placement. Had she insisted upon her involvement rather than deferring to my judgment, I would have had no qualms about declining the opportunity to treat.

Sometimes I have found that while I can arrive at a sound diagnosis, I am not always in a position to treat. Perhaps I am unqualified, perhaps *any* treatment is inappropriate. Have the courage to tell your patient the truth as you see it. It is a sign of accomplishment to know when to act (as well as how), and when to be silent and still. All of us are growing to include a larger view. Have the courage to see yourself in the place you exist, and do not feel less or more for it. Use your energies to do quality work at whatever level. No one benefits from overextension or lack of humility, and many suffer from it.

A treatment system may purport to deal with a specific level in the bodies, but since none of the aspects of a person can be separated, we must realize that our actions have far larger scope than we often believe. Just because we cannot prove it via scientific method, or because we aren't yet expanded enough to appreciate it, the effect is there. Know that many things exist beyond our perceptions.

In every acupuncture class, there are those who swear on their lives that acupuncture is a technical procedure with measurable and predictable effects. There are others in the same class who see the energetic changes in the bodies when the needles are placed. And there are those who perceive the emotional changes. A few can see alterations in the karmic program of the patient. It is a question of expansion, of spiritual developmental level. None is wrong in her/his assessment, but some can see larger than others.

Many treatment modalities exist ranging from surgery to crystals to herbs to foods to chemical medicines to manipulation of energies by spirit or incarnated entities. The vast array exists because the need is there. If any one system took care of it all, the others would be rendered obsolete. A system is as good as its usefulness. Techniques do exist that contradict Natural Law, but most problems stem from inappropriate application of adequate systems.

Unfortunately, technologies and exposure to tools and techniques have developed faster than the consciousnesses of many who use them. This is obvious in areas such as genetic engineering or nuclear development. But identical is the case with many treatments and tools (considered to be benign) which are gaining in popularity in alternative medical communities. Popularity is not necessarily indicative of wisdom. The problem is not with the methods (many are extraordinarily useful), but with the lack of consciousness and appreciation for total impact of such methods.

Innocent or benign treatments do not exist. True, our intentions are important, as are the ideations which we take into our actions. But we are either naive or irresponsible if we think that intention and ideation are the totality of our involvement, or make up for inappropriate action. As patients and as practitioners we are responsible to know the alterations we agree to, to know the treatment and its effects on all our bodies, and to know with whom we interact.

Energetic systems which rearrange polarities, charges or directional flows using the energy of or accessible to the practitioner and the energetic climate of the patient are quite prevalent. Benign? No. Where specifically does the energy come from? Where does it go? What are the precise effects on all the participants? In fact, who *are* all the participants, and how many are there? What are the karmic situations of all involved people, and how does the rearrangement affect each of them? Who takes on what from whom?

Crystals being very powerful, produce easily recognizable effects. They offer a big splash quite effortlessly, and many are enamored by the power they wield. "Oh, but they work" is a pretty irresponsible attitude. Do you know what the *specific* effects of a crystal are? Can you direct the amount, kind, and location (depth, width, and concentration) of the energies precisely? Do you feel you know enough to control the integrity of your systems to the extent that you can allow or disallow your interaction with the crystal as the practitioner or user? What precisely does the crystal do to all the bodies, the physical, mental, and spiritual aspects of your patient? These are not unreasonable questions, and can easily be answered by a sufficiently expanded individual.

Who is the authority behind a book? This is especially important when dealing with material that has much power, yet is quite unfamiliar to many of us. We are traveling in some pretty new territory and there are plenty of incompetents traveling with us. Just because you read it in a book, doesn't make it true.

The reason I bother to mention even specific treatment methods is because your responsibility increases with your development. Likewise do your capabilities. Commonplace are massive healings, the prolongation of life, the "saving" of lives, and the removal of suffering among advanced entities. And equally commonplace is abstinence from involvement in the ways one imagined previously one would act if only she had the power or ability. Why do you suppose this is? Something is gained in the expansive process which changes such plans, and this something I think is perspective. Everything exists in context, like a massive game of standing dominos. Knowing this, we should not move into a realm of fear, where we hesitate to take action or to decide. But there is an increasing amount of criteria to consider and to enter into that decision to act. I want to be careful when I push that first domino that the chain reaction follows a desirable course.

An argument goes that if the person isn't meant to get well, the treatment, any treatment won't work. This is true provided the practitioner's spiritual development is at such a level that she is not capable of overriding the condition. As the entity's vibration becomes more subtle, the extent and degree or depth to which she can influence another entity also increases. Ideally her consciousness should be in alignment also, but practically speaking, this is not always the case.

You must know your abilities, and take responsibility for your increasingly effective actions. You are responsible whether you choose to acknowledge it or not. If you are able to alter or remove a karmic debt, a pre-decided condition, and you do so, it becomes your problem, your debt. Meanwhile the person has just been deprived of an important and necessary lesson. You do effect specific changes on many levels. Please continue to grow to come to understand the vastness of your choices. And, continue to grow so your actions can do wonderful things for all of us.

MAJAI

The essential energy of all women is the same. Because of our commonality, none of us exists in isolation, so imbalance of an individual means comparable imbalance of the collective. Thus treatment of a specific entity directly impacts upon the group. Healing of an individual needs to occur in the context of the collective.

For example, a treatment resulting in the removal of necessary or instructive physical pain clearly has repercussions for the group. Likewise, the failure of an individual to take responsibility for the removal of her own imbalance or obstacles affects far more than just herself.

So even as you journey on your respective paths, try not to see yourself in isolation.

GRACE

I want to talk specifically about crystals. I have worked with crystals for many, many lifetimes, on the earth and elsewhere, and am just now beginning to feel my competence with them.

Crystals wield tremendous power. They are capable of causing major change in the earth itself. They grow of the earth for cause, and in response to vibrational counterparts elsewhere. Balance has been made between them and the environments in which they grow. Their removal from their birthplaces necessitates rebalancing—rebalancing *far* more extensive than most of us, even in spirit, appreciate.

It makes me sick to know that commercial interests have been served to the detriment of the earth and to many of those who now possess crystals. Crystals should be used in their natural environments. It has taken me a long, long time to come to appreciate this. Healings should happen at *their* place, not at a place convenient to a healer or to an ailing person. Respect for the integrity of the earth is *elementary* learning. And so, even on such an elementary level, all of us should understand why the removal of crystals from their natural environments is wrong. (Crystals in their birthplaces have grown in harmony with their surroundings, and the surroundings have come to accommodate their presence, both of which took a terribly long time to happen.)

Learning about crystals happens from the inside out. It does not occur from someone telling you what to do or how to use them. The vibrations of each type vary, and extend far beyond the physical plane. In fact, their existence is perhaps 95% in the non-physical. Those of you who think *you* know their effects and what *you* are doing with them, yet who are not now capable of communicating with non-physical entities, had best re-evaluate your conclusions.

Entities of small expansion use these powers in the name of healing. Their intentions are good. And sometimes the results *are* positive. Usually, however, the results cannot be measured by the users for the effect of the crystal is well beyond the earthplane and the abilities of those who live on the earth.

There is anger in my words. Anger comes from pain, frustrated in its resolution. I hurt from the affront to Natural Law that has resulted from the use of crystals on this planet. I hurt because I am made of the same essence of which the earth is made. And I hurt because I now live in the non-physical realms and see firsthand what the abuse of crystals on the earth has done there. The imbalance hurts us all, especially women.

This is not the first time crystals have been misused on this planet. In previous civilizations such as Atlantis, the inappropriate use of the technology of crystals caused much destruction. Today, luckily, consciousness has not developed to the extent that similar technology has again been created. Destructive use of crystals extends into all the vibrations in which the crystals live.

Ellen spoke a bit about the interaction between the physical and the non-physical when the two are placed together. Because crystals exist so much in the non-physical realms, and in physical realms less dense than the normal functioning place of incarnated beings, crystals actually bring the non-physical into play with the physical. The presence of crystals causes lots of disruption of physical vibration, the grosser the density, the greater the disruption.

One of the reasons people have concluded that crystals are effective is because they do indeed cause change. Change, especially dramatic change, is noticeable, even to relatively unaware entities. When a vibration is more subtle than the norm, it can be very attractive initially. So people leave a session with crystals feeling good and feeling that something has indeed happened.

For some people, the disruption and change is bigger than they can use. It is not a question of their unwillingness to participate or their resistance. It is simply too much energy of a vibration they have not had experience with to result in positive effect. And further exposure will cause much damage.

But the momentary contact a person has with a crystal is like the tip of an iceberg. The rest of the iceberg lives in places inaccessible to most people on the earth. And so it will be a long, long time before those crystal effects can be appreciated, and longer before they can be evaluated.

Vibrations are fluctuant, thus those associated with a particular crystal also fluctuate. Crystals are alive. They change. They at times access much energy, and at others little energy. And the specific vibrations of that energy also vary. Therefore, a particular crystal is not constant or predictable in its effect. And because entities also vary in their stamina, toxicity, ability to accommodate various vibrations, and growth potential, an entity in the presence of a crystal is a very unstable mixture. Do not be fooled into thinking that bigger is more powerful. Even a tiny little peanut of a crystal, with lots of impurities or cracks, can wield tremendous power. And some of the monster crystals are relatively small in terms of their non-physical presence.

(Note: Obviously crystalline forms are very common on the earth. When we speak of "crystals" we do not mean all that has crystalline form. And certainly table salt is not the subject of our discussions. Neither are synthetic crystals.

Because of the fluctuant nature of certain crystals in terms of their accessibility to various vibrations, and because individuals differ developmentally, we cannot reliably predict which crystals might be detrimental to an individual. We will say however, that all of the varieties of quartz (including amethyst) and of tourmaline are likely to be beyond the scope of most people on the earth. Other minerals must be evaluated on an individual basis, and should not automatically be assumed to be benign or beneficial in application.)

ELLEN

Grace and I found some crystals that had come loose from their birthplaces and had been carried to shore by the sea. I was leery of

111

even picking them up, as my knowledge of crystals is less than basic. Grace had a bit more confidence in my abilities than I, and recognized a good use for them.

I had been working with a wonderful friend, a child who was born with facial deformities (manidbulofacial dysostosis). He was, at the time, undergoing extensive reconstructive surgeries including bone and skin grafts. This child (a category III entity) has incarnated specifically to teach via his physical condition. His awareness of his own situation is quite clear, and his willingness to honor his feelings excellent.

Grace felt that he would be able to use one of these crystals during and after his surgeries, as it would be able to help with regrowth and new growth of tissue. Since I knew this child already knew how to use the crystal, my role was someplace between Grace's knowledge and his knowledge, hopeful to see firsthand what was possible.

I am timid about what little understanding I have of crystal function, and keep what little I know filed for future use, I think for good reason. I have witnessed some disastrous mistakes made during supposed healings. And they are not the kind to be easily forgotten. I am afraid of what I do not yet know about crystals. And until such a time when I am expanded enough to have knowledge in excess of any application I might have in mind, I will keep this knowledge on hold.

While I do wish to learn more, I do not feel that the direct pursuit of knowledge of crystals would be beneficial. As I continue my overall expansion, that knowledge will grow to find its rightful place naturally within the realms I expand to include. My feelings of fear reflect the inappropriateness of pursuit of such specific knowledge out of the context of my total expansion. And all this, I believe, is what Grace means by saying that the way to learn about crystals is from the inside out. (Obviously, she concurs or I wouldn't be writing this!)

ANJA

This child is an extraordinarily bright child by intellectual standards, but his operational level is within the yin range, *if* he is effective. He is a male who is learning his way of harmony with the yin. His travels and his understanding, thus what he will teach, are not the same as a woman's. But he is willing and able to make use of the yin in order to do his work as a male. He is not threatened by opening to an energy other than his own. His successes as a teacher reflect his ability to harmonize and feel.

ELLEN

Smiley is the name of the crystal, because of the face that was left after the work of the sea.

A year before the arrival of Smiley, this child had surgery for the construction of an external ear. Because the predominant energy universally is yin, for any new growth to occur, influx of yin must be allowed. (Examples of this principle, repeatedly demonstrated, can be seen in the case of the sweat lodge. The branches used for women's sweat lodges will grow new leaves if the women properly maintain their connection to the yin.) At the time of surgery, in a moment of panic, he called to me for help. I represented yin connection to him. My presence (not in body) allowed him to open to the yin as he went into his day-long surgery.

A few days post surgery, in his sleep he proudly came to me to show me his new ear! It was a couple of months before I had occasion to visit him in person (as we lived several hundred miles apart), and at that time he still wore an ear guard which obscured clear view of the new ear. His mother asked him to remove the guard to show me the ear. Typical of a five year old, he exasperatedly answered, "I told you, I already showed her!" Eventually I did get a peek, and it was quite the same ear I had seen in the dreamtime.

A year later, for the second ear construction, Smiley was on the scene. Just prior to surgery, again he panicked. His mother reminded him how he had called me the last time, to which he quickly responded, "Go get Smiley. Now I have Smiley." And Smiley accompanied him throughout his hospital stay, as a vehicle for his opening to the yin.

Smiley is also a crystal, a vehicle to deliver to this child the necessary energies for regrowth and growth of new tissue. Smiley's function is twofold, and the two should not be confused. (Crystals do not bring in yin. People do.)

ELLEN

Ordinarily Smiley lives on the windowsill to bathe in the moonlight and in the sunlight, but occasionally gets called to the scenes of emergencies.

Nelson is a guinea pig. One Saturday a chain of calamities occurred, culminating in the toppling of a very thick pile of sheet rock onto Nelson. Nelson's leg suffered severe bruising and a compound fracture. Unsuccessful attempts were made to heal the leg with topical treatment and bandaging for several days; Nelson's future on the earthplane looked grim. Suddenly Smiley was remembered and called to action. Off the windowsill and next to Nelson's cage went Smiley. By the following day Nelson had taken a turn for the better. The leg was healed and Nelson returned to normal.

In this case the presence of the crystal effected most of the healing, although certainly Smiley's owner didn't hold back on love, concern or energy. (In fact, it is by special request of Smiley's owner that Nelson has a place in this book!)

GRACE

While on the subject of crystals, I should like to tell another story. It is an example to back up my warnings, now that we have first shown examples of appropriate use.

Many of us, myself included, did some of our training in crystalwork in civilizations of the past on the earth. One such, quite advanced in stone and crystal application, was Egypt. Appropriately gems were placed in patterns around the body to redirect energies and to facilitate the entrance and exit from the system of others.

As crystals gained in popularity, some adventurous albeit ignorant entities began the application of crystals similarly. They were unaware that the effects were far different (although not always apparent) and more extensively involving of other realms.

On one such occasion, a woman suffering from emotional disorders presented for treatment. One crystal was placed on her head, at which point the connection between her bodies loosened. Carried farther, she would have died, leaving her body altogether. However, enough dissociation occurred that she could neither leave nor remain sufficiently connected to function. Today her condition would fit a comatose category. And there she remained for many, many years. And following the death of her physical body, the dissociation between her other layers remained even longer.

The dissociation occurred because of the extensive existence, thus involvement, of the crystal in non-physical realms. In that particular case, the energies drawn upon were sufficient to override all attempts by spirit and incarnated people to the contrary. She was not able to maintain connection to her physical body while accessing so extensively non-physical realms.

This is not an isolated example, unfortunately. Nor is it a particularly dramatic one. I speak of it to point out the damage that can be done in ignorance or arrogance.

ELLEN

Grace has been badgering me for years to tell the women I work with to forget crystals. So, contrary to popular preference, I have repeatedly suggested that the use of crystals be eliminated from the daily spiritual diet.

We do not know what we do not know until we know it. So suggestions of this kind can only be taken on faith. But faith or not, we are still responsible for our choices. A decision to inaction is equally as weighted as is a decision to action.

I don't believe, however, that we are completely left to choose on faith, for we have our own awareness of our ignorance to work with. When I don't know something, or am treading on thin ice, the situation smells suspect. I may not know what it is that I don't know, but I certainly recognize my ignorance. If I can think up a list of questions that could be asked of me that I could not satisfactorily answer (and this I can sometimes manage within a matter of seconds), I know that to move into action is a dangerous proposition. With a choice not to act, what is the risk? Loss of speedier progress? Probably loss of recklessness, and loss of a very slim chance of making progress in spite of my ignorance. Not a good gamble, it seems to me.

If my decision of inaction proves eventually to be hesitation or timidity, at least I own it. And I have not moved into territory I do not yet have the vision to see clearly or confidently. Perhaps in my inaction, I have made a choice not to involve others in my suspected ignorance.

GRACE

Crystals are particularly powerful objects, therefore dangerous in the hands of ignorance. With most things we travel in our learning for a time, then begin to apply that knowledge, just a bit of it. We travel more, evaluate the application of that initial little bit, and eventually feel comfortable applying a bit more.

With crystals, the same is true, yet their scope is so vast relative to earthplane perspective, that the time for conscious application is quite a long way down the road. It is still time to travel the road of learning.

Approximately one handful of people incarnated now have sufficient knowledge, in my judgment, to be able to use crystals without causing harm.

One such woman is a musician. She arrived on this earthwalk with extensive experience with crystals. Her orientation is sound, and by listening to the crystals in their environments, has come to understand deeply their harmonious and disharmonious interactions. Music is her tool to heal. And gradually she is incorporating crystals into her existing framework.

Her experience is her own and cannot be shared with others. She is coming to know her connection to the yin and within it finding that crystals have a place. Just as she cannot teach her yin connection, she cannot teach her understanding of crystals. Perhaps she can lead others to the threshold of making their own discoveries, from the inside out.

ELLEN

Playing with or the knowledge of tools does not measure or equal a person's spiritual growth. There are many little old ladies living in huts in the mountains who understand universal harmony and balance enough to live it every moment. Many do not even know of the existence of the toys of "civilized spiritualists." Obviously they didn't reach their developmental level by playing with these tools. They did so by going inside.

Some objects have function independent of their interaction with people. And they also have function as a result of their interaction. So it is important to recognize and separate their essential capabilities from their interaction capabilities.

As spiritual seekers, we *can* make use of objects in the natural world to facilitate our connectedness. If so, it is important to keep perspective on the value of these objects. They are only tools to assist us in knowing our connection. Once we know it, they cease their purpose. To increase any connection, you have to do it. An object can't do it for you.

Further, be it sage, stones, music, animals, drums, medicine women, or whatever, the object has a life separate from you. If relevant to your path, that function can assist you. But again, only to help you know your point of balance *so that* you then can undertake your travels.

Once we realize life exists beyond the physical plane, we necessarily gain perspective on the relevance such objects have to us. There comes a point in a woman's development when she outdistances the usefulness of these objects. Still, however, sage for example, can be used to purify the environment. But no longer is it, or any other object, necessary to her. She can do her work without them. She can go to her center regardless of external conditions. Objects and rituals help at the beginning. Then aside from their essential function, they cease relevance.

It is also not necessary to ever be involved with tools. Plenty of women have figured out how to make their connection purely and simply without these trappings. In this technological and material world, it is easy to confuse the path with the scenery.

ELLEN

Chosen paths are in a perpetual state of becoming; choices need to be made nearly every moment and travel follows each of these choices. All this happens even while you stay on the main avenue of your journey.

Thousands of side streets join this avenue, some with tempting displays or luring excitement. Each side street leads away from the avenue, either temporarily or permanently. There are dead ends and loops. Some return after a time to the avenue, while others maintain a direction perpendicular to the avenue. It is not possible to know in advance where a choice to diverge from the avenue will lead.

A possibility to learn new things exists on each side street, as it does on the avenue, but efficient forward motion happens best on the avenue, and scattered, undirectioned movement best on the side streets. Major opportunities for change in direction present at intersections. Some offer routes not in your best interest, while others can take you a different or better way to the same goal.

It is important to remember that what we are learning is how to *let go* of everything extraneous to our centers. We are not trying to accumulate some magical or special information. A specific technique, for example, is only good for you if it can help you release and simplify, to grow closer to your essence. What you see on the side streets may indeed be very interesting, but does it help you with your process?

The distractions along your goal directed avenues, as well as the opportunities to take side streets are plentiful. When you come from your heart, the signposts announcing distractions or vacations will be very easy to read. Fast food magic miles contrast clearly with the country roads over natural terrain. As momentum builds on your rightful course, it will take effort to slow down to turn into a distraction. Until then carefully and quietly listen to and follow your heart.

KIOKA

There are dangers to be found on our spiritual journeys. The spiritual path has been described as walking on a razor's edge. I don't believe it is quite that gruesome, or the consequences of poorly placed steps or choices lethal.

The greatest danger comes to us when we walk beyond our means. If we tread without solid foundation we will be sure to fall through the ice, all the way to sturdy ground. It is necessary, not bad. And we are not injured by the process. If we make such a "mistake," we will only return to where we can appropriately function. Unfortunate it is for women who gamble a bit, and apparently survive the gamble for a time, only to fall through the ice after many years.

We wish to warn you of territory that is beyond your means. That is why we bother to give the example of the crystals. There are others. And you are smart enough to recognize them. Have the courage to make your actions harmonious with such recognition. We want you to move forward, but only to the extent that you are able without compromising the quality of your journey.

MAJAI

Throughout a woman's journey she must strive to be solid and strong on her own. She works to perfect herself for the good of the group. But never should she assume anyone will do her work for her, or carry her work into its potential. Her successes are only what *she* accomplishes.

We make ourselves vulnerable by *relying* on the collective. The strength comes when we perfect the individual and use such achievement in a collective effort. We are empowered by and sustained through our connection with the group. But if we view the group to be for the purpose of sustaining us, we weaken not only ourselves but the collective. The desirable ideation is one of giving rather than getting, of building and growing from the roots (the individual) upward rather than from the branches (the collective) downward to the roots. The flow necessarily is bilateral, but our focus should be from the vantage point of what we have to offer.

It is dangerous to allow the effectiveness of our individual work to be dependent upon the actions or work of others. We, and the products of our selves, need to have endurance in isolation as well as in union with others and their efforts.

KIOKA

Formation of the group to which she belongs occurs spontaneously. Creation of the group follows from the development of individuals. Those individuals unite *because* they have commonality of vibration; that union is group.

Groups with solid foundations are formed of women with commonality. The individuals join to pool their strengths to create something greater than the individuals alone could create. Groups formed for the purpose of establishing commonality are operating in reverse. They begin with nothing and hope to create something. The motivation for these groups comes from a need to merge.

From growth mergence follows. Very unlikely to succeed is grouping in order to grow. This is thin ice territory. When the group fails, the individual will fall back onto herself, and there she will begin again the process of growth, possibly with the support of women to whom she has previously bonded. If, on the other hand, she is part of a group which has formed as a result of commonality of vibration, and the group were to fail, she would be left standing exactly where she was, and still self-reliant. With growth she recognizes sameness around her: other women of comparable vibration. The bond occurs spontaneously, and absent of neediness. Through their common development, alignment is a given.

How many times have you tried to work with a man, only to find that it is necessary to fall back onto other women to receive support in order to be able to sustain that connection with the man? Without their support, you lack stamina or motivation to continue the constant uphill course. This is falling through the ice to the place where the foundation is solid, followed by repeated returns to thin ice territory.

I see that a lot of women on the earth receive sustenance and growth through their connections with other women. At the same time, they lack it in their relationships with men, yet continue to try to function in male arenas, clinging to women as they do so. Without the support of women behind them, they cannot sustain their efforts with men. What does this tell you about where to find solid ground?

119

MAJAI

Why do you think women are threatened by a separation from men? Why is it a subject many women don't even want to think about? And yet, why are other women drawn to that separation and cannot even breathe without it? What if we were to walk away from men altogether? For some of us, deep in our centers we feel a pulling in several directions at the mere thought of any separation from men.

Some of us operate under an illusory umbrella: that if we cling to others we can negate our isolation and individuality. By pretending that we exist only in terms of others, it is possible to ignore the work and the path of the individual. There must be a context for this pretension to come into being, and thus an artificial group is formed. As we force a "belonging" we force ourselves away from the individual, away from the self. To group, we can rally around sports events, parties, places, activities, or intellectual pursuits. All are degrees removed from the individual. In all cases, focus is far beyond the core entity.

Our journeys are solitary journeys. We obviously must birth and die alone. No one can know or feel our experiences as we do, in the context of *our* journey. We can visit another and temporarily feel the other at a specific point in time. But each of us *is* alone. It is why we journey in the first place.

Acknowledgement of likenesses amplifies our uniqueness. In other women we see ourselves. And there too we see our differences and uniqueness: how we are "the other," how we are separate and not the same. And what are we to make of these differences?

In a man we see the absolute of contrast. We expect to be different from a man, and thus to be unknown to him. (We expect to be known to another woman, and are joltingly shocked and alarmed when we are not.) Merging with a man is an impossibility and comfort arises from the unconditionality of such a realization. A context for rationalization follows. Entire social systems and behavior patterns develop to accommodate and legitimize the discrepancy. In the process, focus centers on the male and ways to hold male-female interaction. Focus is in any direction which serves to bond women and men. Lost is the female in the context of herself.

If we redirect the beam to illuminate woman, visible becomes her connectedness, her likeness to other women, as well as her separation from women. The separation is the problematic spot. It is the awareness of what we are unable to feel and know. It is the sense of failure at our lost access to the universal yin.

Panic results because we know not how to bridge the gap of separation. Easier to deny the existence of this problem and relax into an unsolvable situation: life with men.

Our aloneness is inevitable as long as we remain dissociated from the universal yin. The closer we allow ourselves to get to other women, the closer we get to the larger yin. But also the more glaring our inabilities and inadequacies—the obstacles—become. Obstacles, yes, the old obstacles; all that retard our forward motion. So the points of concern should be the identification of and the removal of the obstacles, rather than the situations and business that are distractions from the problem. To identify the obstacles we must first face squarely ourselves and likenesses to ourselves: other women.

Many of us have come to own our yin natures, and have bonded with women in social collectives and individual partnerships. Those women will be at relative peace with these ideas. In fact, they may think of them as "no big deal." Woman identification is a prerequisite to the owning of our isolation, our disconnection to the yin. And now the job is to decrease the disconnection to the point of its elimination.

ELLEN

Friendships between women are devalued. Assumptions are made that the only real relationships are the male-female ones. And all interactions between women are ultimately to enhance their respective bonds to men.

At the first meeting of one of my women's groups it was necessary to make a pact. And that was that no one would break her commitment to attendance because of a male. It was our statement that we were important in our own right, and did not have to exist relative to any man. Some man's concerns were *not* more important than ours. This happened quite a few years ago, and it makes me laugh to remember that *this* was a serious issue.

And it makes me cry to think that in terms of our spirituality, it still is.

Many of us have wondered what we'd do without a man. (Some of us certainly didn't waste any time figuring it out sexually.) And now spiritually, what will we do without male structures? Everything we always wanted to do and knew we were capable of doing. Luckily our time is not limited to just this little bit of time on the earth.

ELLEN

For so long woman's choice has been to function under a male umbrella even if encircled by oppression. An awful lot of us have been unhappy with this choice, stoically pursing our lips in order to remain standing under the umbrella without verbally shattering the illusion of peace.

The attitude with which we continue standing in the same place does not change our location even one millimeter. To move, it is necessary to lift the leg and place the foot outside the parameters of the umbrella. Doing so breaks the silence.

Our silence as we continue camping under the umbrella is a statement of allegiance to male principles. To change our statement, we cannot simply think it. The body must follow along with what's in the head.

ELLEN

Woman-identification, it seems to me, is not merely the recognition that other women are the same as the self. We must extend that recognition beyond the appreciation of the sameness of essential energy and commonality of spiritual goal (absorption into the universal yin), to encompass the requirements for realization of that spiritual goal.

It follows then, that women bonded with each other by appreciation of essence and goal, yet operating within a male context, fall short of the totality of the *process* of womanness. Realization of the self necessarily is a process of exclusivity. And our silence about our identity and requirements to potentiate that identity keeps us within the male context.

MAJAI

The next story is for the purpose of emphasizing the seriousness of our allegiance to our own natures. It shows the consequences of failure to support the yin, and the power invested in male tradition and male systems by our silence. We tell this story to stimulate you to look at the end result of your actions and your inactions. Know the ramifications of your choices, especially of a choice to remain silent.

GRACE

In a linear time frame, these incidents occurred a long time ago. All of the participants have subsequently changed forms several times, although some are still paying a high price for their involvement. We wish for you to learn from our experiences and so we tell this not so happy story.

She Who Lives With White Eagle came as a gift to the tribe. We were a Plains tribe and followed the buffalo. Much time she spent with the stars and in the night skies. She Who Lives With White Eagle enjoyed many friends who came from the sky. She talked with them and she and they delivered the messages between the places they lived. This was at a time when people did not think the earth was the center of the whole universe! Some of us knew our place in terms of the much bigger picture.

She Who Lives With White Eagle was in a difficult spot, between many worlds. This can be hard on the physical body, and She Who Lives With White Eagle suffered adjustment problems. These were temporary imbalances and would have lasted only a short while, until her system was able to adjust to all the contradictory vibrations.

She Who Lives With White Eagle was quite a young woman, but she knew her purpose. She also knew well what nourished her and sustained her: the company of other women and the natural environment. The plants and the stones were her very close friends. The waterfalls and the springs gave her life. The grasses and winds fed her body and cleansed her mind. Because of her balance and her connectedness, she was a joyous person.

So, I couldn't help but fall in love with her! In those days, women had the option of remaining separate from men to do the necessary work. The tribe sanctioned friendships and bonds such as ours, for everyone knew we did great work and all the earth would receive the benefits.

We lived only among women. The other women saw She Who Lives With White Eagle as their teacher, and a good teacher she was. But they were just beginning to know the power of woman and were not sure enough to trust it completely.

She Who Lives With White Eagle began having much physical discomfort from her adjustments. Sometimes she would cry and I would practice the medicine I knew on her. But she always told me not to worry, that she understood the situation, that she had come on the earthwalk prepared to make the necessary adjustments. She did not have to come to walk on the earth at that time, but did so to help the women learn their medicine and their purpose.

Well, I am a good worrier. And I was not comfortable watching what looked to me like much pain or deep imbalance. Even though she suffered, she released the pain through her practices and her tears. I did not understand this. And so I worried. The more I worried, the more I gave away my power. I began looking everywhere except in myself for answers and solutions.

One day I went to the Chief, who was a strong tribal leader. He did not know women's medicine, but I thought he might know something I didn't because of his tribal position. I spoke to him of the difficulties of She Who Lives With White Eagle. He did not understand either. He knew she had come as a gift to the people, but he did not appreciate the magnitude of that gift until we spoke. And then his fear grew. I did not recognize his fear as any fear I had known, but I could see well that he was afraid. It showed in his eyes, in his hands and in his skin. His color changed and his posture changed. I was sorry I had spoken to him, although then I didn't know why. I had done something very wrong and I knew it. And it was then that I knew She Who Lives With White Eagle knew exactly what her condition was, and how to handle it. I had not listened to her, because I couldn't hear. I needed to see it all for myself, and no one could learn it for me. So no blame.

The Chief saw that She Who Lives With White Eagle had a power he did not have. And not only did he not possess it, her lifestyle and association with only women precluded his getting it. He was afraid too that the power had gone awry, this power he could not control even in the best of times. Her pain worried him, but only because he was afraid bad would come to him and his tribe. Mostly he wanted something he could not have. His fears grew daily, but not a solution could be found, until there was a raid by another tribe. This tribe was known for its brutality toward those it captured and its disrespect for Natural Law.

There was a ceremony among many tribes called the Morning Star Ceremony. It was originally a give-back of something sacred to the stars. Later it was changed to be a way to compensate the Morning Star. Not always did it have a male-female polarity built in, and not always was there a physical sacrifice.

The offering in the ceremony eventually came to be a young girl who had never had sexual contact with any man. She was taken by a rival tribe for their ceremony. Traditionally she was fed well and pampered by the host tribe for one year. She was seen as a sacred being and treated with utmost respect and care, in order to be a valuable give-back. It was intended that she be willing to give her life voluntarily after the year of good care. At the end of the year, she was shot through the heart with one arrow as part of the ceremony.

So, the Chief was increasingly distraught over what to do about She Who Lives With White Eagle. Then the raiding party came onto the land where our tribe was currently hunting. The Chief made a bargain with the raiding party that they could have She Who Lives With White Eagle for a Morning Star Ceremony if the fighting would stop. She Who Lives With White Eagle was taken very much against her will, and very disrespectfully.

The women in our tribe were afraid to offend the Chief so said nothing of their objections. They knew this was all wrong and talked for years of the terrible affront to Natural Law that had occurred. But never were they willing to speak up or defend their sense of knowing.

I, however, caused what commotion I could. The Chief declared me the equivalent of crazy. I was restrained and returned to the women for care. I was afraid to speak further, even to the women, and saw the futility of my actions in terms of having She Who Lives With White Eagle returned. I was consumed too by my broken heart. I was wrong in my silence for the other women as well as myself could have gained strength from the sharing. She Who Lives With White Eagle would not likely have been returned, or even benefited directly, but much could have been gained had I had the courage to speak my mind.

She Who Lives With White Eagle was raped and abused for as long as her body held out. She was left in the care of the women of the host tribe, all of whom saw her as "the enemy." She was tied by the arm to one woman to prevent an escape. And this woman took care to see that she was at least fed and bathed. This woman was split right in half—by her allegiance to another woman, and by her allegiance to tribal policy. She too failed to speak to her sisters of her feelings. She failed to stop them when they harassed or hurt She Who Lives With White Eagle.

The men in the tribe soon realized the powers of She Who Lives With White Eagle and began to fear her. They carved her face to disfigure her in hope that her friends in the sky would not recognize her. Eventually she was killed by many arrows, much like a lynching.

There was obviously nothing sacred about this happening. She Who Lives With White Eagle was greatly disheartened by the lack of support by other women. Her purpose was to teach women to know their medicine, yet all the women she encountered empowered men at her expense.

In all of my walks on this earth as a Native person, women have quietly feared the Morning Star Ceremony, and other comparable ceremonies.

125

But never have such practices been opposed or eliminated through women's efforts. There is something very wrong with a ceremony which sacrifices a woman connected to her power for the benefit of men, or men and women. Even in its most sacred form, it is disempowering to women.

Our message to you is: think seriously about your silence. Who really benefits from that silence?

INYANI

Each of us is an individual journeying. We shall always remain an entity of exclusivity. Yet as we develop, our perspective, thus decisions and actions, come to include the collective. We grow to act in harmony with the common mind of yin. Commonality of consciousness can exist in each of us, thus enabling us to be separate yet one.

It is impossible to simultaneously give up the self and expand the self to be greater. If one lets go of something, one relinquishes access to it. The collective benefits as the individual expands, and suffers when an individual self is denied. *So never do we give up the self in favor of the collective.* Thus the concept of self-sacrifice or risk of self is without relevance or purpose when considering collective benefit.

When an entity such as She Who Lives With White Eagle takes on work for the group, she does not donate herself to a cause. She *is* the cause, and is not separate from the purpose. The self expands to include the interests of the collective. When events unfold as they did in the Morning Star story, the sufferer is not She Who Lives With White Eagle. The lack of growth rests in the collective, She Who Lives With White Eagle being part of that. And each participant experiences pain relative to her awareness and consciousness.

The consciousness and expansion of She Who Lives With White Eagle allowed her to actively and knowingly participate as she did in line with the collective mind. And the lack of expansion and consciousness of the other women disallowed their knowing participation. Nevertheless, no one was actually separate from the collective.

For those of you not yet oriented to the collective, risk of self or feelings of self-sacrifice would exist if you were to take action such as She Who Lives With White Eagle took. For her, risk did not exist. Her only option, given the fact of her expansion inclusive of the collective, was to act in the interest of the group. The presence of feelings of self-sacrifice means that you are not yet oriented to the collective. Thus actions such as hers would be detrimental to your self, and therefore inappropriate.

ELLEN

Transitions can be difficult times. There comes a point when restlessness sets in, uneasiness, and gnawing dissatisfaction. I notice it becomes easier to criticize, easier to discard, and easier to lack patience. Destruction and dissolution are far more appealing than creativity and investment. I want to swing my arms in every direction to clear away debris to make room to breathe.

Deep inside I know something has to change. As I sit with these feelings I lapse into episodes of intellectual self-judgment. I see that I am dissatisfied where others might feel grateful or accomplished. My friends try to persuade me that it's a phase, or that I am avoiding commitment. I know otherwise, and their comments serve only to push my discontent farther ahead. I withdraw to keep myself intact, to protect these budding feelings that I recognize as crucial to my growth and sanity.

I find the courage to say out loud: this isn't good enough, it isn't what I want. I focus on finishing up business to be able to move on. The end of a page has come and it's time to go on to the next, sight unseen and contents speculatable at best.

There are hard truths to face about my dissatisfactions. And what if nothing follows to replace the should-be-adequate discard? The old will not do. I must go on from that regardless of the new. But the new has not shown its face, if it even has one. Void-time: the time between the old and the new.

It is easy to set a goal, reach it, and then fall into ruts of fulfilling others' expectations of what achievement of that goal entails. At such a point we cease to be self-directed. So difficult it is sometimes to up the ante in the face of stalwart status quo-ers. Sometimes it is necessary to insulate yourself in order to follow your heart. There is nothing wrong with doing this, in fact to fail to do it if it is the only way of clarifying your direction and purpose is foolish.

Grace had recently left her Grace Walking Stick body. I knew I could not continue practicing my medicine in the situation I had created. She and I needed to push the limits of our relationship, personally and work-wise. I packed up for a winter on Martha's Vineyard. Grace didn't need to pack.

The location afforded me insulation from mass consciousness (water transmutes energy), and a physical and psychological separation from friends, patients, clients, and distractions. I was truly on an island. This was admittedly a rather severe undertaking, although quite necessary. But then most of what I do is on the edge of usual at best.

Both of us had some remaining work to finish, and as we cleared it away, entered the void-time. And there saw again ourselves and each other in our imperfections. We necessarily faced our inadequacies (what else is there to do on an island in the middle of winter?), and painfully let go of each other over and over, because we knew in our guts that we each had to be willing to go for more.

Our most recent work was just completed. We had been together daily for 36 years. The new was nowhere to be seen. And there I was on an island! The wind was considerable all winter. And that's what it took to blow away the old. The strength in the sea storms egged me on, and helped me know my power. The birds played easily on the wind, and I learned to harmonize better with whatever weather in whatever vibration. The energy rose and fell with the winter solstice, and by spring Grace and I had the courage to take our divergent paths, and to rejoin the rest of the world.

The courage to move on alone into the earth's transition was hard in coming. And with each step into the unknown, onto pages which turned out to be unwritten, I have watched my path go straight to the center of the yin. And too to see the paths of my sisters go to the same place.

Grace and I have learned to trust even more deeply that divergence lives in a greater context of mergence. We need to keep moving, and that sometimes takes a lot of courage. But forward motion in the long run means a coming together. We may need to leave a familiar setting or person or behavior, but try to remember that even if it carries an illusion of separation, it only takes you closer to and deeper into the yin, and ultimately closer together.

GRACE

On several occasions I have mistakenly tried to hold back my sisters when I could see they would likely grow beyond me if given open range. This is stupid, because I, in my smallness, cannot possibly stop a woman's longing for her essence. Sooner or later she will move on if that is her path.

The reason I have felt the need to cling to another woman or to prevent her progress originates in fear of being left behind, forgotten. If I can control her, she *has* to accompany me. Again, this is stupid.

For I have known from my own travels that the closer I move to my essential energy, the closer all women become relative to me. Rather than forget them, I know them and love them more deeply.

Yet with Ellen, especially, I have assumed wrongly that she will move on from me, separation being the inevitable end. All I have succeeded in doing was making her frustrated and angry, and wasting my energy.

As each of us furthers our own connection to the universe, we decrease separations we were too disconnected to even recognize. So instead of allowing separations by allowing the growth of our sisters, we facilitate connectedness and closeness.

Trust in the mergence. And do not fall into competitive or controlling behavior. It only causes hurt.

ELLEN

In retrospect things look small. What stands ahead of us looks large and maybe overwhelming. Our spot in the present is somewhere in between with various shades of comfort and appropriateness. And as we outgrow it, it loses its appeal.

No matter what vibration we travel in, this set of relativities exists. And because of it, there are always feelings of ordinariness and struggling. We are acutely aware of our greenness even in the face of completion. We sit between the things we understand and the things we have yet to understand. We know there is forward motion each time we recognize this cycle of relativities.

No longer do I believe in a concept of struggling to then sit comfortably above, basking in the glow of one's efforts. Our journey is continual, and forever exists between the "where we have been" and the "where we have yet to go."

MAJAI

We arrived into our present forms, ready to adventure, with a vast array of skills and previous experience. As with a plant in a garden, the environment in which we develop can be conducive to our growth or stunting. Many of you have felt like fish out of water for most your present lifetimes. The uniformity of environment has been rather stifling. Your life may seem in retrospect like a battle for survival in unfriendly territory, the weed in the garden which is only a weed because its purpose has yet to be discovered. There has been little or no demand for your talents and perspective. Yet this is the place you came to grow.

Take heart. Arriving is the time when you can be appreciated as a beautiful flower rather than noxious vegetation.

Boundaries limit. By definition, boundaries for individual or collective capabilities limit the scope of performance. The child in school who is labeled a poor reader in first grade frequently in sixth grade has still not been able to grow beyond such boundaries for performance.

Compartmentalization and standardization of our every function is the norm. There is normal behavior, normal feeling, normal thought, normal speech, normal sleep, normal breathing, normal heart rate, and normal body temperature. Many of us know too well how it feels to be "not of the norm." Reaction to us ranges from condescending tolerance to sociopsychological categorization. If we see spirit we hallucinate. If we avoid competition we have poor self-image. If we choose to live separate from men, we are gender disturbed. If we stray beyond the mean greater than the allowable standard deviation, we are thusly maladjusted.

(Certainly there are unbalanced and unstable personalities. Very important it is to be able to control one's functions, abilities and behaviors. Pathological are those who see or hear spirit involuntarily, avoid situations or behavior out of fear rather than choice, or whom life acts upon rather than who acts in the context of life. So it is not the unbalanced or unstable who are the subject of my discussion.)

Unlimited possibilities exist as long as we allow for them. As soon as we define boundaries, our expansion is curtailed individually and collectively. Expansion requires that we surpass *all* existing boundaries. We allow others to grow beyond their present state by accepting them where they are currently. We allow our own growth via self acceptance. The only unacceptable expansion is expansion without a focus or a center. This would be the entity spinning through the universe with wobble, careening out of control or in poor directional focus.

Acceptance of limitlessness—the notion that *anything is* possible— provides the template for its implementation, whether physical or non-physical. We must begin to expand our concepts of what is possible, for we limit our own growth as well as the growth potential of others by adhering to "the norm," scientific method, the laws of physics, the ideas of those who have come before us. The time to risk venturing into new territory has come.

If you'd rather continue on as the weed you certainly can. Or perhaps you'd prefer to be the beautiful flower you can be. The garden fences must come down, and no longer can we be afraid of the power of the wild and mysterious plants that grow in the meadows and in the forests beyond. You who has been the fish out of water merely requires a larger context. You are too big for the mud puddle, so why don't you move on to the seas?

ELLEN

The Dreams are the surpassing of the boundaries made real. Some of us have learned how to push the limits of our assumptions, and once beyond the confines of our belief systems, to create anew. These are the Dreams. They exist to be recognized when you move beyond your boundaries. When you see them you will know you travel. The Dreams are markers on the roads of expansion, and the system of Dreaming is to help us journey.

A long, long time ago, a group of women were taught to Dream. Of the 54 original Dreamers on the earth, there are 21 remaining still attached to physical forms enough to continue dreaming. There are Dreamer women in many places. Majai did her dreaming on other planets, Grace did hers here. Flying Horse is a Dreamer also.

The Dreams hold physical form, and are of physical realities. Their movement is from greater concentration to lesser concentration. Created in relative density, they grow to exist in places of less density. They are expansion at work.

The Dreams, as well as the Dreamers, are of varying vibrations. There are Dreams which support the male systems, as there are Dreamers who do too. And there are Dreams which are purely for women. Be prepared for this. Even some of the Dreamers are stuck, limited by their assumptions. To dream beyond the already-been-dreamt Dreams requires expansion farther into the yin. Attachment to male ways must be released. Continuation of the creation of dreams that accommodate the male can and will happen. But these Dreams are not dreams of expansion. It is time to dream bigger. Some of the Dreamers from other places are here now to help us learn to Dream even bigger, but most of all to help us join in the new Dreams. This book reflects the first Dream that is big enough to go to the end of physical vibration.

INYANI

Do you know how ducks waddle after one another in a line? I need to mention that a lot of us act like a bunch of ducks. Yes, this is a true story. One duck takes the initiative to travel southward around the pond, and the rest busily and orderly follow equidistant behind, usually puffed up with pride at their impeccable obedience.

Do you suppose the number of possibilities might increase if we stopped waiting for initiator duck? Or if we decided not to take a known route? Or even if we set our minds to discovering a brand new path, maybe upstream this time, without tour guide duck?

When you seek to make your own discoveries, the excitement might just surprise you! There is no reason under any sun or moon (depending upon your orientation) to do anything as it has been done before. Unless of course you are a duck.

AMNA

I too was a Dreamer when I held physical form, but not on the earth. All Dreams exist in the eternal present, however, some of mine seem very far away because they *are* developmentally distant. It's hard to believe now what motivated me to dream as I did. Some were great! Others, well. . . it's good that there are other Dreamers to dream on top of those!

My interest in our little project here originates with an old work connection to Ellen. (None of the others have I known previously.) For quite some time she and I helped consolidate and harmonize plans and work completed on an interplanetary level. We tried to fit many divergent yet beneficial efforts into a unified whole. Many of these disconnected efforts followed from the Dreams, yet the Dreams and what was born of them needed to be tied together.

And here with this book, I wish to help pull knowings together into a workable package. Too many of women's feelings and understandings have floated without context, their validity gone unappreciated because they have existed in isolation. The earth is a place that is a jumble of parts because spiritual focus has been lost. The earth as a functioning organism lacks center in much the same way individuals do. A common goal and synchronized efforts are too overdue to benefit an overall collective consciousness here. However, individuals' attunement to the commonality that exists far larger than on just this planet will benefit that larger collective as well as the component individuals.

There are some excellent Dreams on this planet. We need to recognize the points at which they merge. And to know that at those points they connect with Dreams of elsewhere. As all the Dreams fall into their rightful places in the universe, each of us will have an opportunity to feel that commonality. For we *are* one. Now it seems we are disjointed parts, but you will see, it really *is* the case that we are one.

AMNA

An awful lot of you are in a big hurry to move on from the earth. This is reasonable as there are much more harmonious places to live. However, business needs to be finished here before it is time to move on. The Dreams show us some of the possibilities for the future. They exist in all time, but are of forward motion. So to you they mean the future.

Many of you have a large stack of papers in the "in box." They have to be attended to so they can be transferred, once and for all, to the "out box." Then it will be time to follow the Dreams. Do not miss your opportunities to attend to this past business by only focusing on the future. The earth's transformation is providing you with a chance to clean up a lot of karmic business relatively quickly.

ANJA

Some people are resistant to going forward. Others fight the present. And some will do anything they can to deny the past. Resistance can show its face in many places, and most of us have a little bit in a lot of places.

You are here on the earth because you *do* resist. The transformation can help you with that by presenting you with an overwhelming quantity of things to face, rendering your resistance impossible. It is not a question of surrender (a popular concept these days). Surrender implies the giving away of the self to an opponent. What you resist is not an opponent, it is yourself and your previous choices. It is simply a matter of being willing to take a look. The transformation will dump so much material on you that you will just not have the time or energy to do anything except look.

So why not get a head start on the looking? The more you do now, the less you will have later.

MAJAI

Many changes occur as you pass through each layer of vibration. You will transform dramatically at each of the points or levels we identified. Transformation is always for the better, so do not even bother to resist it. You will grow immensely and gain amazing new perspectives. What you left behind will seem in retrospect ridiculously small and you will cringe at the tenacity with which you held to unnecessary things and ideas.

The going is much slower in the lower vibrations. There comes a point when you excitedly release your resistance. Then you seem to fly. So the sooner you decide it's OK to change, it's OK to experience the universe, and it's no longer OK to fear, you can really move. The sooner the better, believe me.

ELLEN

There will come a point in your development when you will no longer need the system of guides (described before) of Path Keeper and Healing Guide to keep you moving forward. It becomes counterdevelopmental to rely on other entities to direct your progress.

As you grow, you learn to trust yourself—to trust your own feelings, knowings, and judgment. You learn to assess accurately what is harmonious and disharmonious to your individual growth, and to feel your place in the collective. Your awareness will be sufficient that you will know what work you have yet to do. The lessons will walk in the door, and you will be ready, willing and able to meet them.

It is important to take both your own initiative and your own power. This insures that development follows what you *know* to be internally correct. Your involvement with your own process serves to carry you even closer to your own nature. There will still be plenty of opportunity to make mistakes, you can be sure. But you will see the obstacles very clearly. And you will know when, where, and how to get assistance from others.

It is not a posture of arrogance, but rather of self-respect and collective respect. Acceptance of our size, in its smallness and its largeness, allows us to proceed with honesty and sincerity. We outgrow the need for direction external to us because we understand and know the processes of the universal flows to be our own. *We have released our resistance and thus can release the external controls* (the guides). We go in harmony because we see absolutely that there is no other way.

INYANI

As per tradition, the more awe inspired we become, the holier we must be. To swoon at the feet of a guru or melt in humility means we are good spiritual aspirants. I think it's high time we honored our universe but included ourselves in it.

Popular is the notion that as we develop what grows is our ability to witness the universe, to see larger, but beyond opening to see, nothing happens to us. In such a case, to us the universe grows larger, we stay fixed in size, and the result is awe and mandatory humility.

If we expand to merge with the universe, our degree of expansion equals the amount of merger. Our vision equals ourself. We are as big as what we encompass because we are what we encompass. Are you often in awe of yourself? I'm not. I'm pretty ordinary to myself. It's similar to the no-big-deal feeling the day after your birthday. So what follows when we merge with the universe is an ordinariness and appropriateness.

Respect for ourselves equals respect for the universe. But respect is not the same as smallness. The more you know, the more you know you have yet to know. But we must not forget the accomplished distance. When the distance traveled and the distance yet to be traveled come into alignment or balance, we feel neither large nor small for our distance or lack of distance. We feel appropriate to our size, because we are the exact size we are.

When we honor ourselves and allow our connection to the universe, eventually there will come a time when each of us will become as great as the universe. Prior to that time, we will not see any larger than we are. Necessary, however, is to admit and accept our existing connection. Do not refuse it for fear of arrogance. You will be neither awed nor arrogant if you take what is exactly yours and refuse to plead more or less than truly is. It is as unworthwhile to classify yourself as too small as it is too large. Neither accepts yourself in your totality, thus from neither can you grow.

ELLEN

A woman can feel like a bumbling idiot until she realizes that the different drummer she marches to is herself. Acceptance of the legitimacy of following herself is magnificently freeing. It is her permission to take her own power.

AMNA

Being truthful to oneself is the first step to merging with the universe. Often we know and recognize what we want or what is, but chicken out when it is time to act on these knowings. It is *easy* to know the right answer, but hard to make good on it. Many of us would rather believe that it is just too hard to know what to do. That way we are absolutely free of responsibility for the next step, the implementation. Every single one of us knows how "to know." So identify your difficulty in its rightful place.

Another way we avoid responsibility is by refusing our connection to the universe. If we refuse the larger view by refusing to expand, life can go on without changes, without the difficult rearrangements that would be necessary if we were to include this larger view.

"What if someone tries to take my power? My protection is not good enough." Such worries surface exactly at the point when we are faced with finding the courage to implement our knowings. Put it on someone else so change can be avoided.

ELLEN

We speak of empowering the self or empowering the other. I think elaboration on these concepts is in order.

To empower herself, she connects with the universal yin. The empowerment of another is something that can happen only from her perspective, but not from the perspective of the other. She sees the other as controller, and simultaneously neglects to make her connection with the yin.

It is a misnomer to say she "empowers the other" for she cannot make the connection with the yin for another. That is something one must do for oneself.

Can another take your power? No. Another can prevent you from taking your own, but cannot make your power hers/his. If it doesn't belong to you, it's nonexistent. There have been countless attempts to "take someone's power." In fact it is commonplace to worry that one's power will be stolen. Much of what happens in the world today are attempts to control others, thereby becoming more powerful? It just can't happen.

The only way to power, or to increased power is the long way: the way of expansion or development. Your power increases as you access the yin more extensively. It's a long process so no wonder people would rather try to find short cuts. This is what we see all around us: people who don't want to do the work but want the rewards or benefits. It seems to some to be easier to rip someone off who has done the work, than to do the work. But because shortcuts are impossible and absurd, all these people succeed in doing is making a lot of folks miserable and wasting their own precious time.

KIOKA

Acknowledgement of and realization that each individual is responsible for her own journey to the yin, illuminates the ridiculousness of power struggles. Since no one can travel for me, and I can travel for no one other than myself, it is ridiculous to even consider trying to take my travel from me.

Later on I will tell more about my past. For now, however, I will mention that for a good part of my journey I was not exposed to entities of essential energies other than yin. It was therefore clear to me that yin was what I was after, and never did I consider that something else might be better. It was also clear to me that if I was going to move as the entities around me were moving, I needed to do the moving. There never was any question that anyone else would do my moving for me. And there never was confusion created by a comparison of worth between entities of different essential energies. Each of us had identical potential, and each was responsible for realizing that potential, for, by definition, we each *were the realization of that potential.*

The situation is no different for those of you on the earth, except for the fact that you share the earth with entities of other essential energies. At times you seem to get lost in confusion when you witness other entities (especially men) pursuing their paths while you are supposed to be pursuing yours. It is important that you remain clear about who is going where—women to one place, men to another. Trouble arrives when clear delineation is lost. Neither is better nor worse, yet many of you have fallen into comparison thought. Failure of realization of self-purpose and self-worth leads to comparison thinking, and this then leads to power struggles.

Suppose there was a field and in it an ongoing egg hunt simultaneously with an ongoing peanut hunt. One group's purpose was to hunt eggs, the other's to hunt peanuts, as either eggs or peanuts were the sole food of the group members. Suppose in the middle of the hunt, some of the egg gatherers decided peanuts were more valuable because they saw the peanut gatherers growing in size from eating peanuts. What followed were egg gatherers gathering peanuts. Eggs and peanuts were mixed in one basket. Eventually the value of the eggs was forgotten, and by eating peanuts, the egg people lost weight. To someone who runs on eggs, peanuts are useless.

Attempted power thefts are nothing more than mixing of purposes as is the case when men try to take power from women or vice versa. In cases of attempted power thefts among those of the same essential energy, all we have are avoidances of responsibility. Attention to the activities of others, be they of the same essential energy as your own or not, is merely a distraction from individual purpose and progress.

MAJAI

There was a man, who for hundreds of years *determined* to make his way through the universe by taking the power of others. I doubt sincerely if he ever did an honest day's work, although he must have or he would not have been the formidable force that he was. Unfortunately for Grace and Ellen, his path and theirs crossed many times, and on several occasions they became his target in his quest for power. You met him already as the Chief in the Morning Star story. In fact, most of you who read this book have had occasion to encounter him, and may come to remember your own experiences as your awareness increases.

In terms of his own growth, his motion was steadily backward. He talked a good line and made noises about mending his ways. But time after time he put his energy into pursuing self-serving goals and stopping others who threatened this pursuit, rather than into making balance for his previous doings. His efforts have always resulted in much chaos and suffering for many, many people.

The time came when a group of women decided to challenge him, our position being that his choices were contrary to the universal flows and thus were counterproductive to individual and group progress. We felt it would be in all of our interests if either his downward spiral could be hurried along or he could be encouraged to restore balance. Because he was insatiably hungry for power, we knew he would jump at any illusion of opportunity for power. Therefore, we made him an offer he could not refuse, knowing full well that it would be impossible for him to take anyone's power. The risk to us was severe suffering, but ultimately we were sure to achieve our aim.

This man played many roles, his favorite being a crafty medicine man.

138

Always ferocious and imposing, manipulative and charismatic, he maneuvered and bullied until he got what he wanted. People cowered under his will and refused to resist his choices. His medicine totem was the black bear, and so our name for him is Black Bear. He traveled among women and men of much power, as power is what he craved the most.

The telling of this story is intended to be illustrative of our point about power: that power cannot be gained via another person. And this too was his lesson. Ellen entered into this situation with the abilities she currently has. Our example is not an ordinary example by any means, yet it parallels the more moderate situations of attempted power theft we all encounter daily.

Our scheme: Ellen would take physical form on the earth. Black Bear would be offered the trumped up position of her Path Keeper. As such, he would have as much access to her as he wanted. He would have full claim on her power, he assumed. *And* he would have ample opportunity to show his intentions to repair his previous damages. A tasty offer for such a man, to be sure.

Grace had several roles in this scheme, all unknown to Black Bear. Her primary function was to allow Ellen access to physical energy and planes. That way Ellen would be able to participate in the formation of a body, and later to maintain that body for as long as necessary. Her other main function was to encourage Ellen to continue in spite of Black Bear's doings and to help her know her connection to the yin. As Grace's vibration was far more subtle than Black Bear's, she could come and go undetected by him. But it was necessary for the lesson on power to be learned fairly by Black Bear, so it was agreed that Grace's participation in this second capacity would be minimal.

Black Bear's strategy was to first block Ellen's access to her own power, in order to undermine her ability to rely on herself. He hoped to make her dependent upon him. He presumed her cooperation with him would follow the established dependence, thereby enabling him to cease blocking her power connection without risk of her desertion of him. He would then be in a position to siphon all the energies she accessed, in order to increase his own size.

Because of her sensitivity to other vibrations, he was able to create confusing scenes, to reinforce her attention to painful and frightening happenings, and to manipulate her interpretation of her perceptions to give her inaccurate or erroneous messages. To remove her sense of control over her body, he encouraged a relative to sexually abuse her. And to these experiences added memories of previous lifetimes of torture.

By this time Ellen was four years old. The memories triggered her longstanding rage and she became angrily outspoken. Black Bear had not anticipated her rage at the prior injustices and made his first major mistake by pushing these memories. Certainly she did not escape unscathed, but his attempts to disempower her were undermined even at this stage by her sense of self-determination and recognition of what was disharmonious with Natural Law.

Her abilities were in areas of feeling and knowing, dreaming and healing, so he steered her away from endeavors which would give expression to or promote the development of these abilities, throwing her instead into situations which venerated the intellect. Beyond Black Bear's reach however, was Ellen's awareness of vibrational states more subtle than Black Bear. He could not touch her understanding and use of color. Anything beyond his vibration did not exist in his consciousness.

Therefore, for Ellen the external world did not synchronize with her internal experience. Her internal pulls were in direct opposition to the external reality he created. The discord made her miserable. Yet implicit in the inconsistency was the existence of at least two divergent points of reference; behind the discord had to be a state of harmony with Natural Law. And in this knowledge lived the motivation to move beyond the chaos Black Bear created. The discrepancy between internal and external fueled her desire to return to harmony.

Grace provided spirit women to encourage Ellen's connection to the earth, unbeknownst to Black Bear because of his limited vision. These spirit women pushed her to increase her time in the garden, and in the woods as well as with animals. Black Bear saw what he believed to be Ellen following only her natural inclinations. He pushed in the opposite direction to try to break her potential for connection.

As a child she developed a particularly open exchange with a beagle. As soon as Black Bear realized that Ellen accessed many places unreachable by him through the dog, he arranged for the dog to be killed. Countless similar incidents of wickedness occurred during the days when he sought to bring about her disempowerment. It was obvious to all of us that he did nothing to compensate for his previous imbalances.

Because of the familiarity of his vibration and association of that vibration with unpleasant memories, Ellen grew very anxious when he neared her vibrationally. He used her recognition of him to create as much fear as he could. However, because he needed access to her in order to pull off his attempted power theft, he was severely limited by her fear of him. Somehow he needed to get her to cooperate with him.

He was faced with a real dilemma. The more power she had (the greater her connection to the universe), the greater was his potential for power (he thought). If he kept her disempowered he equally lost. He therefore needed to risk her re-empowerment.

His loosening of the constraints on her perceptive abilities began when she was 16, traveling in France. Immediately, access to the dreamtime returned, a sense of independence was renewed, and perception of people and happenings in distant locations flooded her consciousness. It was a bit more than he had anticipated, so he quickly sought to reblock. In doing so, he was successful at contributing confusion and distraction, but could not eliminate her awakened memory of worlds previously accessible.

It was four more years before he made a second big attempt to allow her universal connection. With it arrived another flood of abilities and refound knowledge. Again he panicked at his lost ground and stopped his contribution to her opening process. This pattern continued with Black Bear becoming increasingly more desperate for power, and more panicked at his inability to take hers. The saga continued for all of us, seemingly forever.

Her own momentum eventually pushed her into areas such as medicine and healing which further unleashed her access to vibrations far beyond his reach. She, solely by her natural draw toward harmony and away from disharmony, forced him out in the open. He was losing ground rapidly and needed to risk an attempt at her full power before the possibility was lost.

Black Bear made full identification to her with a presentation of himself in his most favorable light. And with it came floods of claims of desires to compensate for his lifetimes upon lifetimes of self-serving behavior. Direct communication between Ellen and Black Bear occurred day and night as need be. As long as he pleaded intent to make balance for his previous wrongs, *and* backed up the pleas with compatible action, she had to put up with him.

Within a matter of two months, however, Ellen caught him in lies and immoral manipulations. He played with others in her environment and with their perceptions of her, all in order to satisfy his own desires. It became clear that he had no intention of compensating for his wrongs. As she became fed up, he began yet another attempt to disempower her.

In just a few more months, his misbehavior had unmistakenly caught up with him. Still his quest for power influenced all his choices, yet after 36 years, and total access to Ellen, he had achieved nothing.

After a restless night, Ellen concluded that she'd had more than enough of Black Bear. Early in the morning she went into the woods, to a spot of mossy ground. It was a place she had been working on healing for some time, even as Black Bear accompanied her.

ELLEN

I collapsed onto the moss, in tears and exhaustion. If it was going to be necessary for me to continue in any capacity with Black Bear, I had decided I'd sooner leave the earth altogether. This I wailed to whomever might be listening. Grace and a group of grandmothers presented clearly to me, engulfing me in their love and in their womanness. The mending had begun.

Black Bear was made to answer to me and to many, many others for his actions, for that is the Law. He then followed the path of his adharmic choices to his involuntary and painful absorption into his essential energy.

We achieved what we wished—that his process in whichever direction be speeded along, as well as to prove to Black Bear and to others that a power theft is ultimately not possible.

ELLEN

Certainly there do exist entities like Black Bear, intent upon running their lives in reverse of Natural Law, and in the process, taking you with them. Our time and concern are better spent making our own tracks and leaving their antics to those whose business it is to deal with them. Please do not worry that anyone will treat you as he did me. It is very unlikely and worries are not at all what I wish you to carry with you from the telling of that story.

AMNA

There is no need for concern that your guides would be like Black Bear. A rather extensive system exists for the appointment of guides to an entity, the basic prerequisite being that her/his developmental level and ability to maintain a growthful course be equal to or greater than yours.

Recognition of those who act contrary to collective development is important. There are many, far more than any of us would like to believe, who fit this category. To knowingly or unknowingly fuel their efforts is detrimental to all of us. Recognition is the first step to avoidance. And avoidance of participation in their choices, by and large, is the extent of your responsibility concerning these entities.

You should be aware that work is constantly underway of the kind that Grace and Ellen did with Black Bear. Individual progress is important, but at times collective progress can be inhibited (even in the face of individual progress), necessitating temporary focus on the group. Those entities who are one with the collective undertake such tasks, owing to the compatibility between themselves and the collective.

ANJA

Actually, as Majai explained earlier, the universe will take care of the adharmic individual itself. There really is no need to intervene when we look at the bigger picture. And time is not a legitimate factor; the universe operates in timelessness.

Nevertheless, to the developing entity, time does exist. Lessons seem to take an eternity to learn, for example. And special events do happen that provide opportunities for growth. The earth's transformation is one such opportunity, an event particularly relevant to incarnated women.

The presence of entities such as Black Bear means that many opportunities could be blocked. So while it is true that eventually everyone will end up merged with her/his essential energy, how long it takes is a variable in earthplane terms.

Many of us felt that the opportunities for women provided by the yin predominance plus the earth's transformation should be maximized, thus the decision to take action with Black Bear was made. Other similar interventions have occurred and are occurring. You are able to move forward even in the presence of adharmic entities, but it is easier without their interference.

ELLEN

Had I not trusted my connection to the yin, I would never have agreed to the scheme for Black Bear's demise. Surprisingly, during the process, my points of connection were illuminated in ways I did not anticipate. So instead of being life saving rings to frantically grasp in times when your connection is threatened, perhaps they can function as tools for the reinforcement of your connection.

There were times during those years when I didn't know whether I was coming or going, you can be sure. Yet throughout, there was someplace inside where an unshakable understanding lived. And with it a dream that refused to die, that shone of realities vaguely familiar and *absolutely* possible, albeit just out of reach. There was something that my focus stuck to like glue. So even in the most nightmarish times, when I felt as desirable and as profound as a fly, I was that fly addicted to the light.

But all these feelings lived in the recesses of subjectivity, certainly nothing I dared share with any other person. I knew I could not afford to risk their loss upon exposure to criticism or lack of understanding. What these feelings amounted to, was trust in myself and my knowing, so even though I could not at the time identify specifically or intellectually explain this vague connection, it was quite real. And with it, my own deep knowledge that there did exist somewhere a life other than I was currently experiencing. Hope? Hope is empty and this was substantial and full.

Frequently we hear that others have our answers, just the solution or approach we need. But rarely are we encouraged to look to ourselves. No matter how off balance we may be, we do have a center. And that center can and must be trusted. This center of mine was at times so very far away, yet it was still there, and was not something anyone could touch. As Majai has said, it was obscured from view, but could not be accessed by anyone other than myself.

Even as a young child I was aware that my ideas were not the same as the ones I read in my Weekly Reader, or heard at the dinner table. I had perspectives on life and everyone in it, that were full of common sense, so very logical to me, yet a foreign language to others. Granted these perspectives were not ones I relished owning, but in spite of extensive efforts to adopt more vogue-ish philosophies, my weird perspectives had deep roots. And these roots were the kind of roots that could grow a new plant even when broken off below ground level. My perspectives, again anchored in my own feeling and knowing, could not be put to rest. I have learned, admittedly too many times, that if I can't put something to rest, I'd best honor it, or sure enough, it will come around and bite me in the back until it receives due acknowledgement and respect.

These unconventional perspectives I now recognize as part of a spiritual journey and definitely of the female way, both equally unsupported and unknown on this planet. Once I was able to differentiate between spiritual and religious, and later was able to narrow it further to women's spiritual, I remembered so easily and well all that was forgotten. And too, the realization that many perspectives, as opposed to one perspective (male thinking), can and do exist simultaneously and *ultimately* without contradiction, opened many doors to the universe for me. So wonderful to thereby be reunited with the other like-minded, like-journeying women!

To be known by another woman, and to know a woman as yourself, can do wonders for self-love and self-concept, never mind for the collective consciousness of women. Regardless of the inclusion of physical or sexual exchange, woman to woman communication is an incredible asset to our growth, and should never be undervalued. Many of us are taught otherwise, or worse, to compete with women. Even the most disbelieving of us take for granted the threads of connection apparently as insignificant as an exchanged glance. So important it is to allow our awareness of our commonality to grow. And how can it even have a chance of growing if we fail to take the tiny threads seriously?

Long ago I realized that I had a deeper connection to the bag lady on the park bench than to any man. I knew I could say something real to her, or to any known or unknown woman, and have my comment understood *and* appropriately responded to. Never have I wondered if a woman would have the *capacity* to connect. Absolutely incredible I find, are women who deny the understanding or the knowing at the very moment it starcs them in the face, refusing its legitimacy and realness. Out of fear of what? It is not acceptable behavior in a male system, *yet to deny it denies the self*.

Rather instructive to me has been the absence of this commonality in interactions with men. At times their lack of connectedness has been so blatantly outrageous that there was no alternative than to accept and trust my understanding. From each such situation in its ludicrousness, comes for me renewed strength and trust in my own knowing. This is similar to the feeling elicited on those occasions when I have been suddenly amazed by my own physical strength.

As Majai mentioned, implicit in the inconsistency between my internal understandings and Black Bear's external creations lived divergent points of view. (Everything distal to my core was external, thus even his manipulation of my sleep states or mental processes belonged to external realms.) The universe is inherently fair and just. There is order and balance in the natural world. "Disasters" or "catastrophes" are always for good cause leading to the restoration of balance, unlike those happenings resultant from abuses of the planet which cause further imbalance.

I think one of the most important recurrent itches throughout the Black Bear years was my discontent with injustice. Repeatedly I was taught by Black Bear that all was *not* fair or balanced or purposeful. I could just not accept this as true. I knew in my heart that the social and political atrocities were not right. I knew women were not substandard beings. I knew the rip-offs condoned by the economic system did not measure success for anyone. These to me told of affronts to Natural Law.

I now believe that my acknowledgement of this discrepancy between my knowing and what I witnessed was the primary motivating force behind my perseverance. My frustration in not being able to escape the discrepancy (and this was largely thanks to Black Bear pursuing his self-serving goals) resulted rightfully in rage. Anger and upsetness are quite unacceptable emotions. "Calm down, sweetheart. Don't get so worked up. No one can understand you when you're screaming." Wrong. The state of disharmony existent behind such extremes of emotion or emotional expression warrant our attention. The words do not change because the volume is turned up. The increased volume to me means intolerable disharmony crying out for rebalancing.

Once I came to appreciate the legitimacy of my outrage, Black Bear and his portrayal of life became unquestionably unacceptable. My own power lived behind the externals, and that power was precisely my understanding of Natural Law. (My understanding was as good as my existing connection to the universe.) Furthermore, disharmonious components necessarily reside in games of manipulation, control and deceit. I learned over and over to pay attention to disharmonies as valuable indicators. Pointless to deny or to block the disharmony; they are true gifts in disguise. They are roadsigns to the return to harmony and balance.

People will tell you anything if they have a reason to. Sound, color, presentation, words and actions should always be in alignment. If what is told and the teller's vibration differ, pay attention. Vibration is truthful, speech can deceive. Whether the speaker is incarnated or in spirit, the vibration is the key. The physical form of a spirit person is readily malleable, thus her form will quickly reflect mental status. Easy to see an incarnated person lying, but spirit will show even the slightest mental hesitation or lack of fluidity of thought. Use this. Approach the person, the thing, the event, whether past, present or future, with your ability to feel, and evaluate any discrepancies using your feeling assessment as the baseline.

Animals do not hide illness, injury, or emotion. Because they come to you in a state of openness, there is ready opportunity for you to know them. They are easy vehicles to help you connect with your center. Watch your hands go to the site of a medical condition unknown to you. Notice too how animals in need of healing will come to you to show you a problem.

I had a dog friend once who was dying of, unknown to me, liver tumors. Upon placing my hands on her, I saw that her color was a murky yellow green, which to me meant extreme toxicity. Black Bear attempted to confuse me by indicating it was a kidney condition. The owners concurred with the kidney diagnosis, for that is what they believed at the time. Yet I knew something was amiss. I did a healing with the dog, and noticed that energy went to the liver area. Fortunately in this case, the liver diagnosis was made eventually, and I had confirmation for my findings.

In many cases, however, you will not have immediate occasion to verify the information that comes via your expansion. And as you move into new territory your knowing and feeling will be all you have to work with to maintain your balance and progress. I can't say strongly enough that lack of verification is not grounds to discount your feelings. Certainly, if *contradictory* information comes your way, you would be foolish not to seriously consider it. But no more can you afford to toss away your gut assessment just because it *appears* to stand alone.

Another opportunity that repeatedly presented to me thanks again to Black Bear was the chance to face my fears. My worst was: What if all those things that contradicted my sense of knowing proved to be right? No matter how ugly the picture before me became, or how painful his maneuvers were to me, I found relief and peace when I dared to face everything squarely and completely. In order to move beyond whatever discomfort, it was necessary to experience that discomfort in its totality, for I was guaranteed continued discomfort if I failed to look. I needed to risk challenging the truth of my center.

Throughout my childhood, whenever I began stepping into my power, Black Bear would show himself to me in a dream. It was a scene from a previous lifetime when he had stabbed me. All he did was show himself as I had known him then. Upon seeing that form, I immediately froze in absolute terror. My only escape, as long as I chose to honor my fear, and my past response to him as a given in the present, was to wake up. He did this routine for years and years. And I responded in fear for as long. One night I simply decided that I'd had enough, and refused to back away from him in fear. At that point his presence ceased to have power. He couldn't make himself ferocious; it was up to me to see him as ferocious.

This example is all too real to me, yet does remind me of my role in perpetuating my own disempowerment. He acted, but I participated by re-acting. Although this situation occurred while I was asleep, it is comparable in principle to situations each of us faces in waking consciousness daily.

I prefer to see the process of facing my fears as incredibly empowering rather than as terrifying experiences. Since Black Bear was invested in keeping me fearful and immobile, simultaneous with my empowerment, he became disempowered. When I dared to investigate my fears, the

147

rug was pulled out from under him secondarily. His illusion of power could only exist if *both* he and I bought into it.

Had I failed to honor my deep feelings, I never would have made it through Black Bear's antics. And had I been afraid to look with both eyes at the dastardly things he did, and to seek until peace was reached where there were painful discrepancies, I would never have moved beyond that nightmare. But a Black Bear or not, I would never make any progress on this adventure of mine without knowing my center and trusting what *I* feel to be harmonious and disharmonious to the balance of that center.

Regardless of where or when you travel, what or how difficult your encounters may be, you will be fine if you seek that center. Even things as large as the earth changes can be handled. No need to worry about the sequences of events or the timing, as all focus external to your center is a distraction. Stay centered and the externals won't be significantly problematic.

KIOKA

We would like to be able to tell you specifically why Black Bear failed in his attempted power theft. Because we genuinely do not understand what he thought he was going to be able to get, we can't. The most we can say, Ellen has said—to the extent that she bought into his illusion of power, that illusion could exist. But even that illusion was quite empty and ephemeral; it could not be sustained for long, for the buying into it contradicted Ellen's knowing.

Neither can we tell you the specifics of his attempts; they were too empty. From my persepective he was very busy doing nothing, and then panicking at his ineffectiveness. He was successful at disempowering Ellen, but that disempowerment did not lead to *his* empowerment. Further, I can think of nothing he might have tried that would have worked to fuel him.

Perhaps this story will help you see the importance of moving beyond your fears, as well as of recognizing the smallness of each of those fears. I would like you to see that your center, your universal connection, is literally your strength, and that your external attachments can evaporate as easily as did Black Bear's.

The earth's crust is changing more rapidly than was originally anticipated.

Anything of the future exists minus the time factor familiar to you on the earth. So "when" is merely a set of probabilities. "What," if inclusive of unmade decisions is also a probability. *The earth changes can no longer appreciably be influenced by individual (or collective) decision making or actions.* Therefore, "what" remains a given, or is fixed. The earth's crust *will* adjust in order to rebalance.

"When" exists in probabilitics. Constraints, in effect from the spirit world, were lifted. Owing to the extent of the degeneration, the irregular use of natural resources, and the concentrations of people and pollutants, unforeseeably rapid progression has occurred. The progression is many, many months ahead of the predicted schedule.

As the physical characteristics of the earth change, economic, political, environmental and health conditions will subsequently change. The unanticipated speed means that *all* resultant changes will occur more rapidly. This then means that more people will be emotionally and physically unprepared for the rebalancing to be able to make effective use of the opportunities as they present.

Remember, however, it is not a question of "saving" anyone. It is not a time when anyone will be able to squeak by or slide under a line. Those who are prepared are prepared, and those who are not, are not. It's too late really to "get ready" or to make big changes. Courses have long ago been chosen. Each of us has equal opportunity to grow from the changes. Previous choices may have compromised individual potential for growth.

I mention the speed only for its impact on the mental status of all of us. Regardless of the work any one of us has to do, or where she will end up during and after the bulk of the transformation, mental preparation is important. It is time now to find your center, to establish balance as best you can with the givens currently around you. Only then will you be able to successfully add the new as it unfolds. And only then will you be able to benefit from the changes.

The increased speed means to all of us working from spirit that emphasis now needs to be placed on individual and collective centeredness. And even more necessary it has become to open the lines of communication between vibrational states. It is essential to communicate directly and honestly, as there isn't time for playing hesitation or resistance games. Individual spirit women are moving into a phase of communication with their respective earthplane entities that they had not expected to do until the beginning of 1990. This means that if you are to receive their guidance, you must hasten your preparedness to do so.

In keeping with the need for direct communication, I will be more specific about what you can expect to see on the earth. Keep in mind, this is not a message of doom. The happenings are necessary to the purification. They are important and for the good of the universe. It will rebalance what is now unbalanced.

Happenings in the earth's crust will initiate, in terms of the individual, opportunity to release unnecessary attachments and assumptions to facilitate the refocus on individual spiritual growth. The opposite will show as fear and panic, and subsequent emotional and mental deterioration. People will "go crazy" to the extent that they cling to the physical, to other people, or to the existing monetary and power value systems.

The crust adjustments will cause destruction of many of the earth's inhabited places. Natural disasters such as earthquakes, volcanos, the rising and falling of land masses are happening now, but insignificantly relative to what will occur in the future. These in turn will cause industrial accidents, fire, explosions, collapse of buildings, nuclear spillage, and extensive human and animal death. Disease and contamination will be widespread, food and water sources limited.

These massive changes will offset the earth's rotational balance, causing an axis shift. The degree of axis shift is variable, depending upon the extent of the earth's crust rearrangements. And with that, climatic changes and electromagnetic field alterations are inevitable. Happenings will eventually quiet, and adjustments on all planes to the new environmental situation will predominate.

Bear in mind that as the purification progresses, individual mental status will continue to deteriorate for those who lack center, and their contribution to the pandemonium will only cause further chaos. Individual reaction to the physical changes is variable, still a probability. Given prior behavior and response, we in spirit anticipate the usual "uncentered" approach.

Predictable is the outcome for many cities and towns, especially those built on unstable earth masses. But variable remains those areas which will be affected secondarily to the crust events. And variable is human response.

Where you should be at any given moment in the process is dependent upon individual lessons to be learned and work to be contributed to the transformation. Generally speaking, how long a person lives (keeps her body) during the process is not an indicator of spiritual development. Specific work can only be done by able women, so obviously vibrational status determines who is where when. Some women have incarnated to do very specific work as the unfolding occurs. With changes of this magnitude, however, accidents are bound to happen, such that even spirit will be ill-equipped to keep someone in body (alive) who is in the wrong place at the wrong time.

Our advice to you, while seemingly general perhaps, is absolutely specific: find your center, learn to keep in touch with it in the middle of chaos, do not cling to anything in fear, and foremost focus on your own spiritual growth. When you learn to trust your feeling and knowing, not only will you know what you need to do for yourself and others, you will render yourself susceptible to the guidance and help from us in spirit.

The catastrophic proportions of the changes are larger than any of us can fathom. What we say is not at all meant as a warning. It is intended to reinforce your confidence in the methods of remaining centered that you have access to as women, to emphasize the urgency in developing these skills, and to give you information in ample time to allow you to do your necessary preparations.

Most of us carry far too much unnecessary baggage. It is time to relinquish it for you can be sure it will be wrenched out of your grip not too far down the road. It's time to focus on what's *most* important: your development.

INYANI

The transformation of the earth serves a multitude of purposes, all of which amount to the restoration of balance where balance has been lost. Your approach to the transformation will determine your individual progress. It is an enormous opportunity!

For those of you who resist the changes or cling to the physical, it is a game of waiting until your bodies are destroyed or can no longer sustain the tension created. Death can come at any time, although I would guess sooner rather than later.

It is possible to view the process as a vehicle to push your alignment with yourself, thus with the universe. As you harmonize with the forces responsible for the rebalancing, as your expansion progresses, and as your awareness grows, you will easily identify your place in the process. You will know where to go, what to do, and most of all, when it is correct for you to take exit from this plane. There is a point in individual alignment where it is contrary to development to remain in physical form.

151

The time of this occurrence varies from person to person.

It is erroneous to hold to ideas that after the chaos a blissful society will form on the earth. Because of disrespect for Natural Law, the earth is an ugly place to live. The rebalancing involves the earth's transcendence of the physical plane, thus it will regain harmony in other realms. The physical aspects of the earth will not provide a desirable environment for those evolved enough to follow its transformation.

The societies to result from the transformation are already forming. Remember, this transformation has been happening for quite some time and is universal in nature. Your individual alignment with the universe allows your placement via vibrational status in these societies. They are quite real, in fact I speak to you from one such place.

My words should in no way imply hopelessness. The earth changes will create the necessary tension for those of you with appropriate consciousness and motivation, to propel you into realms magnificently superior to the earth. It is not possible to go to these places without undergoing realignment or vibrational refining. It is necessary therefore, to remain on this planet until your alignment is complete, until you reach your maximum potential from your given situation.

There is a range of alignment or vibrational possibilities variable with the individual. So do not fall prey to interpersonal comparisons. What is maximized expansion for one person may be grossly inadequate for another.

The earth's rebalancing is a great opportunity for your individual transformation if only you are willing and participatory. You are here at this time because you serve to benefit from this experience. It is quite an enormous opportunity for you, one that can send you many miles farther along your path. Opportunities of this magnitude rarely occur.

ANJA

Relative to the transformation, the area of greatest concern to us in spirit is human response. The technology exists to suddenly stop life on this planet. Unfortunately, there is a competitive mentality in the actors who control this technology. And worse, many have the attitude that "if I can't have it, nobody else is going to either."

So we do worry that there will be an abrupt interruption in the natural process of rebalancing, in which case, individuals' abilities to make smooth transitions will be greatly compromised, and much opportunity for growth lost. You can be sure there are many, many spirit people who are keeping careful watch on these potential problems. Nevertheless, none of us is perfect and sudden annihilation of part or all of the earth remains a real possibility.

Human response in less dramatic ways is also something we are watching carefully. In the natural process, tremendous tension builds just prior to change. During that time of tension, human behavior is exaggerated. Usually there is much agitation, an increase in irrational behavior, much anger and impatience. (This is similar to the tension before a long overdue rain.) With the tension there are many energetic changes in and around the earth, and human response is influenced also by these changes.

With changes of the magnitude anticipated, the level of tension, thus behavioral problems will be equally proportioned. Already there has been a marked increase in industrial accidents due to human choice and error, plane crashes, and disoriented, bizarre behavior such as mass murders.

We purposely have chosen not to give anticipated time frames, because such information induces panic and paranoia. Our intent is not to instill fear, rather to encourage your development (without neglecting to point out the urgency). The best advice we can give you is to make the most of every day, for ultimately you will be better for it.

None of our suggestions would slow your progress if perchance the earth's events are longer in coming than we anticipate. You will lose nothing by heeding our advice. Either way you will end up farther along on your journey. And this is why we have tried to undermention the earth's events and to emphasize the importance of your individual centeredness and growth.

ELLEN

During sleep or meditation, it is becoming common for many women to have experiences of the future—of specific disasters, of human response, of necessary preparations. Spirit women are indeed working with many of us in order to maximize our gain from the happenings.

Very commonly experienced, especially in the dreamtime (which Grace explains later in detail) are light and vibration changes relative to the axis shift. Typically, a peculiar air or feeling surrounds the earth, with unfamiliar colors and lighting. The specific scenes vary depending upon what an individual woman needs or chooses to witness.

These experiences are alarming for many women. They *should* be to the extent that change could be beneficial. But the idea is not for immobilization to occur due to fear. Forewarnings are opportunities.

153

They give you a head start and a chance to make modifications in your outlook or actions. The future I see on this planet is definitely not pleasant, in fact some of it is quite horrible. But it *is* the restoration of balance.

Predictive techniques as well as practitioners of these techniques range from useful and accurate to worthless. The changes and happenings are much greater than earthplane perspective, so while a system or practitioner may be accurate, that accuracy is limited by ability, scope, expansion and vibration. Once a sufficient number of variables change our current situation, all the systems of the earth will become inapplicable. For example, astrology can be a very accurate predictor. Its range is limited to the scope of the solar system, and cannot accommodate major change in the patterns we now witness. Once planetary patterns are altered, astrology will no longer be accurate.

My point is not to criticize an excellent system, but to mention that adherence to any system amounts to walking on thin ice. I think it is a big mistake to cling to a "correct" interpretation, and to then base your choices upon that. As Majai said, the future exists in probabilities. If you rely on yourself, and are flexible enough to bend and change on an ongoing basis, your choices will be appropriate to the moment, and as "correct" as they possibly can be. Evaluate predictions, but do not assume anyone has a clearer or more accurate interpretation than you do. And stay focused on your individual work; that will not change no matter what contortions the earth needs to undergo to rebalance.

ELLEN

Ideally there should exist alignment of the universe, the earth, organized humanity, and the individual entity. Natural Law is that which promotes such alignment. Misalignment produces tension, and that tension forces rearrangement until realignment occurs.

The universe and the earth (independent of its inhabitants and their actions) are in a constant state of fluctuant alignment. Location of disharmony is therefore either with the individual or organized humanity. ("Civilization" rather than "organized humanity" implies exclusion of much of the earth's population, but in fact does point rather precisely to the actual location of the imbalances within organized humanity.) Because of the extent of adverse interaction that has taken place between people and the earth, many specific locations on the earth are severely out of line with the universe. Such places I assume to be included within the problematic organized humanity.

154

The most localized tension is created (and felt) when the individual, the earth, and the universe are aligned, but civilization is not. To live in or even visit places subjected to civilization's abuse has disruptive effects on a person's otherwise solid alignment. Such an individual's participation with contrary-to-Natural Law-organized humanity obviously counteracts her moves toward harmony, expansion, and alignment.

The greater an individual's sensitivity, which stems from spiritual development and evolutionary growth, the less readily she can tolerate any misalignment. As the source of the problem is on the physical plane (the rest of the components being in alignment), that will be the point to break secondary to the tension resultant from any misalignment. In the extreme, dissociation from the physical body (death) can occur, and can occur quite precipitously if she suddenly enters an environment of disharmony to which she is unaccustomed. Harmony with the universe will prevail at all cost, even if it means relinquishment of the physical body.

So not only is it necessary to move to increasingly cleaner and more harmonious places as we expand and align, it is necessary to permanently maintain distance from the previously tolerated chaos. There comes a point when we must step away from people who defy Natural Law, industrial or technological creations that abuse, and physical locations that have suffered abuse. This is similar to our growing intolerance for poisonous or denatured foods that we experience as our evolution progresses.

Actually at greater odds with the universe/earth alignment than the lone aligned individual, are those who live in abused locations, participate in decaying society and its practices, and who are also individually unbalanced. (This comprises most of the world's population, quite unfortunately.) These individuals will be slower to perceive the tension of misalignment. They continually live in an illusion of harmony, or rather, an oblivion to disharmony, as they align themselves with the chaos and degeneration rather than with the order. And when the chaos ceases to be as contained and as ordered as it currently is, they will abruptly move out of their illusion to perceive overwhelming and irreclaimable degeneration.

Many people have made major adjustments in their lifestyle and places of residence in attempts to maintain their centers. Beginning now is a time when volumes of people will be *compelled*, seemingly illogically perhaps, to pack up and go. Please trust these feelings. They are very real, and quite reliable. Your failure to honor them will place you in very dangerous and detrimental situations.

155

AMNA

We are not getting ready for "an event." We exist in process. The universe in its change is the event. You as you change are the event.

Mistaken are those who think that if they can prepare sufficiently their living environments (by collecting food and water, moving to solid ground, etc.) they will be able to live through the changes. This is an end result mentality, irrelevant to the present situation. The changes are larger than this.

The goal is restoration of harmony and balance. Rearrangements in lifestyle and environment are *only* for the purpose of allowing you the room to realign to the best of your ability. When your potential for realignment is maximized, you will leave the earth.

Those who fail to make use of the opportunity will leave the earth also, but unprepared for the transition, thus not ready for the next chapter, and will forfeit much growth. Those who prepare by taking middle of the road postures will likewise benefit only partially from the changes. (This is like going to church "because it can't hurt," while failing to believe in your actions and failing to have the courage to follow your deeper feelings.)

KIOKA

The taking of a pill, the later the better, to produce the necessary growth is the ideal of many women. I don't have time for these women.

Development is much work. The effort expended reflects the growth achieved. In fact, the growth *is* the process of change that each of us undertakes. Our progress is *because* we undergo transformations. Without them we simply aren't "developed." From my vantage point, I cannot understand a desire to avoid change or transformation. It is one of the most empty-headed desires I have ever encountered. Only people on the earth could come up with something like this!

Ellen has been chasing after me to tell some of my past. "A little realness from Kioka, please." My travels have taken me a route very different from the routes of those of you on the earth. Since coming into your territory I am astounded by what I see, and by the contrast to my experience. Thus, I am responsible for encouraging the inclusion of discussions of menlessness in this book: a common topic just about everywhere except on the earth.

My personal journey was in the company of women from the begin-

156

ning. At times I had very minimal interaction with men, briefly at times when male growth paralleled my growth. Interaction is not even an accurate word to describe it. Better to say awareness of men. They simply have never been part of my experience: an animal to be viewed from a distance, as if at a zoo, but never to be taken seriously as relevant to my life.

To watch the empowerment of men by women on the earth, to me is a rather foreign undertaking. I cannot imagine even for a moment how such a state of affairs was born and now how it is accepted as if indicative of some ultimate truth. My amazement cannot possibly be expressed in words, but Ellen would never forgive me if I didn't try.

Because I lack investment in men, I also cannot take seriously the significance women have attributed to them. Women's allegiance to male spiritual development was never a possibility in my environments. I can't imagine having some creature of different essential energy follow me around for lifetimes upon lifetimes, trying to promote my growth at its own expense. And then further, to have it try to become like me! On the earth dogs are less dedicated to humans than women are to men.

As I give this material, Ellen is asking, "So how did you get your physical form? Some immaculate routine?" Some of you are familiar with the capabilities of the mind in the creation of environments in some of the spirit realms of physicalness. There, thought is the primary component determining manifestation characteristics. Similar to this is the principle upon which my physical forms were always created. There are environments where mental clarity is sufficient to establish precision creations such as human bodies of density equal to earthplane density.

The places through which I evolved were void of the chaos and distractions to path that are commonplace on the earth. Expansion was still limited to the current vibration, but absent of clutter. I suppose, this was because the mixing of male energies with female energies never complicated the picture. Clarity of purpose was always a given.

Your resistance to letting go of the chaos is also rather amazing to me. As I watch, I can't decide if the avoidance of taking whatever measures necessary to rectify your course to become consistent with female vibration is due to ignorance or resistance. I don't suppose it is particularly important at this point, since the choice for you now is to move or not to move. All I can say is that you don't need the clutter. You don't need to cling to the chaos. You don't need to cling to men or male spirituality.

I became involved in the book work because Ellen arrived into my vibration seeking support. Many of the spirit women she encountered on her travels on her return to her own vibration after the Black Bear work were stuck in the methodology of the earth, having previously traveled through the earthplanes on their journeys. Her frustration with the absence of perspectives free of the baggage of the earth led to my response. She sought the friendship of women who would understand her exasperation with trying to work on the earth given these conditions. Because the book was in progress, I figured I'd put in my two cents.

I am the last comer to the project. Even so, my heart has been touched by the few strong women on the earth struggling to get out of the chaos, asking and asking. Your requests *are* heard. I hope you acknowledge the importance of speaking out, given the fact that I, anyway, would not have come had you remained silent. If my words reach any of you, I will be very delighted.

MAJAI

It is reasonable to do what you can to prevent compromising your balance. You need to prepare yourself to make the transition. Sometimes you will require isolation, other times the community of women.

This is not a time for heroics. *You will prove nothing and help no one by staying in the chaos.* In the present case, a greater cause to which self sacrifice can be applied to the benefit of the collective does not exist. It is merely a question of providing for yourself the environment necessary to allow your harmonization with the universal flow. If you sit in the chaos, you can only connect with the chaos. If you create a setting where you can maintain balance and connect with the yin, you will harmonize with the universe.

MAJAI

The usual response to difficulties and problems is to create new technology to override them. Oftentimes the problem is the very result of one of these technological creations. If we follow the chain of creations backward, it is easy to see not only our distance from natural processes, but *motivation to defy Natural Law.*

With the new and overwhelming situations presenting in conjunction with the transformation, the tendency will no doubt be to attempt to create further. The answer is simplicity. Break the chain of compounding need and return to basic functional needs: shelter, food, water, warmth and clothes. Simplicity *is* the solution. It eliminates 99% of the problems.

KIOKA

The women who are most likely to have some use for our words are women at or near the end of their need to incarnate. This includes both spirit and earthbound women.

The resistance of the others is too great to allow them the accumulation of momentum sufficient to propel them forward regardless of obstacles or pain. Their fears are too plentiful to allow them to make choices and to act upon them. Their attachments are too strong for them to risk letting go. Their frustration is not sufficient to make them wish to move on into unknown territory.

I say this to prepare you for the isolation you may experience as you dare to risk, to discriminate, to empower yourself. Know that they are correct in their immobility, just as you are correct in your mobility. However, do not let their choices affect yours.

It is important for you to have courage to act on your convictions. It is important for you to initiate your own progress: the way and the speed. Your journey is only as good as your commitment to it. When you take it seriously, you will act with determination and discretion. For it to be a quality trip, you need to make it so.

Upon leaving the the incarnation process, you will be faced with major changes. This is one of the more dramatic transition points you will encounter. It is a graduation from a place of much resistance (thus interference by others in your process) to a place of self-control and self-determination. And again when you move from physicalness to non-physicalness, you will experience a comparable transition.

It is absolutely reasonable and anticipated that you will be laden with emotions of all colors as your prepare to and do make your transition. Facing and accepting your feelings as you transit is important. But for women of the earth, the most difficult hurdle to overcome is that of willingness to become self-determined and self-directed. Taking your power, and recognizing the vastness of your power is terrifying for many women. Over and over women back away from it, preferring to sit in stagnation or denial.

Your capabilities *will* amaze you, but they need not scare you. They can be exciting. They are your wings. And so, you, the woman ready to fly beyond the earth, is the woman this book is meant for.

ELLEN

When you pick something up, then you have to decide what to do with it. So part of taking your power involves using it. How and where will you do that? This is why discrimination and decision making are important.

A choice made eliminates options. A decision to do one thing precludes the doing of others in that moment. And for every choice, reaction will follow. There are natural consequences for all in the environment of that choice since nothing exists in a vacuum. Some of the consequences or reactions we would rather do without. Some we will be glad for.

In decision making lives risks, risks that we may become unloved for our choice, risks that the consequences will be other than we anticipate, risks that the results will be other than we desire.

The alternative is to choose based on the predicted reactions of others who might take back their love, to opt for a reversible choice, or to avoid choice, none of which involves courage, conviction or risk on the part of the decisionmaker.

Without a statement of choice direction is lost. Without direction effort and motion are scattered. Progress is left to blow in the wind.

KIOKA

Many make noises about wanting to grow and change, but when given even special, clearer opportunities, they quickly run the other way. A person determined to grow does not need complicated accoutrements or extraordinary treatment. There are many choices a woman can make, all capable of taking her beyond herself. The key is the wanting to move, and when present, will illuminate the millions of opportunities that exist that can help her develop and that she can use to help others. Want of opportunity is not a viable excuse for avoidance.

It is frustrating for us in spirit to watch the intricacies of avoidance. You can pick and choose, discriminate, reject and accept *while* moving forward. Choice making does not limit your mobility if done correctly. It encourages it by focusing your energies. Refusal to choose is a blatant statement of avoidance.

GRACE

Ellen and I have had occasion to work with a lot of women, and opportunity to work with even more. Usually there is clear benefit for somebody or a request for our involvement would not be made. For everyone else directly affected, including ourselves, would an interaction also be beneficial? As you can probably guess, we have managed to learn what we have about discrimination the long way.

* * *

The woman definitely had the brakes on her development. Her guide, having exhausted all the options she could think of to get this woman moving, frantically pushed us for a reading. Thinking only of the woman's potential for progress, we figured we had nothing to lose. Needless to say, the woman refused to open even enough to hear the words of her guide. The guide learned finally to let go, but for this guide to hear again what was obvious, was not good utilization of Ellen's time or energy. I felt remiss in having encouraged this reading.

* * *

I had a dog once, a cute little dog. She had a wonderful habit of chewing things. I was best at playing with this dog, and not very good at discipline. There was a man I knew who could very quickly teach animals good manners. Instead of asking for his help, I chased the dog out of trouble, rearranged my things so they wouldn't end up half eaten, and spent an embarrassing number of hours putting one band-aid after another on the situation.

* * *

I was asked to do a healing on a woman. Sometimes there are several ways to treat an ailment. She wished for me to do it energetically, although I felt she had other choices. Rather than risk having her feel rejected, I did a long series of treatments. Eventually she was cured. We could have accomplished the same in half the time had I had the courage to insist that she take herbs and to refuse my involvement energetically.

* * *

A woman insistent that her guides would communicate by way of a reading determinedly requested one. The guides did not wish to use this method as they felt the woman was not ready for either the directness or the content (appropriate to her questions). But they decided to go ahead with a reading as an attempt to appease the woman, hoping to satisfy her on their attentiveness and respect. The answers to her questions, although simplified by her guides considerably, proved to be too big for her. She simply could not digest them, so while she did receive answers, was not able to use those answers to her advantage. Other than having been satisfied that she did in fact have guides, the communication was of little value, and frustrating to all involved parties.

* * *

Ellen is very good at holding onto a mere flicker of potential in a person. She is always the last to give up. Worse than last, centuries later she finally concludes that a situation is not worth her efforts. Of course on many occasions she has gotten results where others have not dared to entertain a possibility of growth. But there have also been times when she has come dragging home, exhausted and defeated, having gone an extra 20 miles for a person, only to have been met finally with apathy or deference of responsibility. We are all very relieved that she is finally learning to say no in some places and yes in others.

MAJAI

Discrimination and loving judgment are key to your expedient spiritual progress. In order to foster your own growth, you must be able to identify your requirements and to define your route with precision. You must discriminate to separate what is useful to your growth from what is not. You must be a judge of quality in order that you know to accept the highest quality and to reject the rest. This includes all people, places and things in your environment.

Mistaken is the woman who confuses the keeping of something in her heart with the keeping of it in her life. We need to have compassion and love for all creatures. Never should we put any out of our heart. But to limit the participation of certain ones in your life is not wrong. It is necessary.

Chaos results from the absence of organization, limit setting and clarity of goal. Whom do you serve if you float aimlessly in the cosmos, refusing to avoid being bumped and jolted or worse? Who benefits when you fail to say no? If you expose your true preferences, what will the consequences be?

Lovingly discriminate to facilitate your progress and to help in the maintenance of your balance. *Have the courage to make the statement of decision and choice.*

ELLEN

Once I worked with a doctor who told me she no longer had time to chase medical students who needed to be forced to learn. There were plenty of hungry students who would chase her, allowing her to teach them *while* she did her work.

Just because a need exists, doesn't mean you have to or should fill it. Opportunity is bountifully overflowing. There is no reason why you cannot choose to participate in situations which foster your own growth, the growth of others, *and* which do so expediently.

KIOKA

Each of us, including those of us in non-physical vibrations, has things to learn and things already learned. What has already been learned is what we are qualified to give away, our contribution to the collective. It is our work. What remains to be perfected are our lessons.

The work is easy, the lessons hard. Naturally each of us gravitates toward work and away from the lessons, especially when our resistance to forward motion is high. At this particular time, resistance is very high, and it is not uncommon to see people shunning the importance of the self. It is seemingly easier for some to focus on everyone else's problems in order to take the mind off those pending lessons.

We have responsibility to the collective and responsibility to the self. To do one to the exclusion of the other creates imbalance between the individual and the group. Frequently those who cannot manage to discriminate are those who like the work but not the lessons. But to work on the self and fail to give comparable amounts to others will arrest individual progress also. It amounts to hoarding and is not balanced behavior either.

We discriminate to make sure that individual-collective balance is maintained. That is how we insure that each of us and all of us keep moving.

163

ELLEN

Oftentimes when I encounter a person, usually for the first time, not only do I take in the present situation, but see scenes from other incarnations or times elsewhere. These other scenes can be accurately reflective of the true personality, motivations or evolution. And usually I tap these other scenes when something incongruous exists with the present situation. Discrimination necessarily must surpass the present.

My glimpse beyond the possibly illusory present does not always demonstrate parallelism between the other times and the present. My conclusion to follow necessarily may seem inappropriate to the present, my likes, dislikes, desire to avoid or move closer to the person, possibly appearing unreasonable. Intellectually I find it difficult to explain my conclusions, and especially as a child, even coming to terms with the existence of such unclassifiable information was definitely a project.

I have come to understand that what I look at is the entity on a developmental continuum, the vibration relative to concentration of essential energy. On the earth it is possible to function using criteria usually associated with other realms. Just because it is atypical methodology for the earth, doesn't mean it is either inapplicable or irrelevant.

Judgments made taking into consideration the past as well as perspectives broader than the present can often be made quickly and accurately. Because such evaluations are free of clutter of extensive present experience, they frequently are even more accurate than we think them to be. The validity of first impressions rests in this type of assessment.

However, pitfalls do exist. It is necessary to know what you do in fact view when you take such a look. Just as the present can be small relative to total development, it is possible to see a person in the smallness of an isolated former state, a tiny part of her or his journey. This occurs most easily if we personally have a past with the person. We zero in on the point of common experience, and can be blinded to condemnation or to love or to the range between. In such a case, the person has likely grown beyond that state which was previously known to us. Confusion can also arise when we identify the presence of karmic debt. The presence of obstacles can falsely appear to be lack of evolution. So it is important to always look beyond the karmic situation to see who exists behind it.

There is practical application for collecting such information, in terms of protection, trust, and efficient energy expenditure. We think nothing of collecting information on the trustworthiness of a person from whom we would buy a used car. We can do so with a heart full of love, for the other and for ourselves.

ELLEN

Many of us can do lots of unconventional things, and these things do not always have a slot in what is normal, on the earth anyway. What you can do, perhaps I can't, and vice versa. We do not grow in unison by expanding in exactly the same ways or in the same direction. We will end up in the same place, but our routes and attainments along the way will vary.

With each jump in expansion, those old feelings of unfamiliarity of territory, of isolation in the subjectivity of experience, and of doubts of missteps and weirdness, flow strong. Lack of verification from others doesn't mean your experience is wrong. Try to go beyond your desire for confirmation from others. And see that as you expand all you are doing is learning to add more to *your* existing size without compromising the balance of your totality. Use your abilities, as divergent as they may seem, to resynchronize with the universe, and don't be afraid of what you are able to see around you.

ELLEN

When your expansion becomes greater than what is typically witnessed in society at large, you have a problem. Do you stop your growth in order to avoid uncomfortable experience? Or do you continue to expand, preparing yourself for the consequences of increasing disparity between yourself and society? This *is* a very real question and not always easy to answer.

On one hand, never should you stop your growth. I do not condone the making of any choice in fear. Neither do I think it advisable to lead a responsive existence. And certainly it is important to have the courage to own the consequences of a choice.

Practically speaking, however, each of us has a myriad of things to perfect and learn. Many directions in which you can choose to grow do exist. This means we have options. Thus it *is* possible to make choices in our own best interest, which also minimize unpleasant consequences to us. Some directions are more easily assimilated by society than are others, resulting ultimately in our own comfort.

This does not mean we make decisions to accommodate the wishes of others. Neither does it allow places for avoidance or fear. It is important to make sure we are not fooling ourselves into compromising our growth. Any choice should maximize our individual growth.

Eventually in your expansion you *will* reach a point where all choices in your best interest contradict societal norms. At this point, however, you will find that any choice other than following your heart or any choice that takes you in a direction other than forward, is so uncomfortable that the importance of the consequences easily takes a back seat.

If society were in alignment with Natural Law, we would not be faced with a growing disparity between ourselves and the norm. Feelings of separation, isolation and not belonging are the most common. But please try to remember that your oddness and illusion of distance is only temporary. Soon you will move into societies where Natural Law *is* respected. And then you will know that your path is the path of many.

There is nothing I can say to decrease the disparity. But I do mention it so you will at least know that you are not alone in your realization that as you move into harmony, the disharmony in life around you will scream at you. You will not be wrong in your inability or lack of desire to tolerate it.

Compensation for the disparity can best be achieved by going forward. Maintain your connection to the yin; it is your strength. Keep your contact with the earth; it secures your center. And most of all *do not* resist your expansion. The worst thing you can do is to slow or stop your growth. Only by growing can you move beyond the disparity altogether.

KIOKA

When the scope of operation is confined to the physical plane, expansion possibilities are also curtailed. To me the earth looks like a giant iron kettle with a heavy lid. Under it, a hot fire is burning. Some aspire to become the crusted residue in the kettle bottom. A few allow themselves to heat up enough to change to steam. The sheer force of the heat will give drive enough to push the lid up ever so slightly, just enough for you to slip out from under the lid.

I want to see your eyes peeking out from under that lid very soon. The Dreams are there to greet you. So are we. If you dare let your eyes meet what awaits you outside of that kettle, those timid eyes will certainly sparkle.

MAJAI

On the earth the range of thought is far too limited relative to the vastness and expansiveness of the universe. Reality for some residents of the earth is confined to the densest manifestations of physical, to the extent that realities less dense are doubted and discredited. Anything of less density, thus of less defined form, is unfamiliar and frequently rejected.

Precision equal to that found in the manufacture of scientific instruments, for example, can be found in all other vibrations. However, different principles or laws govern these realms. While in dense physicalness precision manifests as form. In levels beyond the density of the earth, the total environment, including the type of entities in it, is a reflection of mental clarity, attitude, and specificity. With decreasing density, the clarity, organization and one-pointedness of the vibration itself reflects the degree of precision. This is still true at the point of color and sound.

And with further lessening of density, the manifestation moves even closer to the essential energy of the entity, becoming in the case of women, concentration of pure yin. *To the extent that components exist not of pure yin, the precision is compromised.*

As was stated in the introduction, the authors of this book are known or identified by their concentration of yin. And in fact, so are the women on the earth. But by earth standards such a criterion does not even exist. Rather, one is evaluated by one's ability to demonstrate precise manipulation of the most dense physical matter. That skill is all but irrelevant to those of us sitting where I sat.

It is not wrong to perfect what exists on the earth. However, each of you is far more complex than just this aspect. So developmentally, focus limited to only the densest physical is absent of progress. In order to expand, it is mandatory that an entity's involvement in other vibrations occur.

Since your actual vibrational status is a function of your concentration of yin, lack of awareness of your essential nature detracts from its growth. Expansion is gradual, thus precision and refinement through all the densities is necessary. However, awareness of the fundamental process, growth of your concentration of yin, can help direct your focus appropriately.

When viewing the larger picture, it is easy to see the importance of removing karmic and self-created obstacles. Only having done that can exposure of the yin be possible. We then free ourselves to attend to the growth of our essence. Efforts applied to anything short of this essence are irrelevant. Accidentally we may contribute to our essential natures, or on the other hand, we may create more obstacles. Those entities insistent that dense physical existence is the totality of experience and existence merely stagnate and get in their own ways.

MAJAI

See your essence, the yin, as a snowball. If free to roll in the snow (the collective yin) it will grow. If left on bare land, or covered and surrounded by debris, even when more snow falls, it cannot increase itself. For a snowstorm (an influx of collective yin) or the existing snowpack (the yin in the immediate environment) to have access to the snowball (you), the obstacles and debris must be removed.

GRACE

I see that some of us are afraid to root for a losing team. This thinking could use a little adjustment. It is a misfocus of your precious energy to set some quantitative standard for probable success of the yin relative to the yang, and then to wait to own your allegiance to the yin until such a standard is met. (If you are afraid to own yourself in your totality, at least admit it. Any number of excuses will not change this.)

The yin will not grow larger and larger to eventually explode like a volcano out of the top of a mountain. The yin is as big as it's going to get. Certainly it is large enough for you to find!

ELLEN

The losing team is the team which aligns against Natural Law. A view only from the earth leaves us with a mistaken conclusion that those of us seeking harmony and balance are in a minority. And too, that the state of degeneration we witness on the earth is indicative of conditions elsewhere. Given the scope of vision possible from a physical posture, these are not unreasonable conclusions. With expanded perspective however, it becomes very obvious that we actually have the whole universe in support of our choices. Or rather, more accurately, we are choosing to align with the universe in its balanced state. We are part of *the* majority.

ELLEN

Kioka's astonishment at viewing the condition of women on the earth is an indication that individually she has grown many miles since a time when her vibration was comparable. If I suddenly remember an event from nursery school, the distance between then and now seems vast. Spiritual development has equal appearance when viewed from heights capable of encompassing many miles of travel.

Yet, in other ways, when I look from Majai to Kioka, the vibrational distance appears to be no greater than one quarter of an inch. The sense of sameness of essence and the understanding that each of us undergoes identical processes magnifies our closeness to each other. Refining of the self to uncover pure yin is what each of us is busy doing.

In order to effect refinement it becomes necessary to expose all that I carry that is not pure yin. It is the cleaning of the stockpiled closet routine. Soon the trash is scattered all over the room, overwhelmingly present, burdensome and spotlighted. For the process, approach of the goal of elimination of unnecessary baggage is achieved. Yet were one to view only the mess in the middle of the room, it would be easy to conclude a disarrayful life, compounded by accumulation.

I near perfection or purity as I expose and release the extraneous. That process is realness in action. *That process omits censoring or image projection.* Consequently, *woman in process does not appear to be perfection, charisma, smoothness and ease.* What shows is her willingness to let her baggage surface to evaporate. Clarity and perspective is achieved, yet that is not ordinarily visible to others.

So when I see all of us crammed into the quarter inch, it is because each of us is busy allowing her realness to show. Those so busy are not far from pure yin because each moves, thus the distance from one another *is* minimal. She who fails to refine, on the other hand, has not even opened any of the closet doors. She *is* very far away. If, when the doors are opened and the trash pours forth, she busies herself trying to conceal herself in her mess, she keeps herself distanced from the rest of us. Then what is seen is the charismatic, smooth imaged woman void of realness. This is not progress.

So regardless of your vibrational level, until you let go of all that obscures your essence, you will not look particularly fancy or polished. (In fact, how you appear to others is quite irrelevant. Another's opinion does not change your progress at all.) Do not be afraid of your realness. If it helps, remember that some of us recognize you as a moving woman exactly by that realness, and will not even give the time of day to the image makers.

KIOKA

Instead of using the incarnation process as an opportunity to illuminate areas of the entity in need of attention, many have chosen to adopt the disharmonies created as givens and acceptabilities. Refusal to see individual imperfections and their manifestations as contradictory to Natural Law has created the escalation in the earth's deterioration.

Self-responsibility for growth has been denied to an extent that growth as a possibility and a desirable pursuit has been killed. *The earth is a clear picture of a collection of individuals who have failed to seek the elimination of their own disharmonies.* And to think that the presenting picture on the earth is the manifestation of but pieces of the totalities of these disharmonious individuals, is frightening. Unfortunately from my vantage point, complete manifestation of these individuals *is* viewable. (Remember, their mental and vibrational status is manifest without action in other realms, even as they inhabit the earth.)

I would like to be able to convince you of the importance of giving up your allegiance to the chaos on the earth, but it is not up to me to do so. This is something that must be your choice. The Black Bears will remain creating ugly pictures as they pursue whatever, but you don't need to play those kinds of games. You have a choice as to where you live. You make that choice by evolving.

INYANI

The earth is one of the most, if not the most, abused and disrespected environments in the universe at this time. To live here defies spiritual progress. The lack of synchronicity with the universe opposes one's natural development, so efforts to progress necessitate daily struggle.

The problems belong to all of us. Yet some of us are only adjunctive contributors, while others willfully and wantonly perpetuate the abuses. In their pursuit of goals contrary to collective and universal good, many disregard the consequences of their actions. You can be sure, people capable of such knowing disrespect are not, in universal terms, the pick of the litter. And degree of refusal of consciousness concerning participation reflects evolutionary development.

Some of us are quick to turn a blind eye to the problems. All of us are numb and oblivious to the severity of the situation. *Most have forgotten even how to live in harmony with universal laws were an unopposed opportunity to present to them.* Expectations have hit rock bottom. The limited view of the cosmos contributes to the state of resignation to and compliance with the choices of the decision makers on this planet. Too many of us are resigned to our own inaction. Minimal happiness, limited expansion, and little overall progress is so commonplace that we have grown to expect nothing more and to strive for nothing greater.

We want to wake you up to the problems and the solutions. None of the timeworn excuses will work any more. The situation we face is ugly, but there *is* a way out.

We are not unreasonable in our identification of the difficulties and problems existent on this planet. We wish such identification to enable you to better understand the work that awaits you, and that our acceptance and acknowledgement of the state of degeneration will allow you permission to equally acknowledge. Then we will all be better equipped and free to move ahead from the givens.

AMNA

Female experience bears no resemblance to male experience. Our journey amounts to bushwhacking through the universe. It's a lot of work especially when many of us still have to determine not only the route but our methods of travel.

If we try to apply existing male methods to our efforts we will become exhausted very quickly. Having tried their methods time and time again, we *know* that they don't work for us. The evidence is everywhere.

If you insist on taking male ways with you, you will travel as an old, narrow-minded arthritic woman, who can't even lift her head to see the path in front of her. So step into a brand new context to journey as a child, with her magnificent expectations, fantastic dreams, silent innocence, *and* unbounding energy.

ELLEN

Society condones the self-determined, autonomous, physically strong male. Short hair and functional clothing facilitate his mobility. Woman as a product of societal standards, on the other hand, is not a functional being, does not maximize the potential of her physical body, and has dependent personality as well as behavior. (Hairstyles are frequently cumbersome, never mind time consuming or poisonous to maintain.

Shoes deform her feet and spine, and make the act of walking a dependent and dangerous undertaking. I need not go on, for the state of affairs is obvious.)

Certainly many of us have refused to accept these absurdities into our lifestyles and personalities. And lots of us refuse to identify with such a degrading categorization of women. But in some cases, I think, in our refusal to participate, we have let the pendulum swing beyond what is useful to our growth. There has been a transfer of gender behavior: women copying male style and behavior, and men copying women. Are they external gestures hopeful of effecting power or status changes, or effecting the deeper changes needed because both women and men have been stifled in their growth by societal limitations?

Among some women has developed "male to be emulated" thought (and even the gay man who sits at the opposite end of the spectrum, as a model for lesbians). The right to self-determination that society chooses to place in the male domain can easily be adopted by women. It is not *that* he is male that is desirable to woman; it is what the position of maleness allows him to be (an entity worthy of growth) that deserves our notice.

We should, for example, desire to maximize the potential of our physical bodies (if doing so is appropriate to our path), not to look like a man. Male body build has nothing to do with his success as a self-willed being. If short hair allows easier work performance, it is a desirable style to adopt. To look like him will not make you more successful in the workplace. (Short hair will not make you a better carpenter, yet it might help you avoid getting tangled in your saw.) And many of his behavioral choices (while *possibly* appropriate to his growth) do not work for women. His oppression and control of others I certainly do not find to be worthy of emulation.

Maleness or his effectiveness as a male is irrelevant to our connection to our power. His ways will not upgrade our status or growth. (Nor ours his.) *Each must find essential energy appropriate methods of behavior.* Emulation lives in the realm of externalization. It does not address core functioning or being.

We choose to identify with women because we *need* women for our growth. If we carry that identification into separatist or lesbian lifestyle, the basis for that choice also is need. (It is a choice for women, not gayness.) We also desire the right to make choices which meet our needs. And this reduces to the right to self-determination and autonomy of growth producing decisions. These we can have if we aim our efforts *not to externals* but to the attainment of what we do in fact need.

GRACE

If you choose to interact closely with a man, you'd best be clear about the place you want him to occupy in your life. You *do* have needs that he doesn't have and if you intend to do justice to yourself you must find fulfillment of these needs. My words do not only apply to relationships with men. They hold for all relationships, but moreso with men as men are so different from women.

Fulfilling your needs may entail making times and spaces that are for you alone. There is no need to feel by doing this that you deprive anyone else of anything. Women often feel they owe men, children or other people, all their time and energy. This then means that anything they give to themselves deprives everyone else. The basic assumption here is wrong.

First you are a person. Your body, your thoughts, your actions are yours. Determine what you need to grow. Then decide to whom and to what you wish to give your efforts. Decide how much, and when that limit is reached, simply say no. You are responsible for what you take on. If you take on so much that there is no time for yourself, you lose.

Your needs will change as you grow, with the seasons, with your external environment. Room for ebbs and flows and internal changes must be allowed for and respected. Then variability can find its place in a relationship. Sometimes you will need to sleep alone. Important work is done while you sleep. Sometimes to have another body close physically cramps your style in other realms.

Allotting yourself what you need for growth should be very matter-of-fact. You just do it. There is no place for argument, hard feelings, notions of deprivation or guilt. Start with the assumption that you are here to grow, and to that add the rest of your life.

ELLEN

Have you ever needed to put up a mental wall between yourself and someone else just to be able to think? This is not an imaginary invasion of your territory. It does not mean you are paranoid. People's clinging, neediness, love for you can literally encroach upon the more subtle aspects of your being. Sometimes their presence does scramble your thoughts or make you defensive or nervous. They do not act consciously or maliciously, and would be aghast if they knew what they did.

Nevertheless, it is appropriate and *necessary* for you to step away temporarily in these cases. You need a vibrationally clean place to sleep, to think, to communicate with spirit, to work in other realms. To allow someone to mingle in your energy at these times is comparable to allowing them to keep a hand in your back pocket as you weed your garden.

MAJAI

While the spiritual development of all women can happen only in the company of women, women can choose to participate with men in other aspects of their lives. Eventually there comes a point where spirituality cannot be isolated from other activities. Lessons and work merge, and then women will seek and need only the company of women. For them men simply have no function or purpose.

Prior to such a time, however, depending upon karmic situations and choice, men have purpose in women's lives. Never do they have any role in her spiritual development, except in terms of being available to allow her to remove existent karmic debt specific to men.

Therefore, because for many women male presence is necessary and good, a little understanding of the male situation could help clarify and eliminate confusion. I am obviously not male. Consequently my understanding of their process is limited to only the basics.

Their essential energy is what has been labeled yang. To grow in yang they add to themselves quantitatively, in a process of accumulation and externalization. How they actually accumulate yang, I do not know.

Until the energetic change over, when the preponderance of energy universally moved from yang to yin, men sat in a situation of utter saturation of yang. Their potential for power peaked. Whatever they were able to incorporate into themselves was theirs to keep. And whatever they were unable to use remained a potential to be left unrealized until such a time and place where yang again predominates. Some men were left very frustrated. But frustrated or not, the universal flow is now yin, to be worked with or not.

Even as the yang wanes, many men continue to clamor for power. They force it, they demand it, they try to take it at any cost. As women are beginning to feel the increasing yin, men are beginning to feel the decreasing yang. In their mounting panic in response to the waning yang, they focus on the control of other people. They still operate on assumptions that they can add more and more to themselves at will, that they can grow larger. For these men, the process is now extensively perverted,

174

as they act in futility causing much damage and impediment to the progress of others. These men are obsessed with gaining power at a time when doing so is impossible.

Other men have realized the futility of such an approach and have sincerely attempted to come to understand the yin, enough to ride with it and to avoid being in opposition to it. Men can find help from the example of women. From them they can learn to harmonize. Men will not, however, get power from women, from the yin, or from their alignment. Erroneous are beliefs that men get power from women. They sit exactly in the power they attained at the time of the yang. It will not decrease or fade. They should not fear its loss or dissipation. But acceptance that the yang cannot be increased will allow them to get on with the necessary and urgent job of harmonizing with the yin. Their resistance will only get them into difficulty in terms of the purification and transformation.

Remember that you owe men nothing. They are responsible for their harmonization with the yin. You assist them by your example, by taking your own power, and by showing your independence from them.

So if you choose to associate with men, I suggest that you do it on your terms as opposed to theirs. They can take or leave the options you present to them. There is no time or place for games of chase or convincing. Do your work. They are free to learn from you, free to pursue a path of resistance, or free to do anything they please.

ELLEN

A few men do exist who have genuine respect for women and women's spiritual progress. The respect is sufficient that he is not threatened by her choices which do not involve him. In such cases, she is not limited in any way by her participation with him. Her autonomy equals his autonomy. And they appreciate their individual spiritual paths as dissimilar and divergent.

The majority of men do not fit this picture, nor do the relationships women have with men. Because of the pervasiveness of male control and dominance, even at times beyond the will or recognition of individual men, such attitudes and relationships are rare (if not impossible).

We feel it is necessary to point out the problems, and to address the most typical patterns we see. By doing so, however, we do not wish to alienate women who do have interaction with individual men conducive to their spiritual growth. We do appreciate this situation as being a *theoretic* possibility.

When it is time for a woman to move into non-physical realms, she will have found that men have completely ceased to be relevant to her process. We do not wish to propose the adoption of an elitist posture or attitude. This state of affairs simply is. Likewise exist the state of deterioration, the oppression of women by men (and some women), and the predominance of male autonomy with disrespect for women's development.

KIOKA

The male dominance of society with resultant heterosexual privilege makes it hard for earthbound women to imagine any life without men or without oppression. In order to so imagine, it is necessary to go beyond the earthplane givens and knowns. It is one of the ways earthplane smallness of thought can be expanded.

Women who have developed as far as the B category: physicalness of sound and color, have not *had* to align completely with their essential energies, although many have. When it is time to move into the non-physical, however, men cease to be relevant to a woman's personal journey. Certainly the yang energy has a place in the universe and exists balanced with other essential energies.

As you develop you will no doubt find a decreasing importance for men in your life. We don't want you to be surprised, or to think anything is wrong. And certainly, we don't want you to stop your travels in order to cling to men or to try to tote them along with you.

From my perspective, I feel it is advisable for you to let the need for men fall away quietly. There is no advantage to be had from doing it in a way that attracts attention or causes big splash. Unfortunately we do not live in societies that condone either our growth or the choices we make to promote our growth. We do not have to like this fact. But at this point in time, and given the extensiveness of male dominance and heterosexual privilege, it is not worthwhile to fight for our rightful status. It is easier and the returns more plentiful to move beyond the givens into realms where the issues are simply non-existent.

There is very real risk of running up against the Black Bears of the universe if you insist upon confrontational behavior, in which case there is *very* good chance you will lose sight of your greater purpose by becoming too involved in proving your worth, stopping injustices, and defending yourself and others against the beatings you receive. (This is not to say you should defer to men, passively accept what they choose to deal to you, or remain defenseless. I am merely pointing out where I think the primary focus should be.) It is possible to get so consumed by the injustices that you forget even that you have travels awaiting you.

It is wrong to turn a blind eye or a cold shoulder to the injustices. But sometimes the way to success is on an entirely different route than one might expect or than one is familiar with. What we seek to achieve is spiritual growth.

There is nothing we can do to save our sisters who do not choose to walk away from the oppression. All we can do is to let them know of our travels so that they can learn that there *is* a way out. This can be done quietly, by example, and in loving ways.

The more attention we attract, the greater the chance of attack. Freedom is never gained by announcing the time and route of your escape to your oppressors. (There are many women who equal men in their ability to oppress women, so don't make the mistake of thinking, "She's a woman, she must be OK.") On the other hand, your silence will also hurt all of us. Speak of your feelings and knowings, and dare to connect with other women. *This* is the way to help yourself and other women.

INYANI

I thought it would be nice to introduce the next topic by talking about why I got involved in this project in the first place. (This was not Majai's idea for format, and it was a little difficult to twist her arm, seeing as how she doesn't have one. Nevertheless, she agreed to let me begin.) Ellen and I have been lovers for a very long time. But not lovers in the usual sense.

My journeying has never included time on the earth. (I certainly took my time incarnating repeatedly elsewhere, however.) We first encountered each other at A^1 level, the vibration of those in spirit form with incarnation work remaining. It was a chance meeting and grew rapidly into a unique friendship. Or, rather, I'd like to think it was unique, knowing full well that countless other such friendships exist. Following work or project completions, even after the time when we were both in A^1, whenever we have been of the same form in the same vibration, we have chosen to meet in friendship and energetically (which on the earth is thought of as sexually). The frequency of interaction is not as it used to be, but no longer are we confined to time as you know it.

Because of Ellen's need for healing following the Black Bear escapade,

177

I am here to offer her the encouragement of an old, old friend. The book is just an excuse for us to interact. But I always have plenty to say and what better place than in a book! I have worked with Grace quite a few times and am pleased to do so again. None of the other women is familiar to me.

The subject we wish to discuss is the connection between woman's spirituality and sexuality. The two are virtually impossible to separate and are mutually catalystic. It is actually a most serious subject, and does not warrant the sensationalism and perversion it has received.

All of us have had many, many lovers over our times in all the places and vibrations, male and female, so in that sense my experience with Ellen becomes small. However, the fact that it has lasted and grown through many vibrations has taught us things we otherwise would not have known.

MAJAI

At the time of sexual stimulation a woman opens (to the extent she is able) to the yin. She literally allows the yin to flow into her. It accumulates locally until it is released at the time of orgasm, at which point it is dispersed to various parts of her body. Orgasm absent, the accumulation slowly diffuses to the same places.

Her ability to open to or connect with the yin regulates the amount of energy flow into her. Her awareness of the process can increase the flow. It is the one way a woman knows how to connect with *her* essence in a noticeable way. This merging with the yin, even as momentary as it is, affords rebalancing of the yin in all the bodies, and reminds her of her connection. She seeks to repeat the merging, especially if she lacks conscious connection to the yin in other ways, thus sex becomes a valuable occurrence. Her opening and the influx of yin occurs regardless of the presence of a partner. Even with a minimally adequate partner, her systems get replenished at least partially with yin.

GRACE

To understand the flow of energy, it is easiest to think of your connection with the earth, the earth being yin. When you walk upon the earth, the yin enters your body through the soles of your feet. Even the most sensitive of you would likely only be aware of the point of entry during normal activity. This is because the flow is gentle and continuous, the

178

usual influx so ordinary it easily goes unnoticed. With faster entering of greater amounts, you are more easily able to perceive the remainder of the pathway.

From the feet it travels up the inside of your legs to the vaginal/uterine area, and into the lower abdomen. There it branches. One branch takes it back down the outside of the legs to return to the earth. The other branch follows the midline to the chest and breasts. Again the pathway splits, with one branch carrying it down the arms to the hands, where it again exits the body. There is also another entrance through the palms. From there it flows up the arms to the chest where it meets the yin that came up the midline. With ample quantity, perception of its path into the lower face, neck and chin is possible. It does not go into the upper part of the head. However, some women are able to allow the yin to enter through the top of the head. (This is not from a different source, although a few people have sought to differentiate "heaven" and "earth" sources.)

As was stated previously in the book, yin is the most subtle energy that infuses us; it enters and exits though the entire body surface. It is only with sufficient quantity, and more than the usual opening, that the pathways are perceptible or used. Depending upon the degree of imbalance, a woman's need for replenishing and redistribution of yin, these pathways come into play. They follow similar routes to those described in oriental medical systems, but are not identical. Yin is more subtle than the energies that use those routes (although we do find terminology overlap). There are physiological happenings on grosser levels involving blood flow, nervous system stimulation, etc., but these are not related to yin flow.

Most women feel at best only segments of their pathways. Begin your focus in the lower abdominal/vaginal area and expand your awareness from there. It is relatively easy to perceive the point of entry at the bottoms of the feet. Notice too the abrupt dispersion of energy at orgasm. And pay attention to the resultant evenness throughout your body when you have become as full of yin as you require. Mental or emotional evenness also follows from yin replenishing. (Often anger or irritability will be transformed into calmer, more peaceful feelings.)

The surge of yin spreads evenly throughout the system regardless of areas of need. Some areas may still feel in need of more, or there will be an emotional tension remaining. There is not a way to change the distribution pattern, however, as you open more completely, the increased quantity will become more than ample to cover any need.

A useful exercise to do with sexual stimulation and orgasm, is to visualize the energy coming from the earth, perhaps a pine tree, the ocean, a mountain, and into you. The visualization can make the energy more real to you and provide a way for you to participate in the process of flow. The yin will come to you regardless of conscious participation, but can become more concentrated with your added awareness.

MAJAI

The first problem women face is their resistance to opening. The yin will flow throughout the universe, including throughout women's bodies, as long as there are not obstacles of resistance. The only thing that stands in a woman's way is herself.

Secondly, she must then remain open. Of the few who are able to open, too many quickly shut down as soon as the yin, their power, is perceived. Women *are* afraid to take their power, to make their connection to that which is greater than themselves.

Those resistant to opening do not readily exchange with their environments. The barriers they create interrupt the evenness of flow between themselves and the universe. They prevent the honest, open exchange that naturally occurs in all of the universe. Certainly there are degrees of resistance, some resisting only slightly, others as much as they are able. And at times, the relaxation of resistance is easier or harder.

For these women the deeper problem is lack of self-love. Their unwillingness to accept themselves in their totality, then precludes the sharing of that self with any of the environment. The resistance to openness (honesty is openness, yes?) manifests at every moment during the constant exchange with the whole environment. So do not limit your thinking only to relationships with other people, or to sexual exchanges, although certainly the closedness manifests in these areas too.

For those who are able to open but then close at the first sign of increased yin, the situation is more complex. Fear of taking one's power can stem from a variety of sources. All involve a perceived threat. However, I will say directly, none of these threats is legitimate to warrant closure. *Every moment is a safe time to take your power.* And in fact, *to* take your power affords you the capacity to control yourself in your environment.

Actually the perceived threat is a diversionary tactic, a way to take responsibility from the self and place it elsewhere. Such women readily invite their environment to come to them, yet hold back when it reaches a certain proximity to them. They welcome exchange at a distance, but push it away when it touches them too deeply. Quite a few have many acquaintances but few friends. And many are not orgasmic.

Commonly we think of openness or honesty as allowing both good and bad access to us. Failure to be open and honest is *not* how we protect ourselves. To protect we use discretion and discrimination, but maintain throughout our openness and honesty. Failure to open or to remain open merely cuts off the energies that fuel us and with which we fuel our environments. It cuts off our essence, our essential energy, the yin.

So regardless of how our resistance to opening or staying open enough to access the yin manifests, whether in the physical body, mental attitude or spiritual development, try to remember each time you withdraw or close, that you are starving yourself of your essence, and that that is all you are doing.

ELLEN

Somehow I managed to stay open to the yin throughout the three years when I was sexually abused. Apparently it did not occur to me to shut off the yin—due to naiveté, or lack of conditioning, or knowledge that it was my sustenance?

Nevertheless, somewhere I have learned that to close to the yin deprives myself and kills the growth process. This is not the same as preventing things or people you have deemed undesirable to your well-being from having access to you. That is discrimination. It is quite possible to stay open to the yin *as* you discriminate.

So please, no matter what kinds of horrendous experiences you have had, or will have, do not shut off the yin. They are only excuses and your abuser does not suffer in the least for your closure. You do.

You do not need to live in any certain place, or be of particular blood, or have encounters with medicine women to open or remain open. Your connection to the yin is the most valuable asset you have. You alone are responsible for knowing and making that connection.

ELLEN

Women who do not have some form of sexual expression often show many energetic imbalances. But I think rather than "sexual" expression, what they lack is an openness that can allow yin flow in a substantial, even, constant way. If they are able to connect with the earth and exchange emotionally with other women in deep, real ways, the need for sexual activity, be it alone or with a partner, may not be necessary.

Realistically however, I don't think any of us is sufficiently open on a constant basis to preclude even occasional redistribution requirements. Nevertheless, we don't mean at all to imply that it is mandatory to have extensive sexual exchanges in order to know your connection to the yin. Our power can be realized in many ways. Certainly we are far larger than sexual beings. In fact, what we are about is trying to know our connection at every moment regardless of what we may be doing.

MAJAI

At the time of menstruation, the uterus (the cervix) opens ever so slightly to accommodate the blood flow. For every action in nature, there is an equal reaction. As one substance flows out, another flows in, and what flows in during menstruation is yin.

Women are said to be in their power at the time of menstruation. Yes, they are more open, thus more connected to the yin. Psychological counterparts to the physiological occurrences are easily noted. The natural response is one of internalization, possibly withdrawal from the company of others, especially men. And spiritually a connection is made by the internalization.

Interesting that commonly women refer to menstruation as "the curse," as something dreaded, or as an inconvenience?

GRACE

Native women have retained (to some extent) their appreciation of menstruation in the context of the universe. They respect the time as one of need for internalization, and social structures to accommodate this need have long been in effect. (Of course many of the reasons have since been forgotten.)

Sensible it is to use menstruation as an opportunity to separate from the community at large, to go off in isolation or in the company of women. It is a time when it is appropriate to connect in a more complete way than ordinarily with the earth.

Menstruating women have been honored, respected and feared for their power, and rightfully so. Depending upon their evolution, thus access to the universal yin, they could effect greater medicine and they could access far away vibrations to the benefit of the tribe. Specific rituals and ceremonies have come to exist only for menstruating women. These are not commonly known, and those who are aware of them mostly think they were created in response to being refused at male ceremonies.

This is not true. They were in existence long before there were even co-ed ceremonies.

In the past, these rituals and ceremonies offered opportunities for women to come together in their power, and to consciously distribute the accumulated yin at their discretion to areas of need. Perhaps healing of the earth, certain animals or plants was in order. Primarily however, the gatherings were for the purpose of giving a collective boost to the spiritual growth of all the women present.

Concepts of uncleanliness during menstrual flow had no place in the early native societies. That was a male construct, based upon his fear of losing his power. Competitive society grew, and the universally predominant energy changed from yang to yin. Native men recognized long ago that no longer could they accumulate yang. So as they realized that woman was growing in her power, they began fearing their own loss. Further, they worried that women could and would somehow take away their yang. And from this developed social structures to insure that menstruating women would not participate in male activities, especially male medicine.

Traditionally the post-menopausal woman was seen to be constantly in her power. This is why elder women held the positions of spiritual authority. Not until they became firmly established in the yin were they worthy of guiding other women. So a long, long time ago they were treated in much the same way as menstruating women. Often they were the ones to assist a menstruating woman if she went to the woods, or to aid the woman in childbirth. It was not as is assumed, that she filled these roles solely because of expertise gained over the years of experience. Rather she was valued for her necessary and useful connection to the yin.

Of course later, men erroneously associated blood flow with power, thus failed to see the post menopausal woman to be as worthy of fear as the menstruating woman. This mistake should obviously prove that women can't steal yang, but then who am I to say?

ELLEN

Something rather interesting occurred with Black Bear. He and I were accustomed to communicating directly day and night as need be. One half day prior to blood flow, which is when I perceive the power change, and through the rest of my menstrual period, he would distance himself from me. Always he found excuses why I had to work with someone else.

Eventually he actually acknowledged that he was afraid of my power at that time. Rather curious, as he was intent upon taking my power, and then all the more there was! I expect he was afraid I would stand up to him at that time and didn't want to take any chances, for it was then I was most firmly planted in my own territory.

And interestingly, the night I decided finally he was out of my life, was twelve hours prior to blood flow.

ELLEN

At the time of menstruation woman connects more than usual to her power source. Her receptivity is heightened as is her ability to read her harmonies and disharmonies with her surroundings. More difficult it is for her to accommodate the disharmonious at this time, and in some cases she is unable to force containment.

A client, in describing a just concluded difficult time with her husband, said the following: "I just kept yelling at him. It was one thing after another. Of course, I was premenstrual. The poor guy. Luckily I got my period so now he can have some peace."

The poor guy? She had come into her power, thus was unable to tolerate the misalignment between herself and her environment (which included the husband). And after menstruation the pressure was off from the universe, allowing her to return to her usual state of blocking and tolerating disharmonies. His actions contributed very much to the disharmonies, thus he was the likely recipient of her discontent.

Something is terribly wrong when women unable or unwilling to contain the disharmonious environments in which they function are labeled as diseased. Premenstrual Syndrome (PMS), it seems to me, is a very convenient categorization of woman's natural expression, that encourages the elimination of that expression, or if expressed, the illegitimization of it. Labeled as the problem is the woman in her expression rather than her misalignment. And worse, there exists an underlying assumption that she should change to align.

I see woman forced into behavioral, attitudinal and feeling patterns contrary to or divergent from her natural responses. The ensuing tension results in various physiological or emotional imbalances, according to her particular points of existing weakness. With the influx of yin and acuteness of receptivity at menstruation, resident imbalances are exaggerated. Physical and emotional exaggerations (expressions deviant from deemed acceptability) are the natural consequences of denial, suppression, or forced containment of her realness.

The more extreme the premenstrual behavior or physical pathology, the greater her misalignment. The premenstrual status can be very indicative of the degree and type of imbalance normally tolerated. Pay attention to angry outbursts, tears, insecurities, diarrhea, bloating, headaches, etc. They do not speak of alignment or harmony. Make note of the recipients of your feelings or behavior. Learn from your imbalances in order to make rectification. The woman herself is not the place to seek change; rather change should be sought in the relationship between the woman and her environment.

It is good that a premenstrual state has been recognized as real. Unfortunately however, PMS has become a way to excuse or deny the validity of a woman's experience at that time. Once again woman as a natural being has been labeled as diseased. True, her environment is unbalanced and perhaps her involvement with that environment is less than harmonious, however, the uncontrollable reaction premenstrually is quite a natural response to the situation. The exact expression may also demonstrate chaos, however, it contains truth and remains the most complete and accurate expression of the imbalances that can occur.

By the expression of these true feelings, she inconveniences the status quo and her male cohabitants on the earth. A symptomatic explanation is not at all adequate and serves to perpetuate the existing state of affairs while again requiring woman to adapt further.

With balance and alignment, I have found, a smooth transition exists between all parts of the menstrual cycle, absent of symptomatology or extremes of emotions. So instead of the premenstrual time being a time of irrationality and abnormality, it is a time of heightened rationality, with seemingly bizarre expression due to the distance from center woman lives.

MAJAI

There is a natural place in the universe for women who choose to spend their lives and their time with other women. The amount of time and the extent of interaction necessarily varies from woman to woman. But as development progresses and karmic business with men is disposed of, the need for the community of women will increase.

Sexual exchange between women does not warrant the fear and misunderstanding that it commonly receives. If a woman can access yin via sexual activity, it is logical that she can do so more extensively with another woman.

GRACE

Lesbian lifestyles have been respected and honored in certain previous cultures. Many groups of people have recognized the potential contribution women can make to all of humanity if they are genuinely afforded the opportunity to live solely with another woman.

It is just not a big deal. Nevertheless, certain religions have made it a big deal and portrayed sexual exchanges between women as unnatural acts. Obviously we must look once again to male fear as the source for these prohibitions.

MAJAI

Women need men and men need women to procreate. If procreation was our only purpose in this universe, then men and women would necessarily be bound together. However, it is not. Procreation is a choice. And it is only one choice. If it furthers the growth of all concerned parties, then and only then is it appropriate.

There is no point to sexuality between men and women other than to produce children. It may be correct for her to couple with a man for many reasons, all of which are karmic in nature. Please remember that a woman can connect with the yin with sexual stimulation, but she can do this to the same extent with a man as she can without any partner. So a choice to couple with a man does not further her spiritual development in this way.

A choice to couple with another woman *can* promote her spiritual growth. But depending upon the relationship, the openness and honesty, it may not do this. If both women open as completely as they are able to the universe, it serves to reason that the connection between them will also open. The yin is able to flow into and out of each of them as well as between them. It becomes a merging of self with self, and literally their energies can become one.

The existence of another woman offers an opportunity to transcend the self. She is nothing more than a focus to allow your internalization in order for you to meet the collective yin. You are the same for her. You remain separate yet know each other to be one with the self and one with something greater (the collective yin).

The point of mergence is more subtle than the physical. The physical is not even necessary for the exchange to occur. In fact, many women find that the physical body becomes a burden in a way. The actual physical sensations are only a translation of the yin flows. And since the yin flows are far greater than the physical plane, the physical body seems and is relatively too small.

For such a total exchange to occur, openness and retention of openness of both women is necessary. A willingness to know the other as completely as you know yourself, and an absolute trust of the other are absolutely essential. So as you can see limit setting, boundary setting, lack of honesty, conditional opening, failure to remove your karmic obstacles and failure to risk change all block the potential flow of yin between two women.

INYANI

As Majai stated, the point of communion is more subtle than the physical. While you are on the earth, the physical must be considered during any sexual exchange. You simply cannot remove the sensations. However, the primary focus can rest on the energy flow rather than on the physical stimulation. It is easiest for incarnated women to use the body as a vehicle for opening, so do not shun your body.

The exchange actually happens independently of the physical body. Therefore, in theory such exchanges can happen between entities in spirit, between earthplane and spirit plane entities, or between non-physical entities. In all vibrational states it is the extent of opening and willingness to merge that determines the degree of yin flow.

ELLEN

I would like to mention an incident in order to point out that mergence with another woman is not necessarily "sexual." On the earthplane sexual expression is the usual vehicle for opening, thus we sometimes confuse yin flow with the sexual events.

Some years ago (quite in the middle of Black Bear's antics, by the way), I had occasion to be with a friend in labor. She and I were synchronized by having similar but not identical ideations and mantras. More importantly, she was open to her birthing process and I was open to her in whatever experience she would have. This included not being resistant to any pain or difficulty that might transpire.

Mostly I sat across the room from her, although occasionally held the bottoms of her feet. I was dually focused on the ideation of the mantra and on remaining open myself to receive and deliver energy (yin) to her. Each time her uterus contracted I felt the rise and fall of pressure and perceived the intensity of muscle contraction as if it was happening within my body. Yet never did I experience pain, tension, or discomfort as she did.

While we certainly remained separate, and were actually doing and thinking different things, we merged enough to have common experience of yin flow. In this case there was good purpose to our merging, as I was able to offer her a perspective from outside each contraction, as she lived within each one. My assistance was not based on speculation, but on shared experience and my own knowing. I told her when a contraction was beginning, before the tightness was perceptible to her and well before it became pain, and was able to help her let go of a contraction by telling her when each peak had passed.

Interesting that people are so proud of medical technology and think uterine monitors are so clever. Hasn't anyone wondered what the grandmothers did out there in the huts for all those centuries?

Parallel to this labor experience have been my experiences of other women's energy flows and orgasms in lovemaking. And similar is what Inyani and I feel as lovers in the non-physical. The energy exchange necessarily has bearing on whatever vibrational form each woman is in, yet the yin flow exists beyond form.

ELLEN

To know another women in lovemaking, just as to know another woman in labor or through mediumship is not particularly extraordinary. With lovemaking the potential for complete merging is possible, and with the others only partial experience of the other is necessary or desirable.

Openness to each other and willingness to take one's power are all that are required. And then the possibilities for merging become real. So in lovemaking, this is what it means to know another woman as yourself—to feel her feelings, to experience her experiences, to know her thoughts, to feel her yin flow completely—all as she simultaneously knows you as herself.

The absence of physical form or the lack of physicalness allows a more complete merging. The two women have refined their energies to eliminate more of what is other than pure yin. They have let go of more of what causes separation (all that baggage) so naturally they move closer together. In lovemaking there are no role limits to complete merging, or form discrepancies to cause separation.

In mediumship it is possible to experience the other, but not as totally as can happen in lovemaking. We change our vibration to temporarily become the other. This means a temporary forgetting of the self, so that the vibrations do not get confused or mixed. (With lovemaking, we allow the other woman to exist and the self to exist and she does the same. It is a total experience of commonality that we seek.) With mediumship it is not commonality that we seek, but a knowing of the other.

In order for an earthplane woman to communicate with a non-physical entity, the process is a bit different. She exists in purer form than I because I have a physical body. Therefore to connect at all, I need to let go of as much of myself as is necessary to make us equal. Then we connect, becoming aware of each other by virtue of our commonality. Still, I do not need nor desire to allow expression of myself, for temporarily I wish to know her. So again, there is separation, but underneath the separation a mergence or commonality that is required for the communication to be able to happen.

Maybe it is easier now to see why it is not possible to communicate above one's developmental level. There is too much baggage which causes separation, obscuring the commonality upon which the communication would have to occur. In physicalness, communication above development level is also not possible for these same reasons.

KIOKA

Can two women of different form be lovers?

Two women of the same form and same vibration have the greatest potential for mergence. Any discrepancy of form, as Ellen described about mediumship, creates a separation. And that separation cannot be bridged without the two entities becoming the same form.

For example, Inyani and Ellen, given their present forms, only have a very partial potential for exchange, relative to the potential for exchange they have when of the same form. If you will recall, Inyani said that they have always come together when they have been in the same form. No sense bothering at the other times, especially after they have known each other more completely than would be possible at the times of different form. As long as Ellen has a physical body, attention and energy need to be put into the dropping of that form in order to make her equal to Inyani. Necessarily that is limiting as opposed to two entities already in the same form.

Certainly some mergence can occur between entities of different form, but it is not at all based upon common experience with yin flow. Rather it is based upon openness to yin flow as individuals. The emotional closeness they have developed has plenty of room for expression across form. Their honesty and openness to each other allows their individual connection to yin, and there they know again their commonality. But as you can see, it is far different from what has been described as the potential for women in the same form and vibration.

ELLEN

When sexual sharing is open, honest and relaxed, it is logical that awareness of other realms will occur during or after lovemaking. Not uncommon is it for two women to experience similar visions or music. If sleep follows lovemaking, oftentimes both will know the same adventure or "dream." If both are able, they may journey together into the dreamtime or beyond.

Unfortunately because such complete sharing is rare, these happenings seem magical. Actually they are quite ordinary. Their significance is in the fact *that* they happen, rather than so much in the content of the experiences.

GRACE

Where do these experiences come from? Sometimes a woman's guides are responsible. Or the guides of both women act together to create common experience. If it is due to intervention of guides, usually there is a purpose: the release of trapped emotions, reinforcement of a particularly open exchange, or the communication of ideas that the women would ordinarily be unreceptive to but that are useful to both women's spiritual growth. It is a time when receptivity is high, thus susceptibility to the influence of spirit is also magnified.

A woman sufficiently receptive can experience firsthand the environments of the realms she has access to. Then there is no need for intervention by guides.

Each occasion gives a tiny bit of expansion: something to look forward to. Do not, however, make requirements of your guides to deliver spectacular happenings. The reason such events occur is because *you* open. The way you encourage these experiences is to open more completely.

Your contact with your partner allows you to risk opening. Your opening, however, really does not have bearing upon who she is, but primarily upon your willingness to open in her presence. Additionally, her ability and willingness to open can further encourage yours, the result being a compounding effect.

A potential for similar experience does exist with a male partner. Since the energy exchange is limited between women and men, the caliber of experience is primarily dependent upon the woman's ability to open, rather than upon any exchange with him. If a woman has business with a man, then sexual exchange with him can be valuable to her. It is certainly good for her to travel as far as she can in any setting appropriate to her overall development.

ELLEN

Also common in lovemaking is growing awareness of your partner greater than her present physical form. Through your connection, you may come to know her as an entity, seeing her past experiences, usually with you, her other times on the earth, in spirit, or in other densities, or she may see yours. Sometimes it can be a bit unsettling to have another person see things or know things about you that are not currently part of your experience. Verification can only come through expansion.

Especially if you are a bit more developed than your partner, you may suddenly have revelations about your own past or present behaviors, or the future. Your openness is what is responsible for these understandings.

Even as we walk and talk with our physical bodies on the earth, we exist as masses of energy pulsating with our environments. Depending upon your orientation, you may experience your partner as if without her physical body, but as sound or color. As you touch and exchange, specific body parts may also emit or be sound or color, able to be experienced by both of you, by the way. Don't let happenings like these put you off. They are quite normal.

Most importantly, do not confine your lovemaking expectations to what is usual with a male partner. Know that possibilities for expansion are vast and diverse. Experiences are person specific. They depend upon your particular vibration, your existing abilities and experience in other realms, your fears, and your lessons. Therefore, if you fall into thinking that you need to have a particular experience to be as valid as your friend, you will get into trouble. Oftentimes, the higher the vibration of a woman, the less "physical" or concrete are her experiences. Your guides or yourself may put constraints on some of the possibilities in protection of you. So best to just open and let it be. Your expansion will come and it will be good.

KIOKA

If either or both of you do happen to remember other lifetimes, or experiences elsewhere, work with this information. The content (the lessons or behavior) can be instructive relative to your present. The memories can clue you to repeat behavior or can serve as reminders of an outlook or approach forgotten.

Whether the memory occurs spontaneously or through the help of your guides is not important. Use the content to grow rather than let yourself be diverted by the fact of the memory happening. This is an important point. Too often I see women fail to work with their sleep experiences, for a similar example, and conclude "success" if they remember "a dream." The memory is only the first step. There is value behind the memory, be it a sleep experience or an exchange during lovemaking.

(Here I am speaking specifically of memory of other life experiences or lifetimes. This is not contradictory to what Ellen just said about commonality of experience during or after lovemaking.)

There is no point to *pursuing* memory of other life experiences (of times on the earth or elsewhere). Memory of these times only adds irrelevant clutter to your current lessons, and actually may cause unnecessary concern, confusion or burden to the degree that your present learning may be compromised. If a previous experience can help you in some way, the memory of it *is* relevant and purposeful.

So do not pass up opportunities by forgetting to make the analogy to the present. Neither is it wise to let yourself become infatuated by the past or by the pursuit of past experiences.

KIOKA

The incidence of violence against women (psychological, physical and sexual abuse), clearly does not speak of respect for women or of perspectives on sexual exchange free of struggles for power or control. The man (or woman) who sees a woman as a function of his (or her) needs and desires is representative of very contracted thought. Mandatory participation or dutiful servicing, under the auspices of a marriage contract, or the exploitation of others through the control, viewing or use of their bodies do not perpetuate an entity's development or free choice. *These* are unnatural acts.

To label a woman who decides to step outside such abusive situations (and in so doing breaks her associations with men) as the problem is an example of misplaced blame. Especially those of you who have trouble with the concepts of spiritual sexuality or lesbianism, might step back a minute to look at the sexual climate and values around you. Look at the politics of religion, and the whys for deeming behavior immoral, illegal or unnatural. Who serves to benefit from such policy and thought? Certainly not women. These notions were born of minds trapped and fearful on the earth, threatened by the progress or expansion of others, fearful of rejection, and clamoring for power.

Sexual exchange *can* be a means of connecting to the universe and one's essential energy. It *can* be an expression of love far greater than the individual capacities of the involved people. It *can* be an act of energy rebalancing, and *can* allow the expansion of the individuals far beyond physical reality. Certainly in this light it is quite spiritual and very natural.

But without an underlying respect for one's sexual partner, a nonthreatening posture, and the absence of control desires and struggles for power and dominance, sexual expression in harmony with Natural Law is not possible. Women fool themselves when they choose to believe that their partner is respectful *some* of the time. Women are mistaken who think that because their partner is another woman, struggles for control and dominance cannot exist. People who think that heterosexual bonds are by definition sacrosanct wear blinders. Again, look at the incidence of violence and abuse.

KIOKA

Women's expectations for merging via sexual exchange have been far too low. There are women who have realized previously greater expansion than they are now able to live in terms of their connections to other women.

Spirit women have begun to intervene in some of these situations, and more will do so in the future. The idea is for spirit to help raise the woman's expectations for expansion during her close exchanges (sexual or otherwise) with another woman, as one of the problems has been that woman has just not had a spiritual framework within which to place her sexuality. (Societies see sex in rather two-dimensional terms, as lustful and seductive with games of manipulation and control. This doesn't come close to a woman's potential.)

Flying Horse has a spirit woman working with her, *under the direction of her guides*. Their connection (as is typical for such an arrangement) began with a basis of honesty, openness and trust, because she and this spirit woman had been lovers in previous lifetimes. Flying Horse's comfort with the vibration of the spirit woman makes her receptive to and unthreatened by her intervention.

By acting as a bridge during Flying Horse's sexual exchanges, the spirit woman allows her access to increased yin flow. (Of course her presence is known to the guides of any partner Flying Horse has.) She also helps make a stronger connection between Flying Horse and women Flying Horse interacts with in other capacities. Her role is to facilitate yin flow in any of the ways it is possible.

What the spirit woman actually does is to facilitate Flying Horse's relaxation at points where blockages to the flow of yin occur. Ultimately it allows for increased quantity to enter Flying Horse's systems and for more even dispersion.

Many women who have female lovers have similar arrangements. The specific spirit woman is not significant, except for the fact of her vibration being familiar and benefic. She is best seen as one who works with energetic imbalances, but specifically yin.

I mention this because many women are aware of a particular spirit presence during their sexual exchanges. While most welcome the vibration as highly positive, some are afraid to allow their awareness of her for fear it might mean a betrayal of her loyalty to her partner. It is not at all a question of this spirit woman acting as a lover, or causing sensations, or participating in the process of exchange between the two women. She is no different from a guide who decides it is important to be present during a conversation between a woman and a friend. The spirit woman has a specific role which necessarily requires her presence at times of increased yin flow.

My words are intended to clarify for those women who have already detected a female presence during their lovemaking. I suppose it is necessary to say directly that the presence of *any* male at such times is *highly* inappropriate, and is absolutely void of any purpose beneficial to the woman. No matter who he is, he would amount to interference.

In a few cases where two women in a relationship are of very comparable developmental level, a spirit woman will be assigned to each of them. In such a case the two spirit women will work together with the two women. But this is not yet a common arrangement because few women are coupled with vibrational equals.

This stems, by the way, from the incorporation of male patterns into our relationships with women. Typically we see the controller and the controlled, a dependent personality coupled with an independent personality, the supporter with the supported, the decision maker with the agreeable participant, or even traditional male-female roles in our attempts to create relationships beneficial to woman's growth. Until we cease to be threatened by mutuality of strength, vulnerabilities, self-determination and self-control, our relationships will continue to be unbalanced. With mutuality, we naturally seek the companionship of our developmental and vibrational equals. When this happens, the participation of spirit will become reflective of the mutuality.

ELLEN

The shortage of spiritual lesbians disturbs me. Is spirituality thought of as something that would compromise the hard won knowledge of our strength? We live in fear of being trampled if we dare to loosen our postures of toughness. Spiritual work *gives* us our power and strength.

KIOKA

By living for lifetimes in oppressive conditions, the women who have made any progress at all have learned to fight. The struggle to get free is very real. Yet a new chapter has begun. Reason to take the fighting, the distrustful and the competitive mentality into our relationships with our sisters does not exist. She is not the enemy. As difficult as it may be, it *is* necessary to learn to move *with* other women. Do not look at her with fear. Positions of love and trust are what can cause the change from immobility to forward motion and progress.

Old fears based on pasts (distant lifetimes perhaps) with men creep to the surface with lovers. How much realness or vulnerability can I afford to show before *she* does to me what *he* did to me? One day, will she grow beyond me, putting me out with the trash on her way to the next adventure?

Postures of toughness do nothing to make any pain disappear. Nor do they accomplish much in terms of making risk disappear. Showing your realness isn't going to cause hurt. Your realness is there whether you share it or not.

A choice for women allows you maximum potential for growth. But to realize that growth, you need to risk being known. To be known by another woman *is* the ultimate of vulnerability, because she can *really* know you. If she chooses she can use her understanding to hurt you terribly.

Focus on the potential for hurt belongs to the category of fear, while focus on the potential for expansion, to that of love. You have chosen women because you want it *all*. To make that choice, but to live it out as if you are still making a choice for men contradicts the potential. *Don't take male values into your relationships with women. Doing so will destroy the possibilities.*

MAJAI

Obviously most people are not going to welcome you in your efforts to grow. They won't go out of their way to accommodate separatist behavior or thought independent of men. In fact, it is quite likely that there will be mounting resistance to your efforts as the conditions on this planet deteriorate. Many pitfalls and situations in opposition to your efforts await you. I cannot tell you in certain terms what to expect, but a few patterns are unfolding to us already.

There has been a rise in dedication to existing religious and spiritual systems. And with it, increased condemnation of people venturing into new territory. Those open to new solutions will be seen not as the solution, but as the cause for the earth's convulsions. It is to us that blame will be thrown.

In direct proportion to the rise in panic will be rise in condemnation. Further, people who have previously departed from these religious systems will return to them, likely with increased zealousness. They act in fear, not out of love for these systems or love for what these systems teach.

KIOKA

Menlessness is not a topic usually included in discourses by spirit. Unless you hang out with non-physical entities, you will not likely find expansion beyond the established sacredness of male supremacy or heterosexual privilege.

Some of you I can see are reacting to the apparent newness of our concepts. "How come we have never heard them before?" Remember, public religious leaders and "saints" have to date been male. Accomplished women spiritualists have always existed, yet not visibly so to the general public. With male rule, views such as ours have not been welcomed by the controllers. Nor do we expect that they will be at the present time.

If you choose to see only the words of the established male spiritualists as valid, that is your choice. It is also your option to remain fearfully subservient to male theory. Nevertheless, it is time for spirit to speak substantially from the other side of the mountain. And that is why we are here.

ELLEN

There are a remarkable number of people who have tremendous allegiance to a specific spiritual or religious system. In fact, sometimes I wonder if the allegiance to the system hasn't become their purpose. Apparently demonstrative of their dedication to the system, and out of a need to accumulate the support of numbers in their ranks, they make it their business to "save" people like me. Never has there been a shortage of things warranting my being saved, according to some people. Somehow it never occurred to me that I needed saving. Thus, not only have I lost my way, I'm too stupid to know it!

Sometimes folks don't bother "saving," but prefer to withhold love or turn a cold shoulder. So what are we to do about the savers, or those who decide to hate or punish you for your different-from-their path?

As long as you don't need something they have, or as long as they aren't in a position to control aspects of your life, there isn't a problem. A longstanding lesson of mine is how to deal with such people when they have something I want and will give it only if I change my ways. Embarrassingly I can easily manage a slew of ineffective and untogether responses. Usually I get irate that they think I need modification when I am apparently working even harder than they are.

In my clearer moments, however, I do see a way to side step, as difficult as it may be sometimes. And that is to cease needing what they have. Rarely is anything really a need. If I can relinquish my attachment to the coveted item that controls me, I free myself. In theory it is quite simple. In practice it sometimes means rather extensive rearrangement of my desires. Ultimately I am not worse off for releasing the item. In fact, I have thereby regained autonomy and avoided being controlled by someone else.

INYANI

People who worry about the possible missteps of others are so busy they forget to look where they are going themselves. Involuntarily they bump into walls, go down dead end streets, trip on obstacles, and spend their time primping and pruning to convince others they are on the right track. All this at the expense of their own progress.

KIOKA

We need to talk a bit about victimization. It is a concern of all of us and lives because of the degeneration and lost spiritual orientation on this planet. Even without the typical victim mentality, numerous unfortunate and unplanned events can come our way. Owing to the prevalence of entities (in many vibrations) mucking with Natural Law, all of us are recipients of unnecessary pain, inconvenience and abuse.

It simply is. Let it be. Focus your attention on your growth and keep open eyes to the conditions and entities around you. To become paranoid and constantly defensive is counterproductive and detracts from more profitable efforts.

Accidents do happen in this universe. And then they cause effect (as per karmic law). Occasionally a body will die, or an injury will occur, that is extraneous or even contradictory to the plan. In the extreme, the prescribed work and lessons of an entity may be prohibited by uncontrollable or unexpected circumstance.

In this time of extensive earth change, the prevalence of altered plans and intent is going to become very common. If you become a lucky recipient of the unanticipated or the undesirable, continue moving as best you can. Each of us, regardless of our vibrational level or development, has countless things to learn and numerous things that can stand improvement. There is nothing to stop you from learning from Plan B, Plan C, or Plan D just because Plan A was rendered obsolete. Opportunity will again present for you to cover the material contained in Plan A.

With this type of thinking, victimization is without place. Be flexible enough to make use of what exists. This is very important. But it is also important to take the opportunities *only* if they are compatible with your goal. Do not lose sight of your goal to blow in the wind of your surroundings.

ELLEN

One of the things I hope I'll never forget is my *survival* of Black Bear messing with my head and my life. Terrible things can befall us and excruciating pain can be inflicted. But if we can keep moving, all that can be quickly left in the dust. We don't have to know that pain for long if we choose to move beyond it. We may be very victimized, but only momentarily. Survival comes from forward motion.

We will never forget what happened. And we will be changed by the occurrence. To our center we will come to add that happening. And that is the difference between survival and death. Death is immobility and loss of center.

GRACE

So much these days there is talk of protection. Defensive postures take too much time and energy from the business of growing. Do not worry about protecting yourself. Instead focus on creating and maintaining intact bodies with good integrity.

First of all, people are not out there to get you. Certainly there are rapists and other crazies walking the streets. The way to handle them is to well equip yourself mentally and physically in advance. Then go about your business. If someone does attack, use defensive techniques appropriate to the specific situation, along the same principles as Majai suggested with the energy drainers. And most of all get out of the dangerous situation.

Likewise with potentially troublesome situations in other realms, first be prepared. You thereby eliminate your fear and avoid portraying yourself as a victim by sending out messages of vulnerability. Secondly know your enemies—how they operate, where they work, what their strengths and weaknesses are—so you can take measures to avoid them or to deal with them effectively. If an encounter occurs focus on taking steps to free yourself and resist only to the extent necessary.

Your vibration and solidity in the yin are your greatest protection. Secondly, make yourself invisible. To do this, pull in your bodies and attach your consciousness to your center. The more distally you invest energy, the more external and visible you become. When you center yourself, you have balance and integrity. Most assailants in whatever realm lack exactly that: their own center and bodily integrity. If you just stand your ground, chances are they will quickly tire.

Maintain a clear and centered mind, so you can think and act quickly. You will find that those deteriorating are pretty slow on the draw. Use this time to your advantage, to get out of the situation.

The worry about protection stems largely from exposure to spirit people in the A¹ vibration, those between incarnations. Some of these people are full of flash and splash, big on displays of power and control of others, and generally operate from fearful mindsets. They have instilled in many incarnated people fear of being interfered with and controlled by spirit or by other incarnated people. Their displays of invasions of another person's consciousness and manipulations of physical matter have set false examples for spirit of higher vibration or of less fearful approach.

These entities do exist. But as you raise your vibration, your distance from them increases. You have no need to operate on such a base level and your refusal to participate coupled with an absence of fear will eliminate such entities from your field of operation.

With an open, honest, free-flowing relationship with spirit, dramatic physical signs and displays of power have no place. As a spirit person's vibration raises, the interest in manipulating the physical plane will just not exist. There are far more important matters to be concerned with, and such displays are empty of both purpose and proof.

Further, as you can see from Inyani's chart, there is a limited range of operation by spirit according to vibrational level. If I wanted to I could not materialize from my vibration. In previous times/vibrations I was able. For me today, there is simply no point. I have far more effective ways to communicate.

So be leery of entities showing low vibration. And know that those who constantly fear and talk protection, deal with these entities. Keep raising your vibration and the quality of life around you will raise in kind. It has to, for this is Natural Law.

ELLEN

On an unfortunately memorable occasion Black Bear did one such display. It was at a social gathering of a group of women. I was talking with one woman when suddenly there appeared a drop of blood on her white shirt. It was Black Bear flashing his feathers, but at the time neither I nor the others knew this, and a couple of women were quite scared. His aim: to show us a hefty presence was in the room and we'd better bow to his power. Boys like that we can do without.

There is no need to be frightened. Neither should you interact with such an entity for then you invite many, many problems. If you have occasion to get to the bottom of an incident like the above, you will find it is an empty display by one who wishes to be a little larger than reality.

MAJAI

Even though many of you presently sit in the proximity of some of these empty flashers, if you keep moving, you will not see them for long. It is possible to move very, very quickly if only you are willing to remain open, to trust yourself, and to face your fears.

ELLEN

Our greatest protection is the quality of our vibration. With refinement, the clarity, thus brightness of our energy increases, as does the concentration of that energy. The impurities we carry detract from the brightness. As impurities are eliminated through development, naturally we grow in clarity.

Relative to those of lesser refinement, we literally become too bright for their eyes. They cannot see us, who we really are, for our expansion is too great to be incorporated or appreciated by them. Our light would be blinding were they to look.

Such protection comes naturally from our development. Absent is a need to actively participate other than to keep growing. It is much the same as being a good student. With mastery of the material, the A's follow. A focus on the acquisition of A's is off course. So instead of focusing on protection, go after the lasting quality that comes from development. Trust it, for the strength of your connection to the yin is the best protection you have.

ELLEN

How do you differentiate between two people? By their different appearances. Suppose they were dressed and made up to look identical? Still you would be able to appreciate that they were not clones. This is done through recognition of the differences between each one's baggage (all that obscuring their essential energies). The baggage of two entities is not identical. The closer each moves to the essential energy, the easier the differentiation becomes, for that baggage in its scanty surroundings becomes very obvious.

Kioka could not pretend to be Majai and get away with it for long. I identify Kioka's vibration (her essence plus her baggage) as different from Majai's. (Even though the words and the vibrations have been processed through me, Majai and Kioka each retain separate vibrations in this book, for example.) Each could be named Majai, yet the two would not be the same. Whether or not the name Majai was appropriate to either one of them could only be determined by vibrational alignment, but then many people have names that don't fit them. Identity accuracy can only be ascertained by comparing prior experience to present experience in light of consistency of vibration.

When an event has transpired or a probability for a happening exists, that information is available to any and all who have the ability to access it.

Suppose your dead grandmother came to you and said, "I am your dead grandmother, and I will prove it to you by telling you of an experience we had together ten years ago." She tells you accurately. This does not prove she is your grandmother. It proves she accurately accessed that previous happening.

If she came to you and you said, "Prove to me you are my dead grandmother by telling me of that happening." If she could not do it, it would not prove she was not your grandmother. It would prove she could not access or communicate that information, possibly for a variety of reasons.

The only way to make positive identification is to recognize her vibration in spirit as identical to her vibration as you experienced it when you knew her as your grandmother. How would you know that Susie, the checker in the grocery store, is really the same woman you met at the beach who told you her name was Norma? Therefore, what an entity tells you may or may not be true or accurate. The only reliable way to make identification is via your assessment of the entity's vibration.

Proof of the presence or involvement of spirit is another matter. Coincidence lives. Mistaken is the woman who has decided that every tiny event she witnesses has purpose specific to her. Everything does have purpose in universal terms, as everything is a consequence of existing conditions. But life involves far more than just the individual.

Proof of the presence of spirit is frequently accomplished by the creation of signs. A reliable sign is a happening sufficiently unique to easily surpass the realm of coincidence, which includes the realm of the usual. Repetition often serves this purpose well.

The proof of involvement by spirit does not equal proof of identity of spirit. The creation of dramatic signs also does not measure power or development. When Grace has wished to demonstrate to me her sincerity in carrying out a promise, what follows is a series of actions by unlikely people, culminating in the desired result. This is far different from Black Bear's blood on the shirt, or the presence of a bird in a place and time beyond its normal behavior. Signs need to be vibrationally appropriate to the spirit person.

Signs also need to have purpose. Frivolous demonstration of or requests for signs do not serve purpose in terms of a woman's development. If every time a spirit person impresses you to think or to do something, you require a display of signs, the relationship is based upon mistrust and doubt. Perhaps you do have reason to question that spirit person. If so, deal with the cause for the doubt. Displays of signs will not compensate for existing disharmonies.

GRACE

An entity's vibration contributes to her ability to take physical form. We are most familiar with entities who do so for a lifetime, but other arrangements are possible. I have on occasion chosen to do work primarily centered in spirit realms, but which periodically required my presence on the earth. So then I did have reason to materialize.

Materialization is not something done without much expenditure of energy, so I was careful to make each occasion worthwhile. The duration can be variable depending upon the entity's abilities and access to the fueling energy. That such a capability exists is not particularly relevant or instructive. It exists in the context of itself and has bearing only on those connected to the work.

Of course we see entities who wish to demonstrate their new found abilities and portray themselves as someone special. At best they are a distraction, and demonstrate a waste of energy and effort in a frivolous direction. Such displays are becoming increasingly more common, so I would like to mention one of the occasions when I did materialize.

It was the Tlingit lifetime I mentioned earlier, where Ellen was a medium and a medicine woman, I the contact in spirit. Some of the work we did at that time was healing the environment. Imbalances had been caused through the exploitation of natural resources elsewhere on the planet, causing secondary conditions near our village. One of the reasons we chose to incarnate where we did was to give us opportunity to try to restore balance.

We were not particularly successful at it, mostly because Ellen's life ended too quickly. Nevertheless, the story will show you what I feel to be good use of an ability to materialize.

To materialize, it was necessary for me to interact with a physical form (Ellen's). Generally speaking, my own energy coupled with several energies I had access to, joined Ellen's to create form of a density nearly the same as incarnated physical form. The vibration of a materialization is slightly less dense, and the presence of variable densities (as is found with the existence of bones, soft tissue, fluid, etc.) is absent. Nevertheless, when done maximally, the appearance will be indistinguishable from incarnated form.

The work that needed to be done was crystal work, bringing in the less dense but still physical aspects of the crystals to the earth. My intention was to build a new program from which new crystals could grow on the earth. They would then help restore balance in the earth in the needed spots. It was necessary for me to have physical form to do this, in order to have the capacity to extend the territory of my crystals into the denser physical realm.

KIOKA

We have tried to remark effectively on the criticalness of seeing your path from the distractions. As you discover the excitement of new territory, opportunities will present that are distractions. The distractions are nothing more than excitement. They are void of purpose and will take you nowhere. Notice them but try not to lose sight of your business.

Some of what you will find is confusion. This is not the same as distractions, but can be equally effective in steering you in a useless direction. Sometimes the confusion arrives with the unknown. Reduce it. Simplify it. Don't make a mistake of letting anything grow larger than it has to.

Confusion can arise from the simultaneity of experience, but even that can be understood in simple terms. Regardless of your state of consciousness, or the vibrations in which you travel, remember that it can all be very simple, honest and straightforward. As we develop, we move toward simplicity, not complexity. With expansion, increased clarification results, not the opposite.

So many of the activities that people undertake in the name of development and spirituality are distractions. Added to the excitement are extravagant myths and speculations. "If it is beyond comprehension, it must be good." No. No. No. Make life work for you. Don't make it so complicated that you create the perfect excuse not to understand.

Before we finish our verbal ramblings, we will try to return to simplicity a few more things that have been made far too complicated by unnaturally complex societies.

GRACE

What happens when you sleep? There are so many theories and opinions that I think it's only fair to have a chance to give mine!
• Your body rests.
• You process your unresolved experiences.

- You are given assistance or discretion by your guides or other spirit people.
- You may or may not do work.
- You may or may not travel to seek out your own healing, needed information or teaching.

Your consciousness is not the same as waking consciousness, however, as you gain facility in realms beyond the earth, the discrepancy will be minimized. Experiences had during sleep live in different realms. Necessarily they must be translated into familiar terms in order for you to bring them back to waking consciousness (physicalness) to use. Because of this, alterations in these experiences have to happen. Therefore, symbolism becomes relevant and important as a way to carry much material quickly.

All that happens is subjective. My experience contributes to the formation of meaning. And when I simplify understanding by putting it into symbols, behind the symbol exists the original experiential meaning. A symbol to you cannot mean the same thing as it does to me, unless we agree upon common meaning. A symbol is *your* representation of meaning. So obviously, symbolism is not something that can be learned from a book.

A snake to Ellen represents transformation because of her understanding of the energetic function of snakes on the earth. To someone else a snake would represent a terrifying threat. To another it might be sexual.

(Because we do have collective experience and common consciousness, symbolism common to all women does exist. However, until a time when collective consciousness is more developed, group symbolism has little relevance. The current emphasis upon the translation of collective experience into common symbols is grossly overplayed. Consciousness is simply not developmentally ready to make use of such concepts. Furthermore, when that time does come, it will be obvious that co-ed symbolism is an absurdity.)

The usual nightly happenings that we call dreams exist completely where you live them, in mental territory. They may or may not be remembered, but it is here that you process: what bothers you, what you don't understand, your hurts and joys, your fantasies and aspirations. I think of these dreams as garbage, although, like garbage, they are necessary by-products of useful activity.

Also at this location, spirit may be contributory, to help you clear out the garbage, or to give messages. Usually these occurrences are symbolic although they may be literal on occasion. Again, these dreams live where they happen and do not extend beyond the minds of the participants. Symbolism does exist, so if you dream of Myrtle, what she represents is the point of the dream. Myrtle had nothing to do with the dream.

Beyond this place is what has been called the "dreamtime." Here lives the past, present and future. It is a step beyond the density of your arm or a tree, yet is a real aspect of physicalness as is known on the earth. Here you do not dream, you experience. Here you connect with knowings and with events in any time. Because of the close connection to earthplane physicalness, there is much confusion and chaos, just as is the case on the earth. Isolated work such as one-time healings, communication with dead relatives, and inspiration for inventions or the arts all have a place in the dreamtime. To travel here, either you must know how, or another entity must take you. Commonly remembered upon waking is an experience of "flying."

Most people go to the dreamtime a little bit. Others are able to control their participation there, to direct their experiences, or if interrupted, can return to the dreamtime at will. Objects encountered there can be brought back to the physical plane at will (and with ability of course.) Upon awakening, you know the contacts with other entities were real, that you had an experience, not a dream, and sometimes that you are tired from being so busy. Through the dreamtime it is possible contact spirit people or incarnated people. Frightening experiences from the dreamtime constitute those unforgettable or recurrent nightmares.

In terms of the range of experiences possible during sleep, those in the dreamtime are of relatively slow vibration or much density. They can be thought of as experiences in physicalness.

Beyond the dreamtime, the vibration refines, chaos disappears, and order prevails. This is the territory of those who work in their sleep. Free communication between entities occurs, healings are sought and delivered in an orderly manner. Work with the earth, decision making and implementation occurs. This is a place only for women, although connections can be made which eventually lead to men who exist in other places (for a healing for instance).

Non-physical entities do not exist in the dreamtime, but both physical and non-physical, depending upon vibration, can be in the location just described. These places can be accessed in sleep or in waking consciousness. It's just a question of learning how. Much variety of vibration exists within these categories, so with skill, discrimination of quality of vibration, thus interaction, can occur. It's the same as living on the earth and choosing your friends or your workplace.

Differentiation of vibration is a natural quality control. Just as you cannot see beyond your own developmental level in the waking state, you cannot travel beyond your ability in sleep consciousness. With the help of another entity, however, you can temporarily be taken very slightly beyond your normal territory.

ELLEN

You can receive healings in your sleep, although usually they are not brought back to consciousness with you. Energetic manipulations are a common practice of your Healing Guide. She can work in conjunction with your efforts (or concurrent with medical care), or when you are unaware even that imbalances are present.

A lot of people are afraid to sleep. They feel vulnerable and out of control. Because they don't remember their experiences, they live in constant wonder or dread. True, they give rest to the physical body, and the senses are shut down. But actually, there is an acuteness to the beyond the-body aspects of their senses, making for increased receptivity and sensitivity. The fears stem primarily from identification with the physical body.

People also worry if they do not remember their sleep experiences. Sometimes there is reason, other times it is due to self-blocking or abruptness in arising from sleep. If you are busy expanding, don't worry about it. If you wish to do more or remember more sleep work, take a few minutes to reflect before you get out of bed. Writing or speaking of your experiences can be helpful, but those processes are somewhat two-dimensional relative to the experiences. They can help with memory, but frequently reduce the experiences farther than is useful. That is why internal processing is important prior to sharing.

If you travel great distances vibrationally in your sleep, sometimes you will find it is difficult to come back to waking consciousness. Your body may seem tired or heavy until you readjust to your regular vibration. Be determined in your return, but also gradual.

GRACE

There is a lot of talk about "astral travel," leaving your body, and being permanently separated. I thought about not bringing up this subject, but because of the extensive fear, it seems important.

You have many layers of bodies. They function as a unit, yet at times can operate independently. When a part of you travels into a vibration different from the rest of you, you become very aware of the discrepancy.

In most cases you travel as a unit, which is what should happen. There is no point in forcing a discrepancy, which is what intentional astral travel amounts to. It is of no use and causes tension within your unit. With enough tension it *is* possible to cause dissociation sufficient to result in the death of a body. But to do that requires much effort. The few cases of "almosts" are not stories of near disasters, but stories of the tenacity of the integrity of the unit.

Temporary dissociation may occur spontaneously. It is usually the result of a sudden influx of vibration disharmonious with yours. Black Bear used to use his male vibration to produce such an effect in Ellen. She soon realized that by maintaining strong integrity of her system, and focused consciousness, his actions would be rendered ineffective.

If the system is unhealthy and poorly maintained, with unfocused mental activity, a person is more susceptible to discordant vibration. So again, it all comes down to the importance of doing quality work on yourself.

KIOKA

The fascination for occurrences such as "astral travel" indicates the identification with imbalance rather than with balance. Too many seek the bizarre or the extremes. In striving for balance we welcome the pendulum at the midpoint rather than at the ends of its swing range. By identifying with the midpoint we are allowed view of both directions of swing. But identification with one end shuts us off from the other, and from much potential.

We mentioned "astral travel" to allay fears. But others find it exciting instead of fearsome. Experiences far more fulfilling *and* exciting can be had by following a route of harmony and balance. To do so however, more than just the self needs to be accounted for.

To see the self separate from the many collectives within which we exist is another instance of skewed focus. The individual in isolation by importance, by species, by vibration hovers at the end of the swing range.

KIOKA

People are not the only inhabitants of the earth, although it is clear that many of them would like to think so. The attitude that all of life is to be controlled and mastered for the purpose of promoting human interests is hardly expansive. Personally I find the arrogance amazing.

Maybe it's ignorance, artfully placed ignorance, which leads to the elimination of the importance of everything but the self? Sooner or later even that pampered self will suffer starvation of the energies that the other inhabitants bring. Lost connection means no energy flow.

Those who appreciate their fellow earthlings are able to know energetic connections which supplement their own essential energy. Attitudes of superiority and inferiority negate any connection potential, as merging cannot happen without respect. Appreciation for the diversity of life affords context to *your* life. Context is a guidepost to expansion.

INYANI

At any given moment I should believe I am right. I should have that much conviction behind my thoughts, words and actions. However, I must always allow room for modification. I should be open to anything and everything that comes along, *if* it can stand up to my given convictions.

The idea is not to be so wishy-washy and agreeable that you accept everything you see. It is to be eternally open to *consider* everything. If something can shake my conviction and cause me to change, I welcome it, for it means growth. But it does not mean growth if I simply give way to anything that comes down the pike.

We resist easily ideas and words of others. Why is it that we are so afraid to truly listen to what someone says? Nothing is going to befall us by remaining open enough to listen and hear. When we place something new next to our assumptions, *then* there is a chance we will have to change. Never have I seen a time and place so full of people with closed ears (and closed everything else). Maybe the problem is that we don't really want to grow, even as we swear that we do?

Assume you are right until proven otherwise. Welcome the new as it can only benefit you. Either it will strengthen your existing conviction by not measuring up, or prove so worthy of your respect, for it has just defied that stalwart conviction, that you can joyously adopt a new and stronger opinion. Either way you benefit. With closed ears, you have to stay where you are.

KIOKA

For woman to learn about yin, other women can help her. For woman to learn about yang, a man is the logical resource. And for her to learn about other essential energies, she needs to be open to those of the particular energy type.

Humans somehow have developed ideas of superiority to other species and to other kinds of energies. None is better or worse, simply different. And all are necessary for our total growth.

There is much benefit to be had from understanding the essences of fellow earthlings. Animals, minerals, plants, and bugs can teach us so much about ourselves that we cannot afford to shut them out of our experience.

As Inyani said, we need to be strong in our positions, but that does not mean closing our ears to the rest of the universe. Identification with our own essence does not mean dislike for the others. Our essence affords us our own strength, but never does it make any of us superior.

For the most part we have been addressing in this book the problem that women have failed to appreciate their own essence as valid. Yang has reigned supreme to the exclusion of the legitimacy of all other essences. At this point the important thing is for women to grow in yin. But if they do so in a way that tramples other essences, they will repeat the pattern that has occurred with yang.

ELLEN

The subject of animal medicine or animal totems carries with it volumes of misinformation and speculation. The principles are quite simple, the application of those principles more difficult.

Animals are born knowing their connection to their power. Their essential energy differs from that of humans, but is intrinsically tied to the earth's energetics. Owing to a woman's connection to the earth, the potential exists for her to learn from them.

The way an animal makes and maintains its connection to its power is the medicine that animal offers to others. Surrounding that connection are specific behaviors that contribute to the preservation of the power connection.

The eagle knows her power while in flight. Through the use of her voice (sound), encourages the flow of energy into her. Her vocal maneuvers play with the ebbs and flows of the energy allowing her to maintain even access to her power. This is the principle. She was born knowing its application. For a woman to make eagle medicine her medicine, she must learn that application. Once it is hers, she will retain it despite changes in form.

Observation of the behavior of an animal, especially in its *approach* to its power, is the first step to learning. Then you will need to change your vibration to become one with the vibration of the animal, to feel and live that animal from the inside out. When you are able to feel the animal sufficiently to become the animal, you can then make the power connection. The power will flow through you when you are the animal. And the last step is to make that connection real enough to bond with you in your totality, without need for the presence of the animal.

Remember, you are a microcosm of the universe. All that exists, exists in you. That animal, all animals live in you in terms of their essential energies. If you want or need to strengthen that energetic part of yourself, then you have reason to learn that animal's medicine. The animal is nothing more than a vehicle for a specific energetic connection. The animal itself is not what is valued, but the universal energy behind it, or of it, and that animal's knowledge of how to tap it.

The way an animal behaves can give clues to its power connection. It acts in certain ways to preserve its life, in order to make sure it has an opportunity to connect. Observation of behavior will help you attune to that connection, but the behavior *is not* valuable separate from the connection. To act like a rabbit serves no purpose. To know the essence of the rabbit, on the other hand, could be useful. So don't stop your efforts short of the goal by focusing only on behavior.

Traditionally parts of a medicine animal are carried, in honor of and respect for the knowledge of that animal's power, and as a reminder of the importance of its essential energy to a person's life. Part carrying is not necessary. To take an animal's life disrespectfully or to acquire animal parts from animals abused, does not contribute to one's medicine. It detracts because Natural Law has been opposed. If appropriate, an animal part will arrive into your presence as per Natural Law. *No* force will be required. That part should be returned to the earth when its function is terminated, returned in respect for Natural Law and its place in the universe, energetically and physically.

Expedient to the completion of lessons, the learning of particular animal medicine may be in order. Once a woman owns the power of an animal, and if she also is aware of a person's karmic status, resistance and abilities, she may prescribe for that person the pursuit of the animal's medicine as healing. Where there is a hole, fill it. If that animal's behavior and method of connection can fill a gap in a person's development, understanding of that animal is the treatment of choice.

ELLEN

So what do you do with animal medicine once you have it? Needed to say, unfortunately, it is not so you can control or manipulate an animal of that kind for show. It is not to dominate. It is to harmonize.

Whenever you need to reharmonize with the energy of that animal, one of those animals can help. Your request in the presence of need will draw the animal to you. Usually several! Suddenly they will be everywhere! They may come on this plane or others.

When it comes, open to the animal to reconnect with the energy that it is. Allow the animal to bring the energy to you, for it will participate voluntarily with your need when you own its medicine with understanding and respect. Healing does not accompany an animal sought to be mastered or controlled. In fact, that animal is present against its will.

So the animal can be there for you when you need it. But the reverse is also true. Sometimes animals need a bit of yin, and will seek you out to get it. Prerequisite to such an exchange is mutual respect.

Some years ago I was doing some rebalancing of land badly abused by the installation of railroad tracks. I needed the animals to contribute to the reconstitution process, so, with my requests to them, offered healing in exchange. As I made my daily rounds through meadows, woods and swamps, different creatures would approach me.

The snakes made very important contributions to the rebalancing. And one day, a mother garter snake came towards me as I walked. Around her were entwined little ones. Energy exchange accomplished, I prepared to move on. Just then snake number two, a black snake, pulled up parallel to momma snake and parked, not three inches away from her. So I resumed my end of the deal. When finished, I decided that those woods probably housed hundreds of thousands of snakes, and I was not about to service all of them! Nevertheless, a give-back to animals is too frequently overlooked.

ELLEN

Physiology class contained within it the usual frog abuse lab. My choice was participation or flunking, neither of which was acceptably attractive. And so, a quick visit to the Dean of the Medical School for a little chat. Attendance but no participation was the deal. I *got to watch* the day's entertainment.

Several hundred maimed frogs, suffering no consequence, I was assured, involuntarily demonstrated muscle twitch to an obedient, bored audience. Walking from frog to frog, I made eye contact and delivered a bit of energy to each frog to make balance for the choices of my classmates. The human element would be taken care of by Natural Law. The frogs could use all the help they could get.

ELLEN

A particular fondness for frogs was born.

In the spring frogs make quite a lot of music. As I neared their pond, it instantly quieted. I sat at water's edge with my feet on a fallen branch which extended deep into the water. The silence continued. Soon a lone frog approached, eyes breaking the surface. Audibly I said, "Come if you wish." And it did, to place its front feet on the log, inches from mine, but in the water. There it sat as I did the appropriate healing work. As soon as I stopped, the frog opened its eyes. We exchanged glances, and it dove into the darkness of the pond. The music resumed as I reached the requisite distance in my departure.

ELLEN

Animal communication, while not exactly as we have read in Doctor Doolittle, is certainly possible. It is very simple. It is not on human terms. We need to synchronize with the animal to make contact.

Their need, which has vibration, is made public by virtue of their lack of resistance or censorship. Therefore, communication is not specific to any one person. Over time however, by repeatedly having their needs met, they do learn patterns of seeking.

Because I was tuned to the creatures in my environment, I went to the pond aware of need. My actions were in response to frog need. And the healing began long before my arrival at the pond. So that story actually began in the middle, well after events were underway.

But this is the way it happens in real life. As awareness grows, it extends far beyond yourself. You realize more and more that you are a creature in context. Your responses necessarily become appropriate to that context.

GRACE

Because of population patterns and environmental abuses, *all* animals live in conditions of captivity. Their behavior is far distant from their natural tendencies. Extensive accommodation, physically, psychologically and behaviorally, has been required for them to live in the degenerating conditions on the earth.

Humans have been the source for the environmental alterations. Consequently, we must accept responsibility for the results to animals. Healings are *never* out of place with animals. A healing may have to take the form of the most expedient and comfortable death. Animals are no longer equipped to take care of their own needs, so as Ellen said, they can use all the help they can get.

ELLEN

There are victims to any affront to Natural Law. Affronts compounded by affronts is the usual situation we see, with a few escalations, chain reactions and coverups. Sometimes in order to resume course unfortunate by-products result. Really they are a consequence of the original opposition to Natural Law, but this we do not always see clearly.

Because we wish to speak of a complex situation in terms of the rectification of imbalance, a less compounded example should come first.

Hypothetically, consider an animal exposed to heavy environmental toxins. For a time she can adapt, and do her best to compensate internally for the onslaught of external insults. Eventually endocrine disturbances result.

How do we get out of this mess without causing further insults to Natural Law? The responsibility lies in the chain of events and judgments leading up to the presence of toxins and her exposure to them. This animal's dharma is to expand her essential energy. Living is the way she has chosen to follow it.

To allow her to continue to deteriorate avoids responsibility for the presence of the toxins. Yet to intervene, albeit unlikely to reverse the medical condition since the cause remains, would involve further use of products with unnatural results, and her exposure to additional procedures and products foreign to her experience were she in an uncompromised environment (her natural living conditions). Both amount to pushing her into even more disharmonious conditions.

So then a choice to let her die without intervention (or to terminate her life sooner) might be most in line with Natural Law, and might help her return absolutely to complete balance faster.

KIOKA

The primary issue at hand is how, given woman's interconnectedness with men and her involvement in behavior contrary to Natural Law, can she return to life compatible with Natural Law and her pathward motion, without doing further damage. The answer is, she can't. A certain amount of damage is unavoidable, yet in the long run, by rectifying her course, she will come out ahead. (This is essentially the same thing as our discussion of short-term pain vs. long-term learning.)

Thus far we have presented our solution based on simple considerations. Many complexities have been created on this planet, definitely compounded affronts, of which we are quite aware. The solution is the same regardless of the level of complexity one chooses to entertain.

Nevertheless, I wish to point out a situation which may prove to be problematic for some of you. The specific manifestations obviously will vary from person to person and from situation to situation. Remember to cut through the complexity, for if you insist on looking at conditions greatly distanced from the core problem, you will get bogged down.

Your job is to know your path and to follow it. Countless reasons contribute to the failure to identify and the failure to follow that path. Some of the reasons are tied up with male choices and actions, some are not. In the present, because men are also off course spiritually, and women have managed to become entwined in male spirituality, the situation exists of compounded misdirection.

For woman to resume course, she must return to female spirituality, she must cease to participate in male spirituality, and she must reharmonize with Natural Law (which is greater than harmonization with specific female or male path choice).

A choice to leave the male path in favor of the appropriate path is secondarily a rejection of men. A choice to follow a female path is a choice to make her connection resulting in the taking of her power. Secondarily this is a move in deference to male preference, which is to have her remain in pursuit of unattainable male goals. A decision to reharmonize with Natural Law is a refusal of all that opposes Natural Law. Male spirituality has become so extensively enmeshed with defiance of Natural Law that the two can no longer be separated.

At present much of male power illusorily comes from control of women. Therefore, if a woman decides to reharmonize with Natural

Law, to follow her own path and to take her power, men will suffer a loss of what they perceive to be power (the domination of women). They really lose nothing but this they do not know. The rug will be pulled out from under them because of their choice of interconnectedness of issues. And with the removal of women from their scheme of things, they will incur damages secondarily.

Women are not to blame for the consequences of male choices to defy Natural Law or to control women under the umbrella of male spirituality. Women are responsible to move in harmony on their correct path. The consequences of a choice to reharmonize fall within the domain of the original imbalance. As long as she takes care to avoid any additional affronts to Natural Law by her method of reharmonization, she will not hold the responsibility for the natural consequences of male behavior.

Just as with the animal, the best route to resumption of path may involve abstention from activities that continue to counteract your goal. Short term they may not look to be desirable choices, however, if you keep the long term, the need to reharmonize in mind, the choices will be clear.

Our journeys are not free of pain. And at this point, in order to resume course, additional effort will be required. The key is to have the courage to act on your knowings. Knowing is the easy part, unless you let yourself get consumed by the complexities of the affronts to Natural Law and of women forced onto a male path.

Acting on the knowings takes courage, foresight and strength. The strength will come from the collective of women on all planes. The foresight comes from your willingness to look and to expand. And the courage from survival of your attempts, regardless of their successes or failures.

AMNA

It is foreign to many of us to see women take their power, simply and plainly. Part of why we remain oppressed is because we know neither how to accept nor claim that which is ours. Further, we have been taught to undervalue our capabilities and to hold postures of unworthiness in deference to men.

A woman bold and courageous in her realism and truthfulness is not part of the male plan. She is foreign to our ears, a threat to the systems. Seeing and loving the (sometimes) hard truth will be a challenge for you. She is a truth in her totality. She is real. And you can be real also.

KIOKA

After you have done all your work, made good on your responsibilities, and determined that you have outgrown your situation, articulate it. Entities of appropriate vibration will arrive momentarily to take your hand, to go with you into your next adventure.

Every time you genuinely get to a point of wanting more from the bottom of your heart, know that you are well heard. If you do not speak, how can you be heard? If you act in fear, avoid embracing in its totality what you wish to leave, or are looking for a way to abdicate responsibility, they will not come and you will not be answered.

Each woman on the earth is being watched carefully to see if she has the frustration and the vision to make her a potential escapee of the physical plane. This is true in all time. Frustration is high now. Desire for more should be equally peaked. If you have the courage to feel both, and to feel your love and longing for your essence, you can only progress.

Move into yourself to know your essence. And there you will find the community of like traveling women. Keep going no matter what you find, and trust that if you misstep, eventually you will, by your own feeling and knowing, rectify your course. Learn to depend upon yourself, even as you recognize the quantities of women who walk with you.

Take responsibility for finding, holding and using your own power. When each of us does this, the potential of the collective becomes limitless. The universe will live in each of us. And life, wherever any of us is, will be just as each of us has known it could be.

MAJAI

Now it is time for me to tell you why I am here. I have come to make balance for my previous doings. At the time I did not know any better. Now I am appalled at the injustices against Natural Law I committed. This is the way it is with all of us. When you don't see, you don't see. And when you finally do, you really do. So I will tell my story with compassion, hoping that you will have compassion for yourself when you one day see what you have done that will seem to have been so wrong.

I spent many lifetimes in the same communities as Grace and Ellen. Our roles changed, our interactions being more or less depending upon the time. I am here now because I was, throughout these incarnations, a staunch supporter of Black Bear. For a long time I believed in his power,

I believed in male superiority, and I wanted to align with the "winners." Later I discovered there were better ways, although I still broke under his direction and feared to resist his choices. Eventually, I learned to stand up to him. I suffered as those had suffered when I facilitated his abusive behavior. This was a long, long road, believe me.

At the end of it I still felt I needed to make compensation. Karmically I did not owe. But my conscience could not let me walk away without at least telling my story and my learned philosophy. What I learned is nothing new. It is older than the hills, but it was new to me. I love my sisters dearly now, and perhaps even just a few of you can benefit from all our words. I want nothing more than for you to move beyond the hell you now live in to see the possibilities that await you.

You must give up much in your current lives in order to experience these other worlds. And I know, even a disliked thing can be hard to let go of. I hope my words will give you hope and courage to try something new.

In the Morning Star story, I was one of the women in Grace's tribe. I was in charge of keeping Grace quiet after the abduction of She Who Lives With White Eagle. Black Bear put me in charge because at that time I still would not resist him. And now I write this book because of the cooperation and work of She Who Lives With White Eagle. No longer does that name even remotely fit, for long ago she soared beyond the eagle. Come with us beyond the eagle. We love you and we want you out of your current struggles. There *is* a better way, we know. All of us have journeyed long and hard *to* know. Much love, Majai.

GRACE

When you get to the point where you've had enough, *then* you are ready to risk the unknown. So you can see, it is important to face the totality of every situation. You will gain nothing except a slowed pace by pushing what is unpleasant under the rug. How can you know that it's time to move on if you are too chicken to face squarely what it is you need to outgrow? Or, worse, to face your contribution to a mess you wish to leave behind?

I made some pretty big mistakes working with Ellen on Black Bear's finale. So many in fact, that I was afraid Ellen would send me away forever. This is not funny. It was *big* pain, I think the biggest pain I have ever known.

When she completed her part of the work, it was time for me to let Grace Walking Stick die. And then to follow, because that is the Law, was the disclosure and viewing of the recently completed events. With terror at the possibility of losing her love and friendship, I prepared to die.

She told me so many times I can't even count, "Gracie, if you tell me the truth, everything will be fine and I will always love you. If you go chicken on me, and give half the story, *then* there will be trouble." Worse than the words was that I knew she meant it. And I couldn't believe *anyone* could continue to love me knowing the complete me.

I think I have learned finally, from surviving intact my mistakes and the judgments of them, as large as they were, to trust more completely the love of women who are unafraid of reality. The truth is never so bad. But anything short of it is terrible. So courage to face the truth, should be so much easier in coming than attempts to see anything less.

And when you can accept what exists around you, *and* yourself in it, *then* you can move on. When you get saturated with yourself in the moment, it is time to awaken as a new woman into the next moment. Big hugs, Grace.

ELLEN

I am sure that for a long time I will mentally accumulate miles of things that should-have-been-put-in-the-book. There are so many things my big mouth could find to talk about. Luckily it's impossible to make the non-physical physical! I do hope so very much that we have made even a dent in the sorry state of affairs on this planet for women. The end of women's spiritual starvation is long overdue.

Unfortunately, many of our past experiences have been as the passive element in an active society. It is hard for us to initiate and pursue, but women need no longer play passive roles spiritually. We do not need to sit in the chairs where we get victimized, abused, denied, and neglected. And no matter how many or few of your sisters stand up with you, you *can* move on.

Do not be slowed by your discoveries of your previous indiscretions, sufferings, or abuses. I have done many things I wish I hadn't, as is the case with all of us. But *nothing* is sufficient reason to slow your progress. There are quantities of women in many vibrations reaching out to you. If you make even the slightest motion in their direction they will easily go with you the next five miles.

I hope so much that from all our words you have come to know deep within your beings that you *are* powerful, that you are *not* alone, that your efforts *are* worthwhile and that there are some *magnificent* Dreams for you to discover. But most of all, that soon you will easily make real your own dreams. My deepest love, Ellen.

INDEX

This index is for the woman who has already read the text. It is intended to give help in finding discussions temporarily lost.

NOTES

explanation of our understanding of yin; the relevance of philosophy to our growth with the analogy to electricity and the light switch, 4
on crystals, 111

ANJA

on fear and love; on persecution for our attempts to grow, 10
on the importance of the recognition of the sameness of other women in spirit and incarnated, 20
the outline of the continuum of development with Inyani and Kioka, 22
introduction of and comment on Grace, 29
on respect in terms of group; women's groups as reflective of women's processes; an example of Grace and Ellen's group work, 38
on developmental gaps and functional misalignment, 60
on being a yin entity within the macrocosm, 64
on avoidance of confrontational behavior while maintaining forward motion, 76
on the difference between guides and other spirit entities, and the importance of discrimination, 86
an example of a male (the child) harmonizing with the yin, 112
on resistance to development, 133
on the adharmic entity, 143
on earth changes and human response, 152

KIOKA

on the intellect/logic killing what exists beyond the physical; an example of communication between two women; mention of feeling as the basis for social interaction in other societies, 5
why women have incarnated on the earth; lessons to learn given the state of disharmony; the response of spirit to requests by women for help, 8
the reason for the presence of *Beyond the Eagle*, 12
on the predicament of women on the earth and how to grow beyond it, 14
the outline of the continuum of development with Anja and Inyani, 22
discussion of the outline, 24
on growth as a process of refining to uncover one's essence, 26
on being realistic vs. limiting one's growth, 41
on meditation, 67
on the use of *Beyond the Eagle*, 68
on women censoring other women; on the necessity of loving other women in order to love the self, 70
on concepts (higher self, etc.) that limit women's growth and self-determination, 79
on group consciousness and genderlessness of an entity, 87
the analogy of spiritual expansion to the growth of physical height; the impediment to the perception of other realms caused by the accumulation of baggage, 89
on the reason to incarnate; the advantage to being on the earth; on the differences in vehicles for the expression of imperfections according to plane, 91

AMNA

MAJAI

GYTA

DYTOIANTA

ELLEN

GRACE